SELLING TELEVISION

SELLING TELEVISION

British Television in the Global Marketplace

Jeanette Steemers

 Publishing

First published in 2004 by the
BRITISH FILM INSTITUTE
21 Stephen Street, London W1T 1LN

The British Film Institute is the UK national agency with responsibility for encouraging the
arts of film and television and conserving them in the national interest.

Cover design: Mark Swan
Cover image: *Bob the Builder* © HIT Entertainment plc and Keith Chapman 2004

Set by Fakenham Photosetting Limited, Fakenham, Norfolk
Printed in the UK by St Edmundsbury Press, Bury St Edmunds, Suffolk

British Library Cataloguing-in-Publication Data
A catalogue record for this book is available from the British Library

ISBN 1–84457–055–x (pbk)
ISBN 1–84457–022–3 (hbk)

Contents

Acknowledgments

This book would not have been completed without the assistance of several organisations and numerous individuals, for which I am extremely grateful. My thanks goes to the British Academy, whose provision of a research grant allowed me to initiate this project between June and September 2001 with a series of preliminary face-to-face interviews in Britain and the United States. I also wish to offer my gratitude to the Leverhulme Trust, which awarded me a Research Fellowship between October 2001 and September 2002. This enabled me to undertake my core programme of research, including face-to-face interviews in the US, Germany, France, Italy, Spain, the Netherlands and Sweden. I am also extremely grateful to the Arts and Humanities Research Board and De Montfort University for funding study leave in 2002–03 that allowed me to complete the writing of the majority of this book and undertake further enquiries on markets in Australia, New Zealand and East Asia. Two other institutions should also be thanked. The British Television Distributors' Association allowed me to attend three research seminars on the Far Eastern, Japanese and North American markets between November 2002 and January 2003, and numerous members of the BTDA have provided immeasurable support in accessing information and contact names. At the British Film Institute I owe a sincere debt of gratitude to Andrew Lockett, the BFI's former Head of Publishing, who commissioned this volume and also to the two readers, whose comments proved invaluable and insightful in revising my original draft. For advice in the early stages of this project I would like to thank Professor Peter Humphreys at Manchester University and Roger Laughton at Bournemouth University. I would also like to thank Sophia Contento, my editor at the BFI.

I should also of course declare an interest. My fascination with the performance of British television programmes overseas stems from the time I spent working at HIT Entertainment plc as Research Manager between 1990 and 1993 before becoming an academic. I am extremely grateful to Peter Orton, the Chairman of HIT, for instigating my interest in the world of international television sales back in 1990, and to my former HIT colleagues, who have provided invaluable support in the form of advice, contact names and background information.

A substantial proportion of the research for this book is based on interviews with television buyers and executives, and I am extremely grateful to them for sparing the time in their busy schedules to talk to me. In particular, I extend my thanks to the following individuals, whose positions were current at the time of interview:

France: Nathalie Biancolli, Fiction Acquisitions and Isabelle Queme, Documentary Acquisitions, AB Groupe; Annette Blicq, Head of Acquisitions, Canal Jimmy; Emmanuelle Bon, Head of Acquisitions (Europe/Asia), Canal J; Christine Cauquelin, Head of Documentaries, Canal Plus; Hélène Coldefy, Conseiller de Programmes, France 3; Pauline Dauvin, Programme Advisor for Youth Department and Fictions Acquisitions, France 3; François Deplanck, Directeur Général and Valérie Bruschini-Voyer, VP Programming and Acquisitions, Teletoon; Ann Julienne, Acquisitions and International Co-productions, France 5; Francis Kandel, Programming Manager, Planète; Sophie Leveaux, Creative Director Service Acquisitions, TF1; Dominique Poussier, Head of Children's Programmes, TF1; Tim Muff, Head of French Speaking Markets, BBC Worldwide; Emmanuelle Petry, Vice President Europe, Nelvana International.

Germany: Nadja Anan, Head of Series and Animation, ProSieben Television; Jobst Benthues, Head of Entertainment, ProSieben Television; Hans Wolfgang Herfurth, Head, International Relations/Programme Purchase, WDR; Manuela Huhn, Program Acquisitions Executive, RTL Television; Dieter Kaiser, Editor, Natural History, WDR; Hildegard Kunz, Acquisitions, Bayerischer Rundfunk; Volker Lehmann, Director Acquisitions, ZDF Enterprises; Renate Marel, Manager, Health and Nature Department, ZDF; Suzanne Müller, Head of Children's Programmes, ZDF; Ruth Omphalius, Editor, Culture and Society Department, ZDF; Catherine Powell, Television Manager, Germany and German Speaking Territories, BBC Worldwide; Suzanne Schosser, Programme Director, Super RTL; Sabine Tettenborn, Director of Co-productions, Kirch-Media; Thomas von Hennet, Head of Documentaries, ProSieben Television.

Italy: Giovanna Arata, Head of International Productions, Mediatrade, Mediaset Group; Fabrizio Battocchio, Head of Format Department, Reti Televisive Italiane, Mediaset Group; Mussi Bollini, Head of Children's Programmes, RAI; Laura Di Nitto, Children's Programmes Public Relations and Promotion, and Annalisa Liberi, Children's Programmes Acquisition, Rai Tre; Piero Corsini, Acquisitions, Rai Tre; Luca Macciocca, Acquisitions Executive, RaiSat; Fabiana Maraschi, Sales Manager, Videoshow; Francesco Mozzetti, Acquisitions

Manager, Children's Programmes, Mediatrade, Mediaset Group; Lorenzo Pinna, Acquisitions Manager, Rai Uno; Guido Pugnetti, Head of Acquisitions, Rai Cinema; Claudia Sasso, Children's Department, Rai Due; Zelda Stewart, Acquisitions Executive and Giorgio Grignaffini, Head of Programming, Mediatrade, Mediaset Group.

Japan: Jim Weatherford, Director Asia Pacific, Nelvana International.

Netherlands: José Distelblom, Editor and Buyer of Current Affairs, KRO; Mignon Huisman, Head of Programme Acquisitions and Co-productions, KRO; Els Kuiper, Programme Buyer, Youth, VPRO; Frank Mulder, Director of Programme Acquisitions and Sales, NOS; Frank Peijnenburg, Head of Acquisitions NPS; Caro van der Heide, Head of Programme Acquisitions, VARA; Lisette van Diepen, Acquisitions Manager, Programme Affairs, Endemol International; Suzanne van der Wateren and Francine Boske, Programme Buyers, NCRV; Yvonne Willemsen, Project Manager, Teleac/NOT; Nathalie Windhorst, Programme Buyer, VPRO.

Spain: Pedro Erquicia, Director of Current Affairs and Investigative Programmes, Televisíon Española, TVE; Susana García, Observatorio de Mercados, BocaBoca Producciones; Tamara Misert, Acquisitions Manager, Telecinco; Carlos Martínez Ramos, Fiction Series Acquisitions, Televisíon Española, TVE; Inés Ramos, Programmer and Carlos Ortega, Managing Director, Fox Kids España; Sonia Salas, Director of Odisea, Multicanal; Gloria Saló, New Projects Manager, Telecinco; Isabel Varela, Acquisition Division, Sogecable, Canal Plus España.

Sweden: Annika Cederborg, Acquisitions Executive, Children and Youth, SVT Programme Acquisitions; Olof Dahlberg, Executive Editor – Documentaries, SVT News and Factual Programmes; Elaine Hellstadius, Business Executive, SVT Programme Acquisitions; Gudrun Kjellberg, Acquisitions Executive, Fiction, SVT; Maria Lidén, Acquisitions Executive, Documentaries, TV4; Jan Lundberg, Acquisitions Executive, Documentaries, SVT; Robert Norman, Acquisitions Executive, Drama and Entertainment, SVT; Eugen Plym-Forshell, Acquisitions Executive, Nature Documentaries, SVT.

United Kingdom: Lucy Brodie, European Manager, Seven Network, Australia; Charles Caminada, Chief Operating Officer, HIT Entertainment; Melissa Caron, Head of Iberian Territories, BBC Worldwide; Marie Chappelow, Head of Sales for TV and Video (Europe, Middle East, Africa), HIT Entertainment;

Sarah Diggins, Territory Manager, Television and Publishing, Scandinavia, BBC Worldwide; Rupert Dilnott-Cooper, Director, Carlton International Media; Jane Dockery, Vice President Sales and Genre Executive, Children's Programming (Europe and Scandinavia), Granada International; Ben Donald, Territory Manager Italy, BBC Worldwide; Stephen Driscoll, Senior Sales Executive, Carlton International Media (Asia); John Drury, Head of Factual Programming, Granada International; Geraldine Easter, Head of London Office, Holland Media Group and European Representative, Nine Network Australia; Angus Fletcher, President, Jim Henson Television Europe, the Jim Henson Company; Matthew Forde, Territory Manager, Television and Publishing, Benelux, BBC Worldwide; Matthew Frank, Managing Director, RDF International; Peter Grant, Senior Sales and Marketing Executive (Asia, Australia, New Zealand), Chrysalis Distribution; Glen Hansen, Vice President Sales (Australia, Latin America), Granada International; Noel Hedges, Senior Sales Executive, Carlton International Media (German-speaking territories; Scandinavia, Benelux); Sue Holbrook, Consultant, Trade Shows and Markets, HIT Entertainment; Alison Homewood, Sales Director, EMEIA (Europe, Middle East, India and Asia), BBC Worldwide; Judith Howton, Head of Sales, Carlton International Media; Henrietta Hurford-Jones, Head of European Acquisitions, Fox Kids Europe; Colin Jarvis, Director of Programming and Operations, International Television, BBC Worldwide; Cathy Laughton, Managing Director, Nelvana International UK; Andrew McBean, Former Chief Executive, ITEL; Toby Melling, Vice President, Sales (German-speaking territories, Central and Eastern Europe), Granada International; John Morris, Sales Director, HIT Entertainment; Mike Morris, Marketing Director, Channel Four International; Tim Mutimer, Vice President Sales and Genre Executive for Entertainment and Formats (France, Italy, Spain), Granada International; Peter Pas, Vice President, Sales – Factual, Northern Europe, Granada International; Mike Phillips, Director of International Television, BBC Worldwide; Jayne Pitts, Sales Executive – Factual, Southern Europe, Granada International; Amanda Pratt, Project Officer and Policy Advisor, Strategy and Sponsorship, and Linda Dworowski, Policy Advisor, Broadcasting Policy Division, Department for Culture, Media and Sport; Jayne Redpath, Vice President Sales (UK, Ireland, Scandinavia, Benelux, South Africa), Granada International; Patrick Roberts, Senior Programme Sales Executive (Australia, Japan, New Zealand, North America, South Africa), Channel Four International; Hans Schiff, UK Vice President, William Morris Agency, London; Adam Selly, Director of Asia Pacific, HIT Entertainment; Sally Shell, Commercial Director, Wall to Wall; Paul Smith, Chairman, Celador Group; Jocelyn Stevenson, Creative Director, HIT Entertainment; Caroline Torrance, Head of International Drama, Granada International; Chloe Van den

Berg, Sales Director, Entertainment Rights; Peter Van den bussche, Director of Sales, Endemol Entertainment UK; Christina Willoughby, Managing Director, Chrysalis Distribution.

United States: Joel Andryc, Executive Vice President, Kids' Programming and Development, Fox Family Channels, Fox Kids Network; Candace Carlisle, Senior Vice President Co-Production and Sales, BBC Worldwide and Chief Operating Officer, BBC Sales Company; Stephen Davis, President and Chief Executive Officer, Carlton America; Rebecca Eaton, Executive Producer *Mystery!* and *ExxonMobil Masterpiece Theatre*, WGBH; Tony Egger, Vice President – Development, Discovery Health Channel; Mark Fichandler, Senior Director, Development and International Co-Production, Court TV; Delia Fine, Vice President of Film, Drama and Performing Arts Programming, A&E (Arts and Entertainment) Television Networks; Susan Finlayson-Sitch, Director, British Film Office; Brown Johnson, Executive Vice President, Nickelodeon (Nick Junior); Peter Koeppen, Project Manager, Program Development, TLC (Discovery Networks); Suzie Kricena, Head of Acquisitions, Comedy Central; Paul Lee, Chief Operating Officer, BBC America; Charles Maday, Senior Vice President, Historical Programming, the History Channel; Jill Newhouse Calcaterra, Vice President of Marketing and Colin Garrity, Manager of Marketing and Sales, Nelvana Communications; Kelley Oien Perez, Director of Children's Development, the Jim Henson Company; Antony Root, President, Granada Entertainment USA; John Willis, Vice President, National Programming, WGBH.

I would also like to thank colleagues at De Montfort University, particularly Professor Tim O'Sullivan, for their support during this project. Finally I owe the greatest debt of gratitude to my husband Koen, and my two sons Kai and Finn, who have put up with all the highs and lows of the last two years.

Preface

> It is not the private market which has given the UK a broadcasting industry which is widely regarded as the best in the world. In the language of economists, by a clever mix of the public and the private, the UK has managed to generate for itself a 'comparative advantage' in broadcasting and it would be foolish now to throw this away. (Graham and Davies, 1997, p. 9)

Andrew Graham and Gavyn Davies' comments on why a British broadcasting market run on purely commercial terms would be undesirable, provides a specific view of British television and its position in the international marketplace. First there is the idea that British television is perceived as 'the best in the world', and the implicit assumption is that this makes it attractive to international audiences as well as domestic viewers. The second related point infers that 'the best' is a direct consequence of a mixed broadcasting ecology based on public service principles, and that this mix of public and private has given Britain 'a comparative advantage' over other countries.

Even if there is a notion of British as 'best' it has proved difficult to sustain over more than two decades, which have seen fundamental changes in television cultures around the world, including Britain's. Technological advances, the relaxation of regulatory controls, and consolidation of ownership, across borders and media sectors, have served to strengthen commercial approaches to television at the expense of nationally based publicly owned television, state monopolies and the carefully regulated dual system favoured by Britain. In spite of these profound changes Britain remains a significant exporter of television programmes, albeit at some distance to the USA. Yet both the British government and industry have become concerned about export underperformance.

Within the broader context of globalisation and the transformation of world television markets, this book sets out to address the extent of British television's international presence, and the factors that either promote or inhibit that presence in Britain's major television export markets. Alongside an examination of recent policy debates concerning exports, the research draws on industry interviews and examines television cultures in key overseas markets to pinpoint and assess the culturally specific factors that affect the acceptance of programme imports and British programmes in particular.

Technological innovation and changes in regulatory philosophy have led to a massive expansion in the number of channels worldwide, increasing opportunities for trade in television programmes and formats. In the ranking of television exporters, Britain is assumed to occupy a number two position, neither at the centre nor on the periphery, yet far behind the USA (Tunstall and Machin, 1999).[1] However, the commercial priorities of most new channels demand programming that is quite different from the broad range of content traditionally associated with Britain's tightly regulated mix of public and private channels, guided by public service principles serving the 'public interest'. The mix of free-to-air channels in Britain includes a publicly funded and publicly owned broadcaster (the BBC), a publicly owned and commercially funded broadcaster (Channel Four) and two privately owned, commercially funded broadcasters (ITV, Five). These four broadcasters are responsible for the vast majority of original British productions. All have been subject to public service obligations, with public funding and public ownership underpinning higher standards of public service commitment from the BBC and Channel Four in respect of programme range and diversity.

However, commercial television calls for programming that maximises revenues, through the sale of audiences to advertisers and sponsors, or the sale of subscriptions directly to consumers. There is an international market for programming with minority appeal, particularly on specialist channels, which can be very lucrative. However, the commercial success of mainstream channels (including some publicly owned channels) is based on their ability to provide popular fiction and entertainment programming, rather than the diversity traditionally associated with a public service-inspired mixed system. It is, for example, noteworthy that Britain's most publicised commercial export successes since the late 1990s centred on knowledge-based quiz formats (*Who Wants to Be a Millionaire?*, *The Weakest Link*), children's shows (*Bob the Builder*, *Teletubbies*) and factual event programming (*Walking with Dinosaurs*) whose British origins are masked respectively through local production, production technique and the choice of subject matter. In this situation, a public broadcaster, the BBC, is acclaimed for placing *The Weakest Link* on the NBC network in the USA, but British exporters are criticised for selling 'gritty', 'dark' dramas, which reflect British life (DCMS, 1999a, p. 24).

Yet inasmuch as this is a story about the international circulation of British television, in terms of policy it is also a story about the future direction of British television at home, and the ability of British companies to tap into a globalised communications economy, increasingly dominated by a small number of US-based transnational media corporations (Time Warner,[2] the Walt Disney Company, News Corporation, Viacom, Liberty Media). At this level the book considers what strategies are being considered to enhance British television's global presence, and how these strategies are likely to impact future British production and exports. Underlying the research is the perception of a basic tension between the culturally specific demands of the domestic market, and the demand for internationally attractive programmes and concepts, which need to satisfy a broader range of cross-cultural tastes and circumstances.

Academic debates about the impact of cross-cultural exchange, and the extent to which some countries, notably the United States, dominate this process provide very differing accounts. Chapter 1 seeks to contextualise British television's international presence within debates on cultural imperialism, globalisation and the global trade in television programmes. It looks at how discussion about cross-cultural exchange has shifted from the more narrowly defined confines of the cultural imperialism discourse to the more diverse range of views associated with the process and impact of globalisation. In doing so it seeks to provide a framework for explaining the international presence of British television programmes that goes beyond the explanations of cultural imperialism and globalisation. Instead it is suggested that the international presence of British television is in fact affected by a variety of global and local factors. These include technological change, industry consolidation, policy, levels of local production, the international strategies of key players and perhaps most importantly of all, the very different needs of distinctive nationally based television ecologies.

While Chapter 1 provides the background to debates concerning cross-cultural communication and globalisation, Chapter 2 explains how the export industry operates in practice, the value and volume of British television exports, the economic factors that affect television trade flows, and how and why this trade has become significant. It provides an overview of the background, structure and working practices of the trade in television programmes. It looks at how the markets work, the role of buyers, the type of programmes sold, and the different ways of marketing and funding programmes with international potential.

Chapter 1 and Chapter 2 emphasise the international dimension of television trade with regard to theory and industry practice. Chapter 3 considers domestic influences on programme trade in respect of government policy. In the late 1990s concerns were raised about the growing television trade gap between Britain and the USA. This chapter examines the policy debate that arose around these concerns and the contested view that Britain was failing as an exporter. It explains why television exports emerged onto the policy agenda in 1999, only to almost disappear shortly afterwards, to be supplanted by the Labour government's broader objective of attracting overseas and particularly US investment into free-to-air commercial television and independent production to enhance international competitiveness. Bearing this in mind, the chapter examines the potential impact on exports of the 2003 Communications Act, which relaxes foreign ownership rules for free-to-air commercial television (ITV, Five), and limits the broadcasters' ability to retain secondary exploitation rights to programmes commissioned from independent producers.

Having outlined the policy and practice of television trade, Chapter 4 provides a breakdown of the British distribution sector, and introduces a range of British exporters, their activities and strategies. As Britain's largest television exporter by far, and the only British player with significant global interests in overseas channels, there is a particular focus on BBC Worldwide, the BBC's commercial subsidiary. The role of BBC Worldwide is central because there is a tension between its position as a national champion and purveyor of the BBC as a global brand, and the perception that its dominance is not only at odds with the BBC's public service ethos, but is also hindering the growth of other players. Chapter 4 also looks at other broadcaster-distributors (Granada, Carlton, Channel Four), and a selection of niche players (HIT Entertainment, RDF Media, Wall to Wall Television) which have made an impact in the international marketplace.

Chapters 5, 6 and 7 provide an overview of the circulation of British programming and formats in key markets in Western Europe (Germany, France, Italy, Spain, Sweden and the Netherlands), the USA, and the Asia Pacific region (Australia, New Zealand, Japan, South Korea, China, Hong Kong). Each chapter considers the views of those involved in the selection and evaluation of British programmes. The findings are based on interviews undertaken with television buyers and executives between June 2001 and June 2003. Such interviews provide a unique focus on the overseas presence of British programming because buyers are gatekeepers with specialist knowledge of their own markets and particular views about the suitability of overseas programming. Chapters 5 to 7 also offer an overview of these markets and the industrial, regulatory and cultural factors that affect and shape attitudes and commitment to the most marketable British television exports – namely fiction, factual programming, children's programming and formats.

The timeliness of this study is connected with the Labour government's focus on television exports and its stated objective of 'creating the most dynamic competitive communications industry in the world' in an 'increasingly global' marketplace (DTI/DCMS, 2002a, p. 3). However, although British television exports have been identified as a fruitful source of inquiry, there has been little recent analysis in academic circles.[3] This contrasts with work on Australian exports (Cunningham and Jacka, 1996), and programme flows between countries on the 'periphery' (Latin America, India, the Middle East, China, Australia, Canada) (Sinclair, Jacka and Cunningham, 1996). There have been general studies on the global trade in television programmes (Hoskins, McFadyen and Finn, 1997), specific studies on the international trade in programme formats (Moran, 1998) and work on the relationship between British and US media (Miller, 2000; Tunstall and Machin, 1999). However, most other studies of international television and marketing tend to concentrate on the USA as the world's largest television and film exporter – with particular emphasis on the potentially negative impact of American content on local production and cultures. This volume concentrates on how British programmes and formats are marketed and sold, and on the gatekeeper role of overseas buyers who make decisions based on their understanding of domestic audiences, channel requirements and their own media landscapes.

Having outlined what this book is about, it is also useful to establish what it does not cover. The primary focus is on the marketing of television programmes and formats, and the factors that militate for or against international acceptance, illustrated by examples and case studies, rather than an exhaustive inventory of sales undertaken by each player in the market. Sales of footage, including substantial sales of news footage, which are used to create original programmes in other countries, are excluded. The circulation of news footage from the major agencies and broadcasters does of course raise important issues about Anglo-American dominance, but for reasons of time and space these issues lie outside the scope of this study. The study also focuses on programmes and formats originated for television rather than British feature films sold to television. Unlike the USA, whose films have helped to drive in television product, the business of British television exporters revolves mainly around the marketing and sale of television programmes and formats, because the British television industry has had only limited involvement in film production and its international exploitation. The nature of the study also made it necessary to apply a cut-off point, and it ends with the situation as it stands at the end of September 2003.[4] The international career of British television constitutes the central focus of this volume, a subject meriting closer analysis in view of the growing significance attributed to the international exploitation of content and its implications for domestic television.

Notes

1. See also Nordenstreng and Varis (1974), Varis (1985) and DCMS (1999a) in respect of volume and the ITC (2002a, p. 30) in respect of value. Whether this is still correct in respect of volume is debatable, given that Brazil and Mexico sell many hours of long-running *telenovelas* to Europe, the USA and within Latin

America, and Canada is a successful exporter of fiction to US cable channels and of animation programming worldwide.

2. In October 2003, AOL Time Warner Inc. announced the change of its name to Time Warner Inc.

3. In the mid-1980s, there was some work on British exports/imports arising from concerns that Europe or Britain was about to be 'swamped' with American programming (Schlesinger, 1986; Collins, 1986).

4. Some judgment has been exercised to extend this cut-off point to the end of November 2003, where events have spilled over and where the reader might benefit from additional information.

1

Going Global – Theoretical Bearings

To understand the role of British television in the global marketplace and the extent to which it circulates internationally, it is useful to consider how patterns of television trade have been perceived in the past. This chapter begins by considering the cultural imperialism discourse and theories associated with the concept of globalisation as a means of understanding both international trade flows and changing theoretical perspectives about the nature and impact of the cultural trade in programmes and formats. This provides a starting point for examining the position of Britain in international television markets, a position that within theoretical debates on trade flows, ranges between dominance and dependency, with a variety of positions in between. Ultimately, however, any examination of the international circulation of British television programming and formats demands empirical analysis of its reception in the distinctive national markets where these are marketed, sold and shown. This underpins the final section of this chapter, which explains and outlines the methods used to ascertain the presence of British television programmes overseas and the factors that affect this presence.

Cultural imperialism – from international domination to transnational corporations

When television emerged as a mass medium in the 1950s, the global demand for imported programming was high, because new television stations lacked programmes and the resources to make them in sufficient quantities. Imports were cheaper than domestic production and could be acquired from a more mature American television market (Tunstall, 1977, p. 17).[1] However, the growth in US television exports and US investment overseas in the 1960s raised concerns about American influence, even if the high point of US imports had passed by the 1960s, as some countries began to produce more domestic programming, in what Ithiel de Sola Pool has identified as a natural business cycle of dependency and adaptation, followed by greater domestic activity (1977, pp. 142–3).

The success of American television programme exporters in the 1960s developed on the back of the innovation, experience and earlier successes of American film and radio. Put simply, the Americans were in possession of large amounts of programming and there was growing international demand. However, the American ability to maintain a dominant position in audiovisual trade was enhanced by government legislation that allowed MPEAA (Motion Picture Export Association of America)[2] members to ignore US antitrust regulations in their overseas activities. As a result American companies were able to collude in price-fixing and the co-ordination of overseas sales (see Guback and Varis, 1982, p. 29; Hoskins, McFadyen and Finn, 1997, pp. 46–7; Renaud and Litman, 1985, pp. 247–8).[3]

From the start there has been little dispute about American dominance of the international trade in television and film. Yet there is dispute about its cultural significance, and whether US dominance in some areas of the mass media translates automatically into cultural domination, and from that into domination of the economic and political order (see Tomlinson, 1997a, p. 135).

Concerns about US dominance were expressed in the discourse of cultural imperialism based on the dominant ideology thesis and linked to American supremacy in the production and distribution of cultural goods and services. Media imperialism, a more narrowly focused variation of cultural imperialism, involves a process where media ownership, structures, distribution and content are liable to external pressures from overseas media interests without proportionate reciprocity of influence (see Boyd-Barrett, 1977, p. 117).

Cultural imperialism suggests that dominance of the media and mass culture allows the West, and particularly America, to spread cultural values, ideas and practices that provide ideological support for the dominant order of global capitalism and its emphasis on consumerism. Studies in the 1970s that sought to quantify international programme flows demonstrated American superiority in the television programme export market (Nordenstreng and Varis, 1974; Varis, 1984). These findings reinforced those explanations that argued that American dominance of cultural trade and the spread of Western cultural goods were homogenising cultures across the globe, threatening local identities and reinforcing American hegemony (see Dorfman and Mattelart, 1975; Guback, 1969; Hamelink, 1983; Schiller, 1969, 1976, 1991; Wells, 1972).

Herbert Schiller was one of the first to write about cultural imperialism and its role in supporting the economic objectives of American capitalism. Published in 1969, his book *Mass Communications and American Empire* argued that the export of US television programmes, equipment and advertising was part of a concerted effort by the American government, military and industry to subjugate the world for ideological and profitable ends. Schiller reiterated and reinforced his position in 1991, arguing that cultural domination still persisted in the 1990s, albeit in a different form, because of the possibilities afforded by satellite delivery systems, which undermine territorial controls (1991, pp. 15–16). Schiller emphasises the systematic and integrated nature of global capitalism and cultural domination by a small number of corporations with transnational media interests. These still bear a marked American imprint and set worldwide standards for communications, media and leisure consumption at the expense of citizenship and the public sphere (Ibid., p. 15, pp. 21–2). Television in this instance is but one element, in an all-encompassing cultural package of homogenisation, that helps to promote the free market and the goods sold by multinational corporations (Ibid., p.15). It is not even necessary to do this with American television programmes, because domestic television is 'creolised' to spread the transnational corporate message (Ibid., p. 22).

Cultural imperialism represents one of the oldest models for understanding cultural exchange, but it encompasses a range of contradictory perspectives on media imperialism, national identity, global capitalism and modernity, rather than a coherent set of ideas (Tomlinson, 1991, pp. 19–28). What unifies these different perspectives is the notion of cultural flow as a 'one-way street'. Yet since the 1980s there has been a shift away from this position because reality proved much more complex than the picture painted by this 'total' explanation, which posits the media as a major agency with significant effects. Drawing on the debate surrounding cultural imperialism and its view of the centrality of the media in maintaining dominion, Golding and Harris summarise the weaknesses of the cultural imperialism discourse as follows:

> Firstly it overstates external determinants and undervalues the internal dynamics, not least those of resistance, within dependent societies. Secondly, it conflates economic power and cultural effects. Thirdly, there is an assumption that audiences are passive, and that local and oppositional creativity is of little significance. Finally, there is an often patronizing assumption that what is at risk is the 'authentic' and organic culture of the developing world under the onslaught of something synthetic and inauthentic coming from the West. (1997, p. 5)

If we examine these weaknesses individually we can see that the 'big picture' approach of cultural imperialism has not always taken sufficient account of local production and cultural exchanges between countries other than the US. According to Fejes it neglects those factors operating at the national and local level that both assist and react against external forces to create new cultural identifications that mix local and global influences (1981, p. 286; Hall, 1997, p. 211). Several commentators point out that although earlier research on the trade in television programmes showed US dominance (Nordenstreng and

Varis, 1974; Varis, 1985), the same research also revealed significant regional exchanges among some countries (Tracey, 1988; Tunstall, 1977, p. 40; Varis, 1984, p. 151). According to Tracey the trade in television is therefore not a 'one-way street; rather there are a number of main thoroughfares, with a series of not unimportant smaller roads' (1985, p. 23).

In an attempt to pinpoint these multi-directional flows in television, Sinclair, Jacka and Cunningham write about geolinguistic regions and programming exchanges between countries and communities that share cultural, linguistic and historical ties – ties that are not necessarily determined by national borders or geographic proximity (1996, pp. 12–13). Within each region there are dominant centres of production. Mexico and Brazil export long-running *telenovelas* to other Latin American markets, Southern Europe and to channels serving the Hispanic community in the US. Egypt, Hong Kong and India supply programming within their own regional orbit of the Middle East and Asia respectively, and to diasporic communities around the world by satellite and video (Sinclair and Cunningham, 2000). The USA, and to a lesser extent Britain, Australia and Canada export programmes to other English-speaking countries that share cultural ties and the legacy of the British Empire. Hesmondhalgh and Straubhaar use the modified term 'geocultural markets' to emphasise cultural rather than linguistic connections and the multiple cultural identifications of individuals in a world that has witnessed large-scale migration (Hesmondhalgh, 2002, p. 180; Straubhaar, 1997, p. 291). However, it is also important not to exaggerate the significance of 'contra-flows' from the periphery, which in the case of exports from Brazil and Mexico have been characterised as 'reverse media imperialism' (Rogers and Antola, 1985, p. 33), for the US still accounts for three-quarters of the global trade in television by value (ITC, 2002a).

Rather than dominance Straubhaar refers to *assymetrical interdependence* to reflect the variety of cross-cultural relationships that exist between countries (1991). Similarly Boyd-Barrett's model of generic media imperialism acknowledges that dominance and dependency can vary between different countries, between media and between different levels of activity within sectors of the media industry in respect of ownership, structure, distribution or content (Boyd-Barrett, 1998, p. 159, p. 166).

Second, if cultural/media imperialism underestimates countervailing local tendencies and alternative cross-cultural exchanges, it also fails to demonstrate the extent to which cultural dominance translates into dominance of the political and economic sphere. There is certainly evidence of concentrated media ownership, and US dominance of television trade flows (see Herman and McChesney, 1997). Yet within cultural imperialism there is also 'a definite sense of the conceptual problems of the "moment of the cultural" being forever deferred' (Tomlinson, 1991, p. 40), because of an emphasis on institutional aspects, texts and 'company reports, rather than the realities of individual lives' (Tracey, 1985, p. 45).

Media imperialism assumes that Western/US media have a negative effect on audiences, but there is little evidence of how consumption of foreign television affects local cultures and spreads Western consumerist values in the service of American imperialism (see Lealand, 1984, p. 6; Thompson, 1995, pp. 170–1; Tracey, 1985). It was simply assumed that American television imports had an effect and that this was invariably negative with little consideration of how dominance, resistance and negotiation function in the transfer and consumption of meaning (Sinclair, Jacka and Cunningham, 1996, p. 15). According to cultural imperialism, the process of reception was simply 'a "black box" into which media products infused with consumerist values are poured, and from which individuals oriented towards personal consumption supposedly emerge' (Thompson, 1995, p. 172).

Other studies have shown that, far from being passive recipients of television, audiences actively interpret programmes from within their own distinct local cultures, and that these meanings are shaped by age, class, gender, ethnicity and social experience (see Ang, 1985; Fiske, 1987; Hobson, 1982; Liebes and Katz, 1993; Straubhaar, 2000). Ang's study of the US serial drama *Dallas* found that Dutch female audiences adopted a range of viewing positions and derived pleasure from a programme that was officially derided as 'bad' mass culture (1985). Liebes and Katz' study of *Dallas* introduced a cross-cultural dimension, which established a range of 'referential' and 'critical' readings from among different sub-cultural audiences in Israel, and audiences in the USA and Japan (1993). Miller's work on the US soap opera *The Young and the Restless* in Trinidad demonstrates the importance of the local context of viewing and how an imported programme can be 'localized' by audiences to make it relevant to local traditions, cultural practices and identity (1995).

However, these ethnographic studies tend to be limited in scope and focus mainly on the reception of popular American programming by small groups, which makes it difficult to generalise globally about cross-cultural impact. Moreover, the range of responses is affected and constrained by codes and conventions inherent in the text and the cultural and social context of viewing, which may help to establish 'preferred' readings (Hall, 1980). Such studies also give less attention to wider factors affecting reception, including how programmes are selected, promoted and scheduled. Even if individuals respond to the media in different ways, Sinclair and Cunningham remind us that the media also actively seek out audiences, shaping them 'commercially and ideologically as markets for certain forms and genres by media corporations' (2000, p. 15).

Finally those who detected cultural imperialism ignored evidence that the vast majority of television is still inherently local and that given a choice, most people prefer home-grown entertainment programming (see Morley and Robins, 1989, p. 28; O'Regan, 1993, p. 87; Sinclair, Jacka and Cunningham, 1996, p. 10). The USA might dominate the trade in television programming, but even the earliest studies demonstrated that up to two-thirds of broadcast programmes are locally originated (Varis, 1984, p. 147; Sepstrup, 1990, p. 55). Moreover, the international circulation of American programming does not extend to many parts of the Middle East, Africa, Latin America and Asia because of economic and/or political barriers.

The US is certainly the main source of fiction imports in many countries, but television programmes are still predominantly produced by and for national markets with their own broadcasting systems, regulations, political orientations, class structures and cultural values (see Cantor and Cantor, 1986, p. 510). The strength of national cultures, language and tradition is underlined by the failure to establish pan-European television in the 1980s (see Collins, 1989) and the decision in the 1990s to localise pan-Asian services such as Star TV to attract larger audiences (Chadha and Kavoori, 2000, p. 424). Even with localisation these are not always the most popular channels except with an affluent elite, who possess both the economic and cultural capital that affords preferential access to such services (Bourdieu, 1984;[4] Chadha and Kavoori, 2000, p. 425; Sparks, 1998, pp. 115–16; Straubhaar, 2000; Thussu, 2000, p. 196). Nor are American programmes always the most popular offerings, subject as they often are to poor promotion and scheduling.[5] They tend to do better in situations where domestic television is not producing programming of comparable entertainment value (see Mills, 1985, p. 493). In this context Straubhaar introduces the idea of 'cultural proximity', when he hypothesises that while the US will continue to dominate the supply of high-budget feature films, cartoons and action adventure series, local audiences

> ... will tend to prefer that programming which is closest or most proximate to their own culture: national programming if it can be supported by the local economy. A similar desire for the most relevant or similar programs also seems to lead many national audiences to prefer cultural-linguistic regional programming in genres that small countries cannot afford to produce for themselves. (Straubhaar, 2000, p. 202)

This ties in with Hoskins and Mirus' concept of 'cultural discount', the idea that cultural differences relating to style, values, beliefs, institutions and behavioural patterns will limit the appeal of foreign programmes (1988, p. 500). Audience preferences for home-grown programming lead television industries and advertisers to prioritise national production or programming from within the same region, language group and culture (Straubhaar, 1991, p. 39).[6]

Globalisation and hybridity

> ... in every industry the globalisation concept is happening. ... The trick is can you globalise programming and make it local? You own a lot of formats, you make them in different countries, you take them from one to another. (Greg Dyke cited in Freedman, 2000, p. 321)

An alternative approach to cultural and media imperialism is embodied in those complex processes of integration grouped under the concept of globalisation and its corollary, global culture. Yet there is a bewildering diversity of views on globalisation and very different explanations about what it entails. Like cultural imperialism, there are differences of opinion about globalisation's impact on local cultures, and whether there is such a thing as 'global culture'. However, unlike cultural imperialism, globalisation involves a more unpredictable, less culturally directed set of flows (Tomlinson, 1991, p. 175).

The process of globalisation involves the compression of the world in time and space in respect of its institutions (television, capitalism, industrialism) and economic and cultural practices (Barker, 1999, p. 34). This has accelerated with the instantaneous nature of modern media and communications, so that 'we are no longer able to live our lives entirely "locally"' (Tomlinson, 1997a, p. 118). More recently globalisation has been associated with new communications technologies that create the global information infrastructure necessary for global economies, dominated by a small number of large corporations involved in the global production and distribution of goods and services.

If it is regarded as inevitable, globalisation means that national governments (including the most powerful ones) can do little in the face of technological change and global capital flows that defy the barriers of time and space and favour multinational corporations and integrated international markets (see Freedman, 2000, p. 313). In the case of media and television, if it is accepted that the regulatory role of the nation state is undermined by globalisation, there are ample opportunities for governments to justify relaxing regulations. They may relax national content and ownership rules on the pretext of allowing domestic industries to participate in a globalised economy over which governments are thought to have little or no control (see DTI/DCMS, 2002a p. 3). However, there are strong grounds for arguing that it is perhaps premature to declare the end of the nation state in determining the national economic, technological and regulatory frameworks of national television systems. For content, distribution, regulation and subscriber management for pay television are still geared towards reception by national audiences, not least because exploitation of markets on a national basis is more profitable than one single global deal (see Sparks, 1998, p. 114).

Global television became possible with the emergence of satellite delivery platforms in the 1980s whose transmissions are not confined to national boundaries. The manifestations of global television include the continued push by transnational corporations towards the removal of trade barriers and legislative constraints on ownership and content. This comes on top of the global distribution of television programming, and the worldwide spread of commercial practices in respect of scheduling, formats, funding and regulation. Yet these processes seemed to accelerate with the opportunities afforded by new technologies, leading to the decline of publicly owned television monopolies in the 1980s and the emergence of a greater range of commercial television outlets. Global television is therefore no longer simply about imports and exports, but how local and national media fit into an interconnected, interdependent global media system.

On the one hand there is the 'Utopian' notion of globalisation and global culture where distinct national differences become less prominent with the media contributing to the globalisation of democratic ideas within a global public sphere (see McLuhan, 1962; Volkmer, 1999). However, Featherstone suggests that there is no global culture akin to the culture of the nation state, with its emphasis on cultural homogeneity and integration (1990, p. 1). Rather, he characterises globalisation as a complex set of processes which take place at different levels, take a variety of forms, and go beyond the opposites of 'global' and 'local' (Ibid.). For Smith, global culture is inauthentic, because it is 'essentially memoryless' and unable to draw on the collective history and experiences common to national cultures, which is why it is unlikely to supersede them (Smith, 1990, 179–80). Ferguson challenges assumptions about the meaning, evidence and evaluation underlying the 'myths' of globalisation and suggests that globalisation is neither uniform, universal nor beneficial (Ferguson, 1992, p. 88). In a similar vein Ang refers to a world characterised less by global understanding and unity and more by 'regional realignments and fracturings, nationalist and ethnic separatisms' (1994, p. 325), where global culture is not about the eradication and assimilation of cultural difference, but involves a 'checkered process of systemic desegregation in which local cultures lose their autonomous and separate existence and become thoroughly interdependent and interconnected' (Ang, 1996, p. 153). Rejecting centre-periphery models and linear determinations, Appadurai identifies five dimensions of *uneven* global cultural flows that occur in and through the overlapping disjunctures between ethnoscapes (flows of people), technoscapes (flows of technology), finanscapes (flows of capital), mediascapes (flows of media) and ideoscapes (flows of ideas) worldwide (1990, p. 301). These flows are experienced at a local or domestic level and operate alongside national institutions, underlining the complex, overlapping and 'chaotic' nature of cultural flows and contemporary global diversity (Barker, 1999, p. 41). In this sense global culture is not monolithic at all but 'has its space *between* rather than within cultures' and its '"essential" nature is that of the hybrid' (Tomlinson, 1997a, p. 138).

Others view globalisation as an extension of cultural imperialism and cultural homogenisation because multinational corporations are now able to pursue their commercial objectives on a transnational basis unimpeded by national controls, borders or technological limitations (see Schiller, 1991). This leads to uniform global culture, shaped by corporate values and objectives, and constitutes a reformulation of the cultural imperialism discourse. Herman and McChesney, for example, paint a picture of the global marketisation of communications driven by corporations intent on spreading an entertainment-based culture, which undermines democracy (1997). Manifestations of this type of cultural imperialism as globalisation involve ownership concentration and expansion into new areas of activity through cross-media ownership and strategic alliances. It is a global media market concerned as much with media distribution and access to consumers as with the production or export of content. And it is dominated, according to McChesney, by less than ten largely US-based transnational corporations (TNCs), with a further three or four dozen US, European and Japanese firms serving regional and niche markets (McChesney, 1998, p. 28, p. 31; also Garnham, 1990, pp. 161–2).

The impact of global media is, however, by no means automatic or uniform. To succeed, global media companies require politicians to relax regulations that restrict their operations in local markets. For global strategies to be effective, companies must also work hard to naturalise and indigenise their products and image, taking account of local cultures, social forms and philosophical attitudes (Hall and Jacques, 1997, pp. 35–6). Globalisation and the way it relates to local culture is therefore increasingly as much about heterogeneity, interdependency, customisation, audience fragmentation and hybridity as much as homogeneity, dependency and uniformity (see Ang, 1996, p. 153; Barker, 1999, p. 38; Pieterse, 1995, p. 62; Sinclair, Jacka and Cunningham, 1996, p. 13). This interaction between global and local results in a hybrid culture where differences 'between the modern and the traditional, between the high and low culture and the national and the global culture' are increasingly blurred (Thussu, 2000, p. 197).

Applied to television, global companies customise their formats, channels and products to appeal to differentiated local markets and maximise revenues. Equally, local producers 'draw on the codes and conventions ... of the global popular to stamp their own product, channel, distribution network as "professional", "competitive" and attractive to audiences and, more importantly, advertisers' who sell transnational products (Boyd-Barrett, 1997, p. 16). This overlapping of globalising, regionalising and localising forces is defined by Robertson as 'glocalisation' – or the global production of the local and the localisation of the global in a process involving both homogenising and heterogenising forces, which combine and incorporate the particular and the universal (Robertson, 1995, p. 40; 1994, p. 38).

For instance, local programming is often based on formats originally developed in America – tabloid-style news, 'cop' shows, sitcoms, soaps, game shows, talk shows, action movies. This type of adaptation is particularly important for those producers who harbour ambitions for international exploitation, and Tunstall reminds us that heavy importers of US media have also emerged as strong regional exporters (1977, p. 62). This suggests that US programming models are localised and imitated to create hybrids, which may have a broader international appeal in regional markets and beyond (see Sinclair, Jacka and Cunningham, 1996, p. 13; Tunstall, 1977, p. 129). In this case, Latin American *telenovelas*, European game-show formats, Australian soaps and Hong Kong action movies, which incorporate aspects of American practice, not only invigorate local production industries and culture. They also offer opportunities for wider international exploitation, precisely because they share similarities with US productions, having indigenised elements from US forms, and can act as substitutes in some cases (see Ang, 1996, pp. 154–5).

In this way, national television cultures are affected by external influences and create a reworked and hybridised diversity, alongside more traditional local and national identities, that involves an interplay between the global and the local in television form and content (Barker, 1999, p. 43; Straubhaar, 1997, p. 288). This is a complicated process, but it does provide a more nuanced explanation for hybrid cultures than the centralising explanations of cultural imperialism. However, even if power is diffused or hybrid forms emerge, this does not invalidate the necessity of exploring issues of economic, political and cultural power and the cultural consequences of economic developments and the 'colonization of communications space' (Boyd-Barrett, 1998, p. 157), for some countries or corporations have more power than others to initiate flows and invest in programming and the infrastructure for its distribution, while others lack the resources to produce diverse and more expensive forms of local production such as fiction. This brings us back to the issues raised within the discourses of cultural and media imperialism, including ownership and control, and diversity and plurality.

Britain – between complementarity and subordination

Where then does Britain fit into debates about cultural imperialism or globalisation? Viewed from either perspective, Britain's relationship with the US, its main audiovisual trading partner, remains important in any discussion of the international circulation of British television. Britain is a key export market for the US and the US is a key export market for Britain, accounting for a third of British television programme exports by value (BTDA, 2002). This situation is based on a degree of cultural overlap, shared heritage and a common language, which underpins Britain's membership of the wealthy 'geolinguistic' English-speaking market.

Within the debates, which focus on programme flows, it is possible to ascribe to Britain a variety of positions, which range from dominance to dependency with a number of positions in between. O'Regan writes about a sense of 'complementarity', where Britain and the US operate 'contiguous and connected' television systems rather than irreconcilable models (O'Regan, 2000, p. 309). Miller, in his survey of British television in America, and drawing on the work of Bakhtin, writes about a multi-linear, multivocal relationship between America and Britain, which revolves less around dependency and more around 'assimilation', dialogue, and the negotiation of meaning by American audiences (2000). Collins, Garnham and Locksley argue that there is no one overriding paradigm to interpret trade flows, but that relations are dependent on different contexts, determined by market structures, which in turn are subject to fundamental change from new technologies and ideologies (1988, p. 59).

First there is the notion of Britain as a victim of American dominance, subject to American capital control with large volumes of American television programmes, undermining British identity, homogenising culture, encouraging consumerism and the maintenance of the social status quo. In truth, British free-to-air television (the BBC, ITV, Channel Four, Five) is not overwhelmed by US exports and is extraordinarily resistant to non-US imports. BBC 1 and ITV, the most widely watched channels, rarely, with the exception of feature films, show North American fiction in peak time, although this is not the case with the lower rating Channel Four (*Friends*, *Frasier*, *ER*) and Five (*CSI: Crime Scene Investigation*,[7] *Law and Order*). British terrestrial channels traditionally adhered to a 14 per cent quota on programme imports, and far exceed the stipulations of the European Commission's *Television Without Frontiers Directive*, which demands that a majority of transmissions originate from within the Europe Union (Seymour-Ure, 1991, p. 143; EC, 2002).[8] However, British television (both commercial and public service) is influenced by the US commercial model, programming forms and policy trends, a fact that infers a degree of 'hybridization and neutralization' of British content to meet commercial objectives (see Bil_tereyst and Meers, 2000, p. 397). The relaxation of ownership rules for commercial free-to-air television in the 2003 Communications Act will allow American ownership of British free-to-air commercial channels, ITV and Five. This suggests further emulation of the American commercial model and a shift in audience and regulatory expectations 'towards a more US or internationally focused product mix' (Joint Committee, 2002). However, although the five terrestrial channels meet European quotas, only 53 per cent of all British-based channels satisfied the quota in 2000 (EC, 2002, p. 21). This is because the satellite and cable market remains very heavily reliant on US imports, contributing to Britain's large trade deficit with the US (see Chapter 2).

An extension of the dependency perspective sees Britain not as a victim of US media imperialism, but as 'surrogate Americans', a 'junior media partner' or 'low-profile allies' of the United States (O'Regan, 2000, p. 312; Tunstall, 1977; Tunstall and Machin, 1999, p. 15). This view is attributable to Britain forming part of the Anglophone culture that is believed to dominate media and communications. Possibly disadvantaging its own cultural exports, Britain functions as a launch pad for US international channels (Nickelodeon, National Geographic, MTV, CNN) into European markets. It is an important gateway, providing access for US media first to the lucrative English-speaking markets of Britain's former colonies and Commonwealth, and later as a member of the European Union to a growing market for commercial television (Tunstall and Machin, 1999, p. 259). Britain therefore often sits uncomfortably between European interests, foremost in France, which fears for its cultural independence in the face of a 'modèle unique anglo-marchand' (Anglo-Saxon mercantile standard model), and the perceived 'imperialistic' audiovisual interests of the Americans (Machill, 1997, pp. 494–5; Mattelart et al., 1984).

The idea of Britain as a junior media partner of the US is advanced in Tunstall's 1977 book *The Media are American: Anglo-American Media in the World*, where he argues that Britain and Anglo-imperialism played a crucial role in the global spread of American media and Anglo-American dominance. He points out that English-language media exports and influence predate the emergence of the US as a major economic force overseas. The British Empire established itself as the principal media power in the 19th century through its control of the world's telegraph and cable networks that reinforced imperialistic rule (Tunstall, 1977, p. 95). This ensured that English became the language of international commerce and communications. With imperial decline Britain relinquished its lead in communications to the US in the early part of the 20th century. Thereafter the US, starting with film, managed to impart the imprint of its own popular culture on each subsequent media innovation.

A different view sees Britain less as a 'cadet' to the USA in the imperialism game

(Collins, 1986, p. 77) and more as a complementary public service alternative, as a niche purveyor of 'high' culture in the form of documentaries, innovative 'oddball' comedy, complex thrillers and period drama. This type of programming is 'accessible' and attractive to an elite endowed with educational, financial and cultural capital (Bourdieu, 1984; Miller, 2000, p. 178). It provides 'one international brand image of British television content as a provider of a certain kind of content: middle-class fare skewed in various ways towards the maintenance and reproduction of a literary and cultural heritage' (O'Regan, 2000, p. 304). According to Collins, consistent international success depends on the production of programming which conforms to such internationally current stereotypes as much as the production of product that appeals to international tastes:

> Thus British television presents to the world a costumed image of Britain as a rigidly but harmoniously hierarchized class society: *Brideshead Revisited*, *The Six Wives of Henry VIII*, *Upstairs, Downstairs*; Japan the shogun and samurai pasts; Italy *The Borgias*. *Dallas, Dynasty, Hotel* and *Flamingo Road* represent the United States to international television viewers in contemporary melodrama in which the values of capitalist business and the family are presented both positively and negatively. (1990, p. 158)

The heyday of these 'elevated' types of exports can be traced back to a time when British television itself was perhaps more insular and less subject to external influence. As an 'introverted culture' (Pieterse, 1995, p. 62), British television offered something different. Yet this idea of a complementary, distinctly British 'quality' alternative compared to the broader appeal of American entertainment and fiction has tended to restrict acceptance to the margins. It restricts circulation to those outlets that have been influenced by and share a public service ethos with British broadcasting, particularly with the BBC. Such outlets are exemplified by the geo-cultural and institutional proximity of the minority-appeal Public Broadcasting System (PBS) in America itself, and public service channels in English-speaking countries in the Commonwealth and by the institutional proximity of public service channels in Western Europe and Japan (NHK). But public service broadcasters have come under competitive pressure in the last two decades, and most have lost their dominant market position. Moreover, British television may be perceived as prestigious and innovative by some, but is just as likely to be associated with a 'restrained, stuffy, literary, class-conscious, even paternalist, system' (O'Regan, 2000, p. 317). Tunstall and Machin, for example, argue that the British regulatory framework which promoted public service-inspired programming as a bulwark against imports, actually impeded exports as British television failed to make full use of

the international advantage of the English language (1999, p. 8). British television that was 'inward-looking, parochial, and focused on lovable, somewhat
caricatured, British idiosyncrasy and eccentricity ... did not make for mass
exporting success' (Ibid., p. 8).

Finally there is a position where Britain functions as a supplier of universally
appealing content whose British and public service origins are masked, and
which is 'internationally integrated at a programme inception level' in an interplay of the global and the local (O'Regan, 2000, p. 319). At one level
hybridisation occurs in Britain itself to produce something that is new but also
recognisable in overseas markets. This applies for example to *Who Wants to Be
a Millionaire?* and *The Weakest Link*, which offered new twists on quiz-show formats for peak-time audiences. At the next level there are opportunities for local
adaptation and translation to create something new (Moran, 1998, pp. 171–3).
This certainly applies to entertainment, drama and factual formats, which are
produced for local markets. But it also applies to some straight sales of children's programming (*Bob the Builder*, *Teletubbies*) and factual programming
(*The Blue Planet*, *Walking with Dinosaurs*), which are not recognisably British
and can be re-voiced. These are all programmes that can be indigenised and
adapted by the receiving culture, and in their more 'universal' appeal they are
quite different from the identifiably British historical or literary-based drama on
which Britain's international success was based in the past (see Alvarado, 2000).

However, it is also important to remember that cross-cultural impact in television extends beyond television exports. Sinclair, Jacka and Cunningham
rightly point out that America's legacy in world television is more strongly connected to the implantation of the commercial model and commercial funding
than the supposed ideological influence of American programmes (1996, p. 9).
American imports have often been important for the introduction of commercial television, but as markets mature and produce more domestic content,
American programming is not always necessary to continue the commercial
model. Ang notes that US commercial television has been the prime source of
formats (sitcoms, soaps, game shows, talk shows) and scheduling routines, such
as the stripping of the same series every day at the same time, which have been
accepted as the common-sense way of doing things (1996, p. 154). Similarly
Tunstall and Machin emphasise the US lead in terms of 'genres, formats, fash-
ions, and media policies' (1999, p. 2), allowing the US to set the terms of
television production, circulation and consumption internationally even if other
countries later developed their own 'home-cooked' alternatives (Ibid., p. 23).

Equally the impact of British television is more than simply a matter of television imports/exports. It involves investment in overseas productions and the
establishment of international channels (BBC America, BBC World) and

commercial joint ventures (Animal Planet, People and Arts). It encompasses the emulation and domestication of British formats and production practices; the adaptation of British policy models for regulating and operating television in a dual system of private and public broadcasting; and the use of British creative talent (also O'Regan, 2000, p. 304). The key distinguishing feature between Britain and the US in terms of impact has been the difference between the public service and commercial model. But it is the commercial model that has proved to be in the ascendant in world markets, including Britain itself, with implications for what is produced and exported. This in itself raises issues about identity, and the extent to which British programme exports are tied in to a particular notion of Britain.

National culture and identity

As we have seen, on the one hand exports are linked to stereotypical, 'imaginary' forms of Britishness, particularly in fiction that 'may have little to do with the real Britain and more to do with foreign imaginings of it' (Ibid., p. 318). On the other hand there are those programmes and formats whose British origins are not noticeable to the audience at all. For all intents and purposes these are locally produced programmes. In between lie the vast majority of British programmes with a less certain international appeal – factual programmes and contemporary fiction that deal with a broad range of social, political and cultural issues aimed at a broad mix of different interests in Britain.

For policy-makers there is therefore a tension. On the one hand there is the economic desire to promote the 'British' television brand as part of the 'creative industries' by increasing exports and attracting inward investment. On the other there is the cultural objective of promoting a distinctive national broadcasting landscape that serves socially diverse and multicultural British audiences as a point of cultural identification and allegiance. These conflicting aims are complicated by the dislocation of older forms of national identity and historical 'securities' and their replacement by new manifold allegiances drawn from a range of local and global movements (see Hall, 1992, p. 274; O'Sullivan et al., 1998, p. 282).

Historically, the origins of television are national, starting with the allocation of frequencies and extending to the establishment of the first broadcasting organisations. In Britain the concept of nation and national identity was linked to public service broadcasting from the beginning, and the BBC, as the premier public broadcaster, has always underlined its cultural contribution to the nation. With language as a unifying factor, radio and later television contributed towards the symbolic representation of what it meant to be British through the broadcast of national events, news and programming, which could be enjoyed simultaneously by millions. Yet the concept of a nation state as a specific

historical and cultural formation which promotes sovereignty over a specific territory is relatively new. Nations, according to Anderson, are 'imagined', based
on limited boundaries, sovereignty and a shared sense of community (1983,
pp. 15–16). But nation states are not homogeneous cultural entities.

Indigenous or national culture as a specific form of collective cultural identity is not entirely local, homogeneous or authentic, because it always exhibits
signs of other cultural borrowings, which have become 'naturalised' (Tomlinson,
1991, p. 91; Morley and Robins, 1995, p. 130; Schlesinger, 1987, p. 261).
Schlesinger, for example, reminds us that national identities are contested and
constructed over time and space by the 'continual selective reconstitution of
"traditions" and of "social memory"' (1987, p. 261). Ang also argues that
national identity is not static, but instead involves 'an intense struggle between
a plurality of cultural groupings and interests inside a nation', rendering it 'a
dynamic, conflictual, unstable and impure phenomenon' (Ang, 1996, p. 144;
also Hall, 1992, p. 297). Cultural identity, which is not synonymous with national
identity, shifts around difference from others, and involves multiple identifications based on gender, age, sexuality, class, ethnicity, religion, political position
and nationality, which themselves are unstable and may cut across national
boundaries (see Barker, 1997, p. 194). British identity is not fixed either, but
multiple and changing, involving a mixture of attitudes, beliefs and influences
which contribute to the development of hybrid identities (see Barker, 1999,
p. 85; Sinclair and Cunningham, 2000, p. 17).

Reflecting this diversity, regional and later multicultural differences have been
addressed in British broadcasting to various degrees, acknowledging that Britain
itself has changed. Regionalism was accommodated with the establishment of
regionally based ITV in 1955, but has suffered as ITV has consolidated from a
network of fifteen regional companies to one dominated by two companies,
Granada and Carlton, which announced in 2002 that they too would merge.
Channel Four from its inception in 1982 has been required to serve those minority audiences not adequately served by other broadcasters, but this aim has
arguably become less prominent since the early 1990s when the publicly owned
corporation became responsible for selling its own advertising airtime and commercial priorities become more prominent. In the meantime a huge variety of
satellite and cable channels have been established that cater for particular sec-
tional or niche interests – in film, news, music, sport, children's and lifestyle
programming, home shopping, documentaries, religion, 'adult' content, and
channels catering for women and ethnic minorities.

However, this diversity in terms of audience segmentation and content belies
consolidation at a structural level. Even if most television is still targeted at audiences within specific national boundaries, in terms of ownership it is becoming

increasingly transnational (News Corporation, RTL Group, NBC Universal, Viacom, Disney) with potentially profound cultural and political consequences.

Industry consolidation, and the removal of foreign ownership rules for commercial terrestrial television in Britain, for example, raises questions about what type of programming is likely to be made for diverse British audiences in future. As we have seen, globalisation implies the global production of the local and the localisation of the global. The integration of British television into a more commercial globalised television economy through ownership suggests increased use of imports and imported formats within the British market and further hybridisation. The drive for greater economic efficiency also suggests greater concentration on the creation of fiction and entertainment formats that can be marketed to a wider international audience, perhaps at the expense of less profitable and more locally oriented content. Issues of identity are therefore blurred in this intersection of domestic priorities and the need to satisfy diverse domestic audiences on the one hand and the economic imperatives and strategies of transnational companies on the other.

Mid-range approaches and national markets

There are no audience studies of foreign audience responses to British programmes, possibly because British programming has not played a marked role in most markets, unlike *Dallas* (Ang, 1985; Liebes and Katz, 1993) or the Australian soap *Neighbours* in Britain itself (Gillespie, 1995). Even if such studies existed, their compact nature and focus on particular programmes make it difficult to make extrapolations and generalisations at a broader level (see Schiller, 1991, p. 24). To capture the impact of British programmes one has to look at factors other than those covered by audience analysis (see Cunningham and Jacka, 1996, p. 24). Collecting statistical information on the volume of acquisitions, and the strength of particular forms, like US or even British drama, is useful, but such analysis is often limited to one- or two-week samples (see Buonanno, 2000, p. 22; De Bens and de Smaele, 2001; Varis, 1984). Such information may also appear divorced from local conditions and cultural specificities, which help to explain why particular programmes have been acquired and how they fit into a particular television landscape.

Attributing global success to the universal appeal of particular programmes such as American fiction ignores the extent to which the presence of programming is also affected by sheer availability in the marketplace and promotion (see Cunningham and Jacka, 1997, p. 300; Tomlinson, 1991, p. 53).[9] Britain's success as a television exporter between the periphery and the centre can be attributed partially to sheer availability in the marketplace and partially to British programming's substitutability for American programming. But it is also affected by other locally embedded practices and domestic rituals, such as the rhythms of every-day life, scheduling and promotion or the lack of it, rather than simply its universal appeal. This is what Moran calls national television culture (1998, p. 8).

British programmes and other imports are inserted into a continuous flow of programmes, advertisements, idents and promos, targeted at specific local audiences (Williams, 1974). In spite of claims about globalising processes and the reduction of difference, considerable differences do still exist between national television cultures. In spite of the American influence on formats and scheduling routines, there are local variations in the types of programming shown, the mix of programming on offer, the length of programmes, how foreign imports are adapted (dubbing versus subtitling), and where programmes are placed in the schedule. There are also variations in the timing of significant blocks such as prime time. These traditions are slow to change, and often reflect different cultural practices. To the practical realities of scheduling and promotion one can also add culturally specific and familiar forms of storytelling and routines, which provide 'ontological security' and a framework for understanding the new and unfamiliar (Silverstone, 1994; Tomlinson, 1991, p. 85). Industrial, institutional and cultural conditions peculiar to each territory and the way life is lived and how television is presented to the public therefore affect the circulation of overseas programming even before issues of audience reception and how the audience is constituted can be considered.

But where does this leave the international circulation of British television? Neither cultural imperialism nor globalisation theory can adequately explain the international circulation of British television. The first overplays the economic dimension and too easily 'lumps' Britain together with an overbearing US without adequately explaining the complex relationship between the two. The second tends to underestimate the persistence of the nation state, not only as a political form and cultural and economic entity, but also as the key market for television programmes (see Golding and Harris, 1997, p. 8).

Cunningham and Jacka in their study of Australian television exports point to a form of 'middle range research', that lies between the 'total' explanations of political-economy or institutional analysis and a narrow 'micro-situational' audience approach informed by ethnography (1996, p. 22). This combines industry and cultural analysis with analysis of the reception of programmes through the television systems and cultures of individual territories. This approach not only takes account of the complex characteristics that define different television cultures and their receptiveness to foreign programmes, but also looks at the professional practices and gatekeeper role of buyers and television executives, who are making decisions based on their understanding of domestic audiences, channel requirements, scheduling practices and the prevailing television environment. A shift down to a mid-range level of analysis allows examination of different circumstances in different countries instead of seeking to find generalised global explanations based on universal appeal (Sinclair, 1996, pp. 53–4).

A word on methodology

For an analysis of British programmes a mid-range analysis on a territory by territory basis is useful because it gives greater insight into the different perceptions of British programming in each country – perceptions that are contingent on the particular historical, structural, cultural and regulatory circumstances of each television system. Analysis on a nation by nation basis is also necessary, because programmes and formats are still marketed overwhelmingly to national markets. Within the context of national markets, a mid-range approach allows us therefore to look at how programmes and formats are chosen; who is involved in the selection process; the cultural and regulatory factors that militate for or against selection; and the role of acquisitions in schedules through the eyes of the 'primary audience' of television executives.

For this study, semi-structured face-to-face interviews were first undertaken with executives in British companies to identify buyer contacts, background information on how programmes are traded, and perceptions of British export performance and how this related to government policy initiatives. Interviews with senior executives concentrated primarily on strategic concerns. These were supplemented with shorter telephone interviews with junior sales executives, who provided additional background information on specific territories and further overseas contacts. This occurred alongside the examination of policy documents, government and industry statements, import/export statistics, company reports and secondary sources in the trade press and on industry web sites. Interviewees in Britain were drawn mostly from among the membership of the British Television Distributors' Association (BTDA) and reflected Britain's strengths in drama, factual programming, children's television and formats. Interviews took place with executives from larger broadcaster-affiliated sales organisations (BBC Worldwide, Granada International, Carlton International Media, Channel Four International), as well as from independent distributors and producers (Chrysalis Distribution, Celador, Endemol Entertainment UK, Entertainment Rights, HIT Entertainment, RDF Media, Wall to Wall Television).[10]

Based on contacts and information provided by British interviewees, face-to-face interviews and a smaller number of telephone interviews were arranged, conducted and transcribed between September 2001 and September 2002 in Britain's most important markets in the USA (nineteen interviews) and Western Europe (Germany, France, Italy, Spain, Italy, Netherlands and Sweden – sixty-two interviews). In the case of non-English-speaking territories in the Asia

Pacific region (China, Japan, Hong Kong, South Korea), it proved unfeasible to conduct telephone interviews because sales in these territories often take place through local agents. Instead I attended two seminars held by the BTDA in November and December 2002 on South-East Asia and Japan respectively. These were supplemented by telephone interviews between March and August 2003 with sales executives responsible for selling to these countries.

Respondents were drawn from both public service and commercial broadcasting organisations, and from mainstream and specialist channels. In the case of formats some interviews took place with production companies that acquire formats. When it became apparent that interviews with the US networks about formats would not be possible, an interview was conducted with a representative from the American William Morris Agency in London, which has acted on behalf of British interests for many of the recent format sales to the US networks. Interviews were also undertaken with representatives of British companies based in America (the BBC Sales Company, BBC America, Granada Entertainment USA and Carlton America).

Buyer interviews were structured to the extent that the same basic themes were introduced, but questions were left purposefully open-ended to allow respondents to develop their own line of thought. In addition to background information on individual channels and markets, the interviews sought information on the process of acquisition, the type and amount of programming acquired, why it was acquired and how it was promoted and used in the schedule. Buyers were asked about the factors that influenced their decisions to buy or not to buy, and the extent to which British content met or failed to meet their specific requirements. Acquisitions of British programming and formats were compared with other foreign sources, and trends in acquisitions were pursued in relation to levels of domestic programming and the growing importance of formats. The line of questioning was adapted in each interview to reflect the nature of involvement with British programming in terms of genre, off-the-shelf acquisitions, formats, pre-sales and co-productions. Although this type of material is coloured by personal experiences, there are benefits because themes and ideas emerge, which can be followed up with documentary evidence and other interviews. Alongside an examination of policy debates, the culturally specific factors, which affect acceptance of television imports, can be assessed to address the extent of British television's international presence and the factors that either promote or inhibit that presence.

Notes

1. US television exports only took off in the late 1950s because productions were not recorded before this time (Tunstall, 1977, p. 105).

2. Now known as the Motion Picture Association of America (MPAA).

3. The antitrust exemption was lifted in 1977 (Renaud and Litman, 1985, p. 248).

4. In developing countries, economic capital allows a few to access satellite channels. Cultural capital refers to the education, language, employment and travel opportunities which give the elite preferential access to programming originated overseas (Bourdieu, 1984, cited in Straubhaar, 2000, p. 200).

5. For example, Silj (1988, pp. 36–8; also Rogers and Antola, 1985, p. 30) relates how *Dallas* failed in Peru, because of strong competition from local programming. Yet it succeeded in Algeria not only because of a lack of local competition but because Algerian audiences found that the series' depiction of extended family life under one roof corresponded in some ways to their own cultural experience.

6. However, research on European fiction imports has found that channels rely on either domestic fiction or American imports with limited exchanges of programming between European countries (De Bens and de Smaele, 2001). This suggests that cultural and language differences play a greater role in Europe, a region comprising many geographically proximate single-language markets rather than a cultural-linguistic market.

7. *CSI* is produced by the Canadian Alliance Atlantis entertainment group for the American network, CBS.

8. The European Commission's report on the implementation of the *Television Without Frontiers Directive* in 1999 and 2000, established that 68.8 per cent of BBC 1, BBC 2, ITV, Channel Four and Channel Five transmissions were European in 2000 (excluding news, sport, games, advertising, teletext and teleshopping) (EC, 2002, p. 21). These channels had an 83.5 per cent audience share in 2000.

9. For example, Tomlinson gives the example of Charlie Chaplin, who is known worldwide because his films were distributed worldwide, not simply because he had universal appeal (Tomlinson, 1991, p. 53). Similarly Sinclair, Cunningham and Jacka draw attention to the fact that the international success or failure of the US drama serial *Dallas* in different markets was attributable to scheduling, as much as its universality or primordiality (1996, p. 17).

10. A full listing of those contacted both in Britain and overseas can be found in the acknowledgments section of this volume.

2

Process and Product – The Global Trade in Television Programmes

---

The previous chapter contextualised British television's international presence in respect of trade flows and cross-cultural exchange with reference to debates on cultural imperialism and globalisation. But how does the trade in television programmes function in practice? What are the key trends and where is Britain positioned in a market where sales of completed programming are becoming less important than the ability to fund programming from a variety of sources? This chapter starts with an overview of the characteristics that differentiate the trade in television programmes from other products before considering how that trade has changed as a result of technological advances and the liberalisation of television markets. It then examines how the market functions, the role of buyers, the types of programmes sold and the different ways of funding or selling programming internationally. The previous chapter considered the concerns associated with the US dominance of television trade. This chapter briefly considers some of the economic reasons behind America's success before an analysis of the trends suggested by data collected by the British Television Distributors' Association (BTDA) on British television export revenues between 1998 and 2003.

The nature of television trade

Television programmes and film with their distinctive cultural dimension are not like other products, and Hoskins, McFadyen and Finn draw attention to three attributes that make them different (1997, p. 4). First, enjoyment of a television programme or film does not reduce its enjoyment by others. This affects the prices of programmes, because although the initial cost of producing a programme is high (and may not be covered by the primary broadcast licence), the cost of duplicating a programme for other markets is low. This allows different prices, which are lower then the original cost of production, to be charged in different territories and for different outlets according to what the buyer can afford to pay (Wildman and Siwek, 1988, pp. 3–4). The low price of acquiring a programme as opposed to producing it makes acquisitions economically attractive, allowing broadcasters to subsidise more costly domestic productions and retain audiences at lower cost. In 2001, for example, the average cost per hour of producing drama on the five British terrestrial channels was £344,000 (ITC, 2002a, app. 1, p. 18). This compares with costs of $20,000–100,000 per hour for off-the-shelf acquisitions (*C21*, 2003).

However, the attractiveness and price of an overseas programme purchase is also affected by what Hoskins and Mirus call 'cultural discount', the second characteristic of the trade in television programmes. This is where a programme 'rooted in one culture' will be less appealing elsewhere if 'viewers find it diffi-cult to identify with the style, values, beliefs, institutions and behavioural patterns of the material in question' (1988, p. 500). This cultural discount is likely to be exacerbated by language differences. For example, British, Aus-tralian and American markets are highly resistant to subtitled or dubbed programming because audiences are 'used' to English-language imports and domestic productions. In other non-English-speaking territories, subtitled or dubbed programmes are acceptable, but are not usually as popular as indige-nous programming. Other factors which add to cultural discount include pacing, dress, the foreign 'look' of casts, body language, humour, settings and unfamil-iar forms of storytelling.

Finally Hoskins, McFadyen and Finn refer to the 'external benefits' of tele-vision programmes which, like cultural discount, act as a brake on imports (1997). In theory, it would make economic sense for smaller and/or less wealthy countries to buy in all their television programmes cheaply from larger, richer countries, which can afford to invest in higher 'quality' productions and sell below the cost of production. This does not happen because the 'external ben-efits' of television, including its role in informing, entertaining and educating the public about local issues, culture and institutions, militate against complete reliance on imports. This contribution to national culture is recognised by national governments and supra-national institutions such as the European Union in the use of subsidies and quotas aimed at enhancing domestic pro-duction or stemming imports (Hoskins, Mirus and Rozeboom, 1989, pp. 71–2).

The transformation of the audiovisual landscape and the growth in television trade

How did the trade in television programming come about? The 1950s marked the beginning of the first significant period of television trade, when exporters, primarily from the US, sold recorded programming to emerging television systems worldwide. Demand for imports grew throughout the 1960s because, having introduced television and made a large capital investment, countries needed programming to fill their schedules (Tunstall, 1977). This provided opportunities for American producers, where television was more established, and the US was tentatively estimated to be exporting between 100,000 and 200,000 hours of predominantly entertainment programming in 1973 with two-thirds of US revenues generated in Canada, Australia, Japan and Britain (Nordenstreng and Varis, 1974, p. 32). British broadcasters were exporting 30,000 hours in 1973 in second place after the US (Ibid., p. 33). By 1983, with television established in most markets, it was estimated that one-third of global programming time was devoted to imports (Varis, 1984, p. 147). However, by the mid-1980s it was also shown that the proportion of foreign programmes had declined in *some* countries as maturing markets began to reduce their reliance on American imports (Varis, 1984; Varis, 1985, p. 53).

The second significant expansion of television trade took place from the mid-1980s onwards as a combination of cable and satellite distribution, marketisation and deregulation opened up a range of previously heavily regulated television markets, particularly in Western Europe and Asia. This led to an influx of new commercially funded channels, which needed programming to fill their round-the-clock schedules. Between 1987 and 1991 the average number of channels with national reach in the hundred largest markets increased from 3.54 to 5.21 (a 47 per cent increase) (Hoskins, McFadyen and Finn, 1997, p. 13). This expansion continued and by 2002 an estimated 1,500 channels were circulating within Western Europe alone, compared to only forty-seven in 1989 (Reding, 2002, p. 5).

Satellites promised abundance because they overcame the technical limitations of free-to-air transmission, allowing more channels. They also offered opportunities for the creation of transnational markets because satellite footprints do not respect national boundaries and there is significant overspill. In fact, transnational channels such as SuperChannel, broadcasting in English in Europe in the 1980s, proved much less successful than new nationally targeted commercial channels that met the needs and expectations of distinctive national audiences (Collins, 1989; Tracey, 1988, p. 16). But the arrival of satellites did make it difficult to justify the tight regulatory regimes that had favoured a limited number of nationally based public or state broadcasters. Countries like Sweden and Germany legislated to allow domestic commercial television rather than have this imposed from outside their borders by satellite with the possible loss of jobs, advertising revenues and control. In Asia, governments sought to limit the influence of Western channels through a mixture of restrictive measures (bans on satellite equipment, censorship, quotas) and active support for local production (Chadha and Kavoori, 2000). Regulatory policies, which had been based on the scarcity of frequencies, strict regulation of content and restrictions on ownership, were undermined by technologies, which promised abundance.

The falling away of technological barriers that made an increase in channels possible was also accompanied by an ideological shift in favour of market-led solutions for the regulation of television and the relaxation of public interest requirements (Dahlgren, 2000, p. 25; Murdock and Golding, 2001, pp. 113–14). In Western Europe, market liberalisation in the 1980s not only broke up the old public service dominance in television, but also led to a prioritisation of commercial principles and commercial funding, and a relaxation of rules relating to content and the ownership of commercial channels. In Asia, where media were subject to strict state control in many countries, the commercial drive for audience and profit maximisation served to undermine structures based on a limited number of services and a high degree of state censorship (Cunningham and Jacka, 1996, p. 29). This ideological shift went hand in hand with broader social changes, which emphasised the needs of the individual and consumption rather than the community and society-led principles that underpinned British and Western European notions of public service broadcasting (Dahlgren, 2000).

The new commercial stations were less concerned with schedules comprising a range of output reflecting the public interest or material that served political or state objectives than with attracting subscribers or large audiences, which could be sold to advertisers. Their arrival automatically led to an increase in imports because there was insufficient domestic production of high-cost fiction, feature films and entertainment programmes that were likely to generate new audiences and profits quickly (Wildman and Siwek, 1987, p. 73). Increases in transmission times by both public and commercial stations served to heighten demand for programming. By 1992 it was estimated that the expansion of channels in seventy-five countries had lead to a 40 per cent increase in the hours of weekly programme transmissions (Hoskins, McFadyen and Finn, 1997, p. 14).

Yet the new commercial channels were lean organisations. Unlike their state-owned or public service predecessors they did not have access to large in-house production infrastructures or the means to support them. Moreover, the independent production sector in many countries was often small and fragmented because television production had been dominated by vertically integrated public or state-owned broadcasters. The new stations had to look beyond their borders, to North American, British, Australian, Hong Kong and Latin American suppliers to secure the volume needed to fill their schedules cost effectively. Latin American producers found a market for their long-running *telenovelas* in Southern and Eastern Europe (Biltereyst and Meers, 2000). Australian producers found markets for long-running serials (*Neighbours, The Flying*

Doctors, *Home and Away*) in some Northern European markets, but particularly in Britain (Cunningham and Jacka, 1996). This expansion in television transmissions also benefited British exporters. Even if imports were not always the most popular programming in the schedule, they were cost effective in achieving a balance between programming costs and revenues from advertising and subscription.

However, as Chapter 1 indicated, as systems mature there tends to be a growth in domestic content because this has greater resonance with local audiences and serves to differentiate outlets from rival offerings. Writing in 1977, de Sola Pool referred to the changing flows of television, where imports are highest in the earliest stages of development. Imports remain high from the larger producing nations (the US, Britain and Japan) for the most costly programming, which territories are unable to produce in quantity themselves – notably feature films, animation, some long-running fiction and the most expensive factual programming. However, over time imports have a tendency to shift to the margins of schedules on the highest-paying mainstream channels or are limited to lower-rating niche outlets in the secondary cable and satellite sector, which pay less (see Kapner, 2003; Morley and Robins, 1989; Rouse, 2001; Tracey, 1988).

Two two-week surveys undertaken in 1988 and 1997, although limited in scope, show how the share of US series and films increased at the expense of domestic fiction on thirty-six mainstream channels in six Western European countries as transmission times increased. The share of US series/serials grew from 36 per cent to 64 per cent, while the share of national series/serials declined from 37 per cent in 1988 to 20 per cent in 1997. However, while US series/serials dominated overall with a 64 per cent share in 1997, this did not apply to peak time, when domestic series/serials achieved a 44 per cent share, compared to 39 per cent for US imports (De Bens and de Smaele, 2001, pp. 61–4). The growing primacy of domestic fiction at prime time has also been found in similar week-long surveys undertaken by the Eurofiction project. A Eurofiction survey (12–18 March 2000) of mainstream channels found that domestic fiction accounted for 47 per cent of British fiction transmissions, 36 per cent in Germany, 25 per cent in France, 19 per cent in Italy and 20 per cent in Spain. These levels rose in peak time to 51 per cent in Britain, 56 per cent in Germany, 75 per cent in France, 43 per cent in Italy and 51 per cent in Spain (EAO, 2001a). Elsewhere a decline in the volume of US exports has been detected. Based on a sample of 101 European television networks the hours of transmitted US fiction imports (including films and repeats) fell for the first time since 1994 from 222,884 hours in 1999 to 213,928 hours in 2000 (68.7 per cent of all fiction imports) (EAO, 2002).

What this cycle of dependence followed by increasing levels of domestic production suggests is that exporters need to adopt other strategies than simply selling finished programmes, which are subject to 'cultural discount' against local productions and low prices in an oversupplied marketplace. One solution to this quandary is to sell formats and produce them locally in overseas markets. For example, the Australian production company Grundy (now part of Fremantle-Media) recreated local versions of the Australian soap *The Restless Years* for commercial channel RTL 4 in the Netherlands and RTL in Germany in the early 1990s, when these countries had little experience in the production of long-running series (Moran, 1998), in a strategy dubbed 'parochial internationalism' (Cunningham and Jacka, 1996, p. 82). However, format sales and local production overseas contribute rather less to the financial well-being of the exporter's production sector as opposed to the local market where the format has been sold. Other forms of international partnership – notably co-production funding and pre-sales – have a more direct financial impact on the exporter's domestic production industry. As we will see, co-production finance and pre-sales have become increasingly important in an environment where the funding of programming in the domestic marketplace has become more difficult.

How are programmes traded?
The markets

> ... we found a marketing environment that charitably could only be described as chaotic, unruly, and unpredictable, with no one really in charge and no one knowing, for example, why certain programs sell one year and do not move off the shelves the next. (Cantor and Cantor, 1986, p. 514)

This description of how programmes are traded reflects the charged atmosphere of the regular international markets, where new programmes and formats are launched. For British distributors, the key markets are MIP-TV held in March/April and MIPCOM, held in October. Both take place in Cannes, France. MIP-TV was created in 1963 and attracted 10,217 participants in 2002. It is preceded by MIPDOC, launched in 1997 as a specialist event for factual programming, which attracted 577 participants in 2002. In 2003, MIP-TV was held simultaneously with MILIA, a market dedicated to digital content and interactive entertainment. MIPCOM was created in 1984 to cater for the emerging video, cable and satellite markets, but now attracts the same type of companies as MIP-TV. In 2002, it had 10,294 participants. It is preceded by MIPCOM Junior, a series of screenings for children's and youth programmes, which attracted 689 participants in 2001.

The markets represent only one aspect of programme purchasing and co-production activity. They provide an opportunity for buyers to screen programmes, and an opportunity for sales executives to meet buyers, with whom they are in telephone and email contact throughout the year. The markets are also a chance to strengthen relationships, particularly in the co-production arena. However, detailed negotiations for these usually take place away from the 'chaotic' environment of the larger events. Alongside the main markets there are specialist festivals for documentary programming (the Jackson Hole Wildlife Film Festival, Sunny Side of the Doc), children's programming (Annecy Animation Festival, Cartoon Forum) and formats (Discop). These are less concerned with sales of completed programmes and more to do with locating funding for new projects.

However, there are signs that too many markets emerged in the 1990s. NATPE, held every January in the US, began as a market for US buyers, but in the 1980s became more internationally focused as overseas distributors sought to access the burgeoning US cable market (Schlesinger, 1986, p. 284). However, a global downturn in advertising revenues and consolidation in the US marketplace resulted in under-attendance in 2002. Instead, some British exporters have found it more useful to pursue US co-production opportunities directly through dedicated sales trips, the use of talent agencies, and the establishment of offices in the US (Winstone, 2003, pp. 16–17). MIP Asia was launched in December 1994 as a result of a booming market in the Far East, but by 2002 had disappeared to be replaced by the lower key Asia Forum. The London Screenings were last held in November 1999, and the specialist showcases held by ITV companies in the 1980s no longer take place. The one exception to this trend is the BBC Showcase held every January for over 400 of BBC Worldwide's most valued co-production partners and buyers.

The role of buyers

The key relationship for those wishing to sell programmes overseas is with the television buyer. The process relies heavily on frequent contact, personal relationships and trust, with sales executives visiting the major territories in Europe, North America and Australasia on a regular basis. Sales executives are usually responsible for several territories and, depending on the size and range of the catalogue, may specialise in genres – fiction, factual or children's programming. In smaller, more distant and less financially rewarding markets, such as the Middle East, Africa, the Far East and Latin America, many but the largest distributors employ local agents to keep costs down. Agents may sometimes also be used in territories, where a more permanent presence is deemed desirable, such as France (Howton, 2001), or where the complicated internal politics and rapidly changing personnel within broadcasting organisations, such as public broadcaster RAI in Italy, require it (Maraschi, 2002). The larger broadcaster- distributors, BBC Worldwide, Carlton International and Granada, pursue North

American sales and co-productions from offices in the US. BBC Worldwide has the most extensive international network with local offices in Hong Kong, Sydney, New York, Los Angeles, Washington, Paris, Toronto, Berlin, Tokyo, Singapore, New Delhi and Dubai. The rise in factual co-productions and direct commissions in the US has resulted in a small number of independent producers establishing offices on the East Coast in order to maintain direct contact with American factual outlets, Discovery Networks, National Geographic and PBS.

Within the larger broadcasting organisations, acquisitions departments often have a lower, peripheral status, because the kudos of an organisation derives from its original productions rather than imports, which occupy a less prominent position in the schedules (Huisman, 2002; Mulder, 2002; Tunstall, 1977, p. 275). In the case of an acquisition of a completed programme, the needs of the audience may not be primary if the programme is destined for an off-peak slot. For co-productions and pre-sales of high-profile programming the relationship is more complex, with the buyer risking financial commitment without seeing the final product and without knowing how the programme has performed in other markets. In this case decisions are made on the basis of trust, an assessment of scripts or treatments, casting, the reputation of producers, scriptwriters and directors, or a short trailer in the case of animation (Poussier, 2002). But higher levels of risk and financial commitment are often reflected in better slots and promotion, which are important for tapping into additional revenue streams from video and, in the case of children's programming, consumer products.

In the US the decision to buy off-the-shelf programming or become involved in co-production financing is often made by the same executives, who control large budgets and exercise a substantial degree of creative involvement in respect of treatments, scripts, casting and the production team. Purchases in the rest of the world are less likely to involve creative input, as they are usually straight sales of completed product. In the larger European territories, different departments will handle fiction co-productions as opposed to acquisitions. While some buyers are involved purely in acquisitions, others have broader editorial and commissioning responsibilities for specific slots or strands. Moreover, while some are closely involved in the business affairs aspects of acquisitions, others simply research, screen and select programmes, leaving negotiations about prices to separate business affairs or acquisitions departments. This is the case with public broadcasters in the Netherlands (NOS),[1] Germany (ZDF, WDR) and Sweden (SVT). At public broadcaster RAI in Italy, there is a central acquisitions department, Rai Cinema, responsible for acquiring fiction and some animation for all three RAI channels. Rai Cinema acts as a filter, making the first selections and negotiating on behalf of the channels (Pugnetti, 2002). However, drama co-productions are channelled through a separate department, Rai

Fiction, and acquisitions and pre-sales of factual programming take place directly with individual channels. At public broadcaster ARD in Germany, packages of feature films, usually from the US, are acquired centrally through a separate subsidiary, Degeto, but regionally based ARD affiliates acquire small amounts of factual, children's and fiction programming primarily for the regional channels, which are nationally available on satellite and cable. There are in fact large variations between channels and even within channels for accessing the right person, and it is the sales executive's responsibility to establish a route to those who have the power to make decisions.

Brochures, the trade press, screening tapes and web sites can tell a buyer about particular programmes, but it is a sales executive's job to nurture these relationships through regular contact and information about impending projects, which allow buyers to plan in advance. Sometimes large packages of programmes, particularly from the US, are acquired largely unscreened in order to acquire a limited number of the most highly sought after series and feature films, but the trend towards domestic production by mainstream channels in Europe has led to more 'cherry-picking' and a decline in volume output deals with US suppliers (Jenkinson, 2002; Pugnetti, 2002; Ramos, 2002). Other broadcasters with fewer slots will screen every potential purchase with great care and never buy anything without seeing it first. For example, buyers at public broadcaster NOS in the Netherlands are renowned for assiduous research, and will seek information about forthcoming British productions even before a decision to commission has taken place. There are separate programme buyers for each of the nine main affiliates contributing to NOS' three channels, and several (including NPS, VPRO, Vara and KRO) employ stringers in Britain to ascertain what is in production ahead of both their commercial competitors and competitors within NOS. By contrast, the screening of all British programmes for the Dutch HMG group (comprising three commercial channels RTL4, RTL5, Yorin) takes place through one consultant based in London.

For British exporters the greatest financial rewards come from selling to the longer-established national terrestrial networks that still have access to the largest audiences and revenues. However, as we have seen, these outlets are more likely to be focused on domestic programming, meaning fewer available slots in attractive time periods. The secondary market of general and niche channels distributed via cable and satellite, with the exception of premium film services, to which Britain has little to contribute, offer an alternative window. But these tend to be less attractive, because they have smaller audiences, and less money to spend. For children's animation, which is heavily reliant on ancillary revenues from product licensing, access to channels with significant reach is essential, and this makes some secondary outlets unattractive. However, in cases where some types of programming have almost disappeared from the mainstream channels, satellite channels may be the only buyers. For example, children's and factual programming is largely the preserve of the cable sector in the US rather than the mainstream networks. In Germany, specialist children's channels (KiKa, SuperRTL), which are widely available on cable, have come to dominate children's television. There is also a preference among sellers for sales to national rather than transnational outlets because the potential revenues from individual territories are greater than selling rights on a pan-regional basis to channels that may have quite low audiences (Redpath, 2002).

While domestic productions are increasingly pre-tested, this is not usually the case for acquisitions, because they are rarely the flagships of mainstream schedules. Generally most choices come down to the buyer's experience and intuition. Programmes have to appeal to buyers in their role as gatekeepers, making decisions based variously on assumptions about what their audiences want, their experience of what has worked before, the priorities of their network, their assessment of competing networks, and the target audience for a particular slot. Their decisions will also be affected by the amount of programming in stock, the amount of advertising the programme is likely to attract, and how an acquisition relates to other programmes in the schedule. Decisions are subjective and according to one American buyer are made 'without the benefit of a focus group or a committee' (Eaton, 2002).

In the case of mainstream commercial channels, decisions usually boil down to hard-nosed commercial choices and the need to acquire programming that will deliver audience ratings reliably at a competitive price. Although it is not always the most popular programming, American fiction provides that reliability, recouping the cost of acquisition in commercial revenues. However, among European and North American buyers, for example, there are clear distinctions between public broadcasters and commercial channels. Buyers from the commercial mainstream networks place a much stronger emphasis on the need to locate and purchase programmes that will beat the competition in particular time slots (Grignaffini and Stewart, 2002; Huhn, 2002; Lidén, 2002). A buyer's success is linked to their ability to choose programmes that will achieve good ratings, regardless of their own personal preferences. The connection between the ratings success of a particular programme and its ability to attract advertising revenue is very clear.

By contrast, some buyers from European public service networks, but not all, emphasise their preference for quality, variety and even personal preference above ratings, which leads them to choose from a wider range of programming sources, including more European sources. This tendency is strongest at those public service stations that are less reliant on advertising revenue (NOS in the

Netherlands, SVT in Sweden, BR, WDR and ZDF in Germany). Some buyers at public broadcasters in the Netherlands and Sweden emphasise the importance of experimentation and buying certain programmes on principle because they fit their perception of the public service mission, even if there is no identifiable slot (Kjellberg, 2002; Windhorst, 2002). Those public service buyers who come closest to their commercial counterparts in prioritising ratings success over public service considerations are primarily those who acquire US fiction (but not necessarily factual programming) for stations that are highly or predominantly dependent on advertising revenues (France 2 and France 3, RAI in Italy; RTVE in Spain; CCTV in China).

What kind of programmes are sold?

It has already been noted that the vast majority of television programmes are inherently local in flavour, and that audiences prefer local programmes if these are available (Sinclair, Jacka and Cunningham, 1996, p. 10; Tracey, 1988, pp. 16–18; Wildman and Siwek, 1988, pp. 41–4). But countries will import or co-produce programming that they cannot afford to make in volume themselves – drama, animation and more costly natural history and science programmes. News programmes,[2] current affairs, sport (except for international events) and factual programming about local issues have little appeal to overseas audiences and are subject to high cultural discount. Locally produced game shows, reality programmes and lifestyle shows also have limited international potential, although the formats on which these programmes are based may be very exportable indeed.

It has been estimated that between 10 and 25 per cent of British programmes have potential in overseas markets (David Graham & Associates [DGA], 2000, p. 40; Marlow, 2003a, p. 23). The vast majority of exportable drama, factual output and children's programming is commissioned by mainstream terrestrial players (BBC, ITV, Channel Four), because British-based satellite channels tend to be more reliant on imports, secondary British rights and cheaper domestic formats.[3] So what type of programmes form the core of international trade?

Fiction is the most heavily traded genre, and the US, the world's largest and importantly richest market, dominates the trade in fiction. This is because drama in volume with high production values requires a large and sufficiently wealthy population to support the advertising and subscription base necessary to fund it (Alvarado, 2000). British research found that fiction accounted for two-thirds of the volume of traded programmes in 1996–7, broken down into drama (37 per cent),[4] feature films (23 per cent) and television movies (6 per cent) (DCMS, 1999b, p. 35). In 1996–7 the US was estimated to enjoy a 72 per cent share of the trade in drama, 63 per cent in film, and an 81 per cent share in TV movies (Ibid., p. 34). The most desirable imports have traditionally been visually oriented films, television movies and series focusing on action adventure, crime and fantasy, which appear to be less demanding of cultural capital and language than more culturally specific situation comedies and soap operas, which suffer from a higher cultural discount (see Chapman, 1987, pp. 16–17; Hoskins, McFadyen and Finn, 1997, p. 119; Straubhaar, 2000, p. 206).

Drama is also valuable to British exporters. Yet Britain's share by volume of the drama (8 per cent), film (12 per cent) and television movie market (6 per cent), while more than twice that of its nearest rivals in Australia, France, Canada and Germany, lags behind the US (DCMS, 1999b, p. 34). Unable to use recent film releases to drive in other product, and with a domestic scheduling tradition that favours shorter runs (six episodes and less), the British export focus is different. Although there is a tradition of longer-running action adventure series stretching back to the 1960s (*The Avengers*, *The Professionals*), British drama exports from the 1980s onwards tended to focus more heavily on short-run serial thrillers, detective series with self-contained episodes and literary and historical dramas. According to Alvarado there was a conscious decision in the early 1990s by the BBC, for example, to prioritise literary classics (*Lady Chatterley's Lover, Middlemarch, Our Mutual Friend, Vanity Fair* and *Gormenghast*). Many failed to achieve ratings success at home, but sold in the US and fulfilled a public service obligation in respect of 'cultural heritage' (Alvarado, 2000, p. 315). However, the priority of attracting and retaining audiences in a more competitive domestic marketplace in the 1990s led British terrestrial channels to focus on increasing the number of weekly episodes of domestic soaps (*EastEnders, Coronation Street, The Bill, Emmerdale*), whose international appeal is rather limited, because the most valuable international markets produce their own 'soaps'. In respect of fiction there is therefore a marked discrepancy between what works internationally and what works in the domestic marketplace.

Factual programming is a strength of British exporters, because the free-to-air market, based on public service principles, has always supported the production of significant volumes of factual programming. But factual programming only accounted for 8 per cent of global trade by volume in 1996–7 (DCMS, 1999b, p. 35). Britain had an 18 per cent share of this market, after the US with 37 per cent (Ibid., p. 34). Most factual programming is inherently local, and only certain types of programming have international potential – notably natural history, wildlife and science, but also history, archaeology and travel programmes, which do not focus on Britain itself.

Children's programming accounted for 13 per cent of the volume trade in television programmes in 1996–7, comprising largely animation, which is less culturally specific than children's drama (DCMS, 1999b, p. 35). Britain was estimated to have a 4 per cent share of this market behind the US (60 per cent), Japan (6 per cent) – a prolific producer of animation – and Canada (5 per cent), whose animation industry has benefited from government subsidies (Ibid., p. 34). Britain's position may have improved since that time because of the international success of a small number of long-running pre-school series, including *Teletubbies* (Ragdoll/BBC), *Tweenies* (BBC), *The Fimbles* (BBC) and *Bob the Builder* (HIT Entertainment). Animation (*Bob the Builder*) and some character-based pre-school formats (*Teletubbies*) are ideally suited to inter-national exploitation. This is not only because of the ease of local adaptation through dubbing, but also because properties can be repeatedly sold as the tar-get audience of children changes every two years, making the most successful programming a valuable long-term asset. However, the production of new ani-mation is costly compared to the licence fees that can be secured in the marketplace. For example, *Bob the Builder* is reputed to have cost £65,000 for each ten-minute episode, but half-hour animation can be acquired in the major territories of the US, France, Germany, Spain and Italy for as little as $4,000. This has changed the economics of the business, with broadcast sales now regarded as a platform for generating more profitable revenue streams in con-sumer product licensing and video.

The late 1990s saw the resurrection of game-show formats in prime time, with British exporters scoring successes with the quiz shows *Who Wants to Be a Millionaire?* (Celador) and *The Weakest Link* (BBC). These satisfied growing demand internationally for cost-effective domestically produced programmes in prime time, programming defined by Bonner as 'ordinary television', which is rarely imported in its original form (2003). The success of game-show and reality game-show formats such as the Dutch company Endemol's *Big Brother* boosted interest in other format adaptations that focused on 'real' people in artificial situ-ations. These include factual entertainment formats such as *Faking It* (RDF Media), where individuals are coached to pass themselves off as professionals in a job at odds with their own experience, and makeover programmes centred on the home and garden (*Changing Rooms*, *Ground Force* – Endemol UK).

Raising funding in the international market

The small proportion of British programmes with export potential are assessed by distributors, whose role increasingly extends to raising shortfalls in production budgets from distribution advances, pre-sales and co-production finance, rather than simply selling fully-funded completed productions. For programmes with potential in video and consumer products there are ancillary revenues to consider, and the growth in format sales has necessitated greater attention to the possibili-ties of involvement in local adaptations. The growing importance of raising funding for productions in international markets means that distributors are now involved much more in assessing projects at the earliest stages of production.

Programme sales

For undertaking programme sales, distributors charge standard rates of commission to rights holders on gross revenues varying between 25 and 35 per cent for television sales and 20 per cent for video/DVD sales, subject to negotiation. Distribution costs relating to marketing and the cost of duplicating and shipping materials are deducted from gross revenues, as are any clearances for music/footage/stills and payments to talent, unless these have been bought out at the outset. What is left after deductions is referred to as the back end or net receipts, which can be quite low depending on the level of deductions. Typically independent producers making fully-funded programmes for British broadcasters used to receive 30 per cent of the back end, with the commissioning broadcaster receiving up to 70 per cent. However, by investing in their own programmes independent producers could raise their share of back end to 50 or 60 per cent. As we will see in Chapter 3, the limited rewards for independent producers from overseas sales and the perception that broadcasters were abusing their position in the supply market to hold onto rights became hotly disputed issues. This resuted in changes in 2004 that give independent producers a greater share of the financial rewards from international exploitation. Before these changes a typical reward pattern for the sale of a fully-funded British programme overseas, where talent and materials have not been bought out beforehand, might have looked like Table 2.1.

Table 2.1: Reward pattern

	Gross sales price	Benefit (per cent)
Actors	Shared in line with original payment	17
Writer(s)	Shared in line with original payment	5.6
Musician(s)	Shared in line with original payment	
Director	No benefit beyond original contract fee	4
Footage/Photographs/Music	Negotiated separately	various
Distributor	Commission on sale	25–30
	Net Profit	
Broadcaster	Share of back end profits	50–70
Producer	Share of back end profits	30–50

Source: Price, 2002, p. 328.

Programmes are sold to different territories and different outlets or windows within those territories. In most territories the most important outlets are the free-to-air terrestrial channels, followed by cable and satellite channels (which may be categorised as 'premium' or 'basic' depending on the level of subscription charged) and home video/DVD, which is particularly important for children's programmes (Doyle, 2002, p. 84). Windowing involves charging different prices to buyers from different outlets for the same product, with distributors planning the release of material across different windows to maximise revenues. The free-to-air channels with the largest audiences and revenues usually pay the highest prices ahead of cable and satellite outlets, except in the case of feature films, which air first on premium satellite channels ahead of terrestrial transmission. The size, wealth and competitive situation in each territory also affects prices. For example, a small wealthy territory like the Netherlands pays less per hour for television acquisitions than a large wealthy territory like Germany, but considerably more than larger, poorer territories such as India or China.[5] A typical broadcast licence will allow a broadcaster to transmit a programme for a fixed number of runs in a specific territory over a fixed time period.

Distribution advances

If there is a deficit on a production budget a distributor will sometimes offer an advance to partially fund a programme before production begins in order to secure distribution rights (Viljoen, 2002, p. 228). The advance is recouped later from gross sales after deducting the distributor's commission and distribution expenses and ahead of any back end share in profits. For a significant advance, a distributor might receive a share of back end. The risk for the distributor is that the programme will not sell sufficiently to recoup the advance. The risk for the producer is that they will only see a small share of back end after the advance, commission and other costs have been recouped. For the most internationally attractive fiction and factual programmes, British distributors were prepared to invest the following amounts as advances in 2000–01 in return for worldwide rights excluding co-production investment (Phillips, 2000, p. 6):

High-budget natural history series:	£100,000–130,000 per hour
High-budget factual serials:	£35,000–55,000 per hour
Science programmes:	£35,000–70,000 per hour
British TV movies:	£100,000 per hour
Period drama serials:	£65,000–100,000 per hour
Contemporary drama serials:	£40,000–50,000 per hour
Contemporary drama series:	£20,000–35,000 per hour
Situation comedy:	£15,000–20,000 per hour

Pre-sales

Pre-sales involve the purchase of programme rights for a limited period by an overseas broadcaster at the treatment or script and casting stage, and are usually contingent on a firm expression of interest from a British broadcaster (Viljoen, 2002, pp. 178–9). In cash terms these tend to be more valuable than a straight sale, but do not contribute to higher profit margins because the money is needed to fund production. Distributors source funding for pre-sales in return for distribution rights for the remaining territories and a share of net receipts or a finder's fee (Viljoen, 2002). Pre-sales tend to be used in a small number of the more competitive markets in Western Europe, North America and Australia where a broadcaster wants to prevent competitors from acquiring the best programming. They are particularly important for children's animation, and more expensive and prestigious factual and drama productions where budget contributions from British broadcasters are too low to cover costs. For children's animation the budget contribution by the BBC can be as low as 8 per cent or 18–28 per cent in the case of ITV, making pre-sales and co-production finance essential (DCMS, 1999b, p. 25). Unlike co-productions, a pre-sale does not usually involve any editorial contribution by the purchaser, but depending on the level of financial contribution may apply to a wider range of rights (video, licensing). In some cases the buyer may agree to purchase a certain amount of programming in advance based on a minimum spend per year as part of an output deal (Redpath, 2002). In return the buyer gets a first look at new productions, and can negotiate lower prices for a bulk purchase. This reflects the risk taken by the buyer.

Co-productions

Co-production is a much more fluid term and easy to confuse with pre-sales. It can range from co-financing to full co-productions where partners contribute production resources and share the division of labour on a production. Like pre-sales, the contributions are higher than for a straight sale and go towards making the programme, leaving fewer territories for international sales, but this has to be set against obtaining the funding in the first place. Like pre-sales, co-productions are important for children's animation and the most expensive factual and fiction productions.

Most co-productions represent the collaboration of a project-initiating company with a funding and/or facilities partner. Joint ventures in co-production involve longer-term international partnerships with projects submitted to the partners for joint development, thereby reducing the risk of developing a programme with no assured market.

American channels will refer to their involvement in co-productions, when their participation is primarily about substantial cash investment rather than direct involvement in the physical production process. What distinguishes such co-funded productions from pre-sales is that the financial contribution allows extensive editorial and creative involvement. At the very minimum this will be on a consultation basis, but co-funding agreements increasingly include co-producer approvals on script development, casting, the choice of director and writer, rough cuts, and the final version for that territory.

A co-producer will usually acquire all rights in a programme for its home territory. Depending on negotiations and the level of financial commitment it may also secure some overseas distribution rights or a back end share of profits from sales of broadcast and secondary rights in overseas markets (such as publishing and merchandising). For example, in the case of the US, buyers are often assigned North American (including Canada) or western hemisphere (including Latin America) rights for a specified period of at least five years or for the full period of copyright, leaving the rest of the world for further sales.

Only very small proportions of British programmes are co-produced, and these tend to be high-cost drama and factual productions, initiated in Britain. The Eurofiction project established that co-productions only represented 6 per cent of first-run television fiction (totalling 536 episodes) in five European countries in 1999 including Britain. But they did account for 14.6 per cent of total production value (400 million euros), indicating that co-production is used for more costly programmes (Jezequel and Lange, 2000, p. 4). France, Germany and Italy had the highest percentages of co-produced episodes at 17 per cent, 10 per cent, and 7 per cent of first-run fiction respectively, with Britain and Spain trailing at 3 per cent and 0.5 per cent respectively. However, French and German co-productions with same-language smaller neighbours constitute a high proportion of such collaborations (see also De Bens and de Smaele, 2001, p. 69; Buonanno, 1998, p. 18), while British drama co-productions occur predominantly with US partners (see Chapter 6).[6]

The advantages of co-productions include the ability to pool finance, raise budgets, and gain better access to a partner's markets (Hoskins, McFadyen, Finn and Jäckel, 1995, p. 240). Collaboration can help to minimise cultural discount, and the level of commitment to such high-profile projects presupposes a degree of promotion and scheduling which can prove helpful for video/DVD and ancillary rights exploitation. The main drawbacks include the increased financial costs associated with co-ordinating a project involving more than two countries, and the need to compromise resulting in less control and cultural specificity (Ibid., 1995). The need to alter cultural parameters to fit in with others constitutes one of the main limitations of co-productions and for this reason they tend to be focused on a small range of high-cost projects with transnational appeal, which no single territory can afford.

Ancillary/tertiary rights

Revenues can also be obtained from the exploitation of programme-related goods in publishing, video/DVD and from licensed merchandise (toys, games, clothing, food products, online games). However, only a small number of programmes have any value in ancillary markets. Examples include cookery and lifestyle programmes, entertainment formats (*Who Wants to Be a Millionaire?*) and landmark factual series (*Walking with Dinosaurs*).

Ancillary revenue streams from publishing, video and licensed merchandise are especially important for children's television programmes. Here low licence fees in the domestic market have become increasingly predicated on the expectation that production budgets require pre-sales and co-productions in North America and Europe, and that profits will stem from video/DVD and licensed merchandise. However, this is a risky strategy if the programme is not successful on television and fails to function as a platform for promoting other revenue streams. In rare cases the focus of companies has been transformed because of an international hit. For example, HIT Entertainment has built a global consumer products and video business on the basis of in-house hits (*Bob the Builder*) and acquisitions (*Thomas the Tank Engine, Pingu, Barney*) which now outperforms its revenues from television sales (see Chapter 4).

Formats/local production

The sale of formats is quite different from the sale of programmes, based as it is on the sale of a programme concept for production in different territories with local settings, casts, contestants and hosts. Viljoen makes a distinction between 'low-concept' and 'high-concept' formats (2002, p. 79). The latter group includes drama, sitcoms, game shows and 'reality' concepts, which are based on scripts or detailed 'bibles' where the show's narrative or distinctive elements (rules, catchphrases, prizes, sets, artwork, computer graphics) are described in detail for adaptation in other markets. Bibles will also include information on how to make a show, the production process, scheduling and budgetary information (Moran, 1998, p. 14–15), and crucially the mistakes to avoid (Frank, 2001). A bible for a quiz show will contain information on how to select contestants and hosts, the rules of the show, how to deal with the audience, the selection of questions and sets. Low-concept formats include magazine shows, chat shows, cookery shows, and interior decorating and gardening shows, often presenter-led, which have no unique elements, features or structure to distinguish them from other forms of the genre produced around the world. For the most successful formats the returns are considerable. Hat Trick estimated that it generated £1.1 million over five years from sales of its topical news format *Have I Got News for You* to seven countries (Keighron, 2003, p. 14). BBC

Worldwide expected to earn £50 million from format and ancillary sales of *The Weakest Link* (Ibid.).

There are no set ways of selling formats. The simplest deals involve selling the format for a fee based on a percentage of the production budget (5–15 per cent per episode), which will vary according to how many shows the broadcaster agrees to make (Frank, 2001; Jarvis, 2001). Other variables relate to the value of the format in particular markets, the sophistication of the market, the amount of income generated in a particular slot, the contents of a format package (scripts, visuals, clips, music, questions and software), the level of backup provided and market demand (Smith, 2001; Van den bussche, 2001). For a hit show such as *Who Wants to Be a Millionaire?* or *The Weakest Link* the concept of pricing according to budget is not appropriate and broadcasters pay licence fees determined by market demand. In these cases broadcasters are sold complex packages and computer software with little opportunity to deviate from the format in the interests of maintaining control over the brand (Keighron, 2003, p. 18).

In return for committing to a format, the broadcaster gets access to varying amounts of consultancy to guide them through the production process. For increasingly complex 'reality' formats involving 'real' people and prime-time entertainment formats, the value of a show rests on production expertise and know-how rather than the format itself. This has led to a shift where some format owners either end up producing their formats for overseas broadcasters (for example RDF Media's production outpost in the US) or seek to co-produce their formats with local broadcasters (for example BBC Worldwide with *The Weakest Link*).

Why does the US dominate the trade in television programming?

We have already seen that fiction constitutes the largest proportion of the trade in programmes and that the US accounts for between two-thirds and three-quarters of the trade in fiction by volume. Trade data is not the most reliable information, but the US is also estimated to account for three-quarters of the value of trade, with Britain coming second with a share of just over 10 per cent (see Table 2.2).[7] Yet while the US may dominate the trade in programming, it does not dominate transmissions as a whole.

For example, 62 per cent of transmission time within the European Union was devoted to European programmes, excluding news, sports, games, advertising, teletext and teleshopping in 1999 and 2000. The inclusion of the excluded categories would drive levels of European content up still further (EC, 2002). Moreover, US sales are confined primarily to feature films and television series, where 'cultural discount' is lower than for other types of programming.

Table 2.2: The value of the world television export market in 2001

Territory	Value (£m)
US	3,000
UK	430
Australia	50
France	50
Rest of World	470
Total	**4,000**

Source: BTDA, cited in ITC, 2002a, app. 1, p. 30.

Even so, there is a large trade imbalance between the European Union (EU) and North America. The European Audiovisual Observatory calculated a trade deficit between the EU and North America in films and television programmes of $8.2 billion in 2000 (EAO, 2002). Television accounted for just under half of US audiovisual revenues in the EU in 2000 at $4.38 billion (total revenues $9 billion), more than double the revenues of 1995 ($2.06 billion). The imbalance of trade in television programmes is aggravated by the rather stagnant performance of European audiovisual exports to North America (including film and video), which rarely exceed 10 per cent of US imports and amounted to $827 million in 2000.

Various economic reasons have been proposed for the USA's strength in international markets, particularly for fiction (see Dupaigne and Waterman, 1998; Hoskins, McFadyen and Finn, 1997; Hoskins and Mirus, 1988; Wildman and Siwek, 1988). However, it would be a mistake to think that the US dominates simply because it focuses on international trade. This does not happen, because American producers are primarily interested in their own market. But the US does enjoy advantages at home that benefit its export activities. A large and wealthy domestic market with a wide range of available outlets, encompassing network television and secondary outlets in local syndication, cable and satellite, allows US producers to take greater financial risks with larger budgets, because production costs can be recouped across a number of domestic windows.

The failure rate of fiction series on mainstream American networks is very high, but those series that survive rigorous testing and stay on the networks for at least three years (sixty-five episodes) can recoup deficits and make substantial profits in the secondary US market (Hoskins and Mirus, 1988; Hoskins and McFadyen, 1991). The promise of these revenues encourages US producers to invest more in star casts, special effects and scripts, which enhances the series' exportability over exports from smaller or less wealthy countries with fewer domestic funding opportunities (Doyle, 2002, p. 91; Hoskins and McFadyen, 1991; Wildman and Siwek, 1987, p. 74). The American ability to fund long-running series also enhances exports because it meets the scheduling needs of commercial networks in other countries, which strip programming across a week.

But size and wealth alone do not explain the American position of strength. The advantage also extends to a commercial system that promotes mass-appeal fiction programming – which is just as likely to work with an international audience, long acclimatised to Hollywood feature films, as it appeals to the multiculturally diverse US market (Hoskins, McFadyen and Finn, 1997, p. 44; Hoskins and Mirus, 1988, pp. 505–6). The natural advantages of a large domestic market and a language, English, which is spoken in other important and wealthy markets (Canada, Australia, Britain) have been reinforced by access to production expertise, talent, resources and investment, which built on the earlier strengths of American feature film production. Access to these resources gives the US 'first mover' advantages in programme innovation and technological developments (Hoskins and McFadyen, 1991).

However, American dominance of international trade has been undermined by a shift towards local and regional production in many markets, which has affected the ability of the US to sustain high volumes of trade and export revenues (Kapner, 2003; Rouse, 2001, pp. 38–9).[8] At the same time, the fragmentation of audiences and advertising revenues in the US market is making it more difficult for US producers to recoup costs from domestic sales (Collins, 1986, pp. 75–6; Hoskins and McFadyen, 1991). Technological advances have brought down the cost of production and dented US share in areas such as animation, where Japanese and Canadian producers are now active (Hoskins and McFadyen, 1991). Finally, the small but growing tendency of US channels to collaborate with overseas partners allows non-US producers to customise programmes for the US market, reducing resistance to overseas players and programming (Ibid.). This became evident in the late 1990s, when European players, including Britain, gained access with entertainment formats (*Big Brother*, *Survivor*, *Who Wants to Be a Millionaire?*, *The Weakest Link*) to the mainstream US networks, outlets that had previously been largely closed to foreign interests.

Yet the tendency since the 1990s to merge and consolidate into mega-corporations suggests that the US advantage is likely to be sustained, in an environment where the US broadcast networks are just one element within vast horizontally and vertically integrated transnational empires. The US may be taking a smaller share of an expanding trade in programming, but it is likely to continue to dominate trade in the most expensive form of programming, fiction, in the wealthiest of the world's markets in Western Europe, North America and Australasia (Hoskins and McFadyen, 1991).

How much does the UK export?

After America, Britain is often cited as the world's second-largest exporter of television programming. This position as 'number two' certainly owes something to the English language, which gives Britain preferential access to the wealthy American, Canadian and Australian markets. In a 1983 study, Britain was estimated to account for 16 per cent of the one third of transmissions devoted to imported programmes in Western Europe, after the US with 44 per cent (Varis, 1984). Although only 2 per cent of US transmissions came from overseas, Britain accounted for 25 per cent of US imports ahead of Mexico with 24 per cent (Varis, 1985). Britain also came second to the US in Asia and the Pacific, but failed to secure second place in Canada, Latin America, Eastern Europe and Arab countries.

More recent studies for the period 1996–7 have given Britain a 9 per cent global share by volume, and a 13 per cent share for prime time, the most valuable day part in second place after the US with a 68 per cent share in both cases (DCMS, 1999b, p. 33). However, based on a limited number of territories and channels and confined to a single year, the data needs to be viewed as indicative rather than as an accurate assessment of the presence of British programming overseas.

Other data suggests that the British position as 'number two' may be under threat at least in respect of the volume of trade, notwithstanding the limitations of trade data, which make international comparisons difficult (see Acheson and Maule, 1999). The volume of *telenovela* exports from Latin America to Hispanic channels in the US may now exceed the volume of British exports. One study stated that Britain came third as a source of imports in Italy, Spain and France, but without specifying who came second (DCMS, 1999b, p. 33). However, other reports on fiction imports in Europe show that transmissions of European fiction (including British programmes) are exceeded by transmissions of Latin American *telenovelas* in Spain and Italy (Buonanno, 2000, p. 22; De Bens and de Smaele, 2001, p. 65).[9] The rise of strong regional production centres in Hong Kong, India and increasingly China, and the performance of Canada in animation and drama for the North American market, are also likely to affect Britain's position as the world's second-largest exporter of television programmes.

Since 1998 the BTDA (British Television Distributors' Association) has collected statistics on the value of British exports, which break down export

Table 2.3: British television exports by territory 1998–2003 ($ million)

Sales by Territory	1998	1999	2000	2001	2002	2003
USA	142.5	165	167	199	284	399
Canada	13.7	14	16	22	30	31
Germany	48.4	47	59	59	44	68
France	33.7	33	50	37	40	50
Spain	17.8	23	28	22	23	32
Italy	15.6	18	16	19	18	25
Scandinavia	21.4	24	29	29	27	36
Rest of Western Europe	46.4	45	43	38	73	69
Eastern Europe	12.0	13	16	18	19	18
Australia/New Zealand	52.2	64	65	59	73	76
Latin America	17.1	15	22	24	23	16
Asia	50.1	47	50	46	59	62
Not elsewhere classified	32.9	42	55	53	39	39
Total	**503.8**	**550**	**616**	**625**	**752**	**921**

Source: BTDA, 2000; BTDA, 2001, p. 2; BTDA, 2002; BTDA, 2003; BTDA, 2004.

revenues according to sales by type and territory. These provide a useful overview of Britain's export performance (see Table 2.3). However, the size of overseas revenues, £430 million in 2001 ($624 million), needs to be set against total industry revenues in Britain, which are almost eighteen times larger. In 2001, total industry revenues were approximately £7.7 billion, with £4.4 billion attributable to the free-to-air channels (ITC, 2002a, app. 1, p. 3).

In terms of territories, the USA is the single most important purchaser of British programmes, accounting for almost 43 per cent of sales in 2003. Combined, the Western European territories, led by Germany (7 per cent), account for a further 30 per cent share ($280 million) in 2003. Sales to smaller territories in Scandinavia (4 per cent) and the rest of Western Europe (mainly the Netherlands with 7 per cent) are also important. Sales to the other English-speaking territories of Canada, New Zealand and Australia account for almost 12 per cent of sales, and combined with the US account for 55 per cent of sales. Asian territories including Japan, account for a further 7 per cent share. Sales to North America, Western Europe, Australia, New Zealand and Asia account for more than 90 per cent of sales. Between 1998 and 2003, sales to North America (including Canada) grew by over 175 per cent, fuelled by successes in formats, co-productions and licensing revenues associated with children's programmes. Sales to Western Europe grew by only 53 per cent, based largely on

Table 2.4: British television exports by type 1998–2003 ($ million)

Sales by type	1998	1999	2000	2001	2002	2003
Television	378.5	348	339	352	333	371
Videogram/DVD	25.8	39	41	54	117	128
Co-Production	43.3	40	58	61	84	115
Format/local production	10.0	15	23	35	39	63
Licensing/miscellaneous	46.2	101	149	118	176	239
Commission on UK sales	–	7	7	4	5	4
Total	**503.8**	**550**	**617**	**624**	**754**	**920**

Source: BTDA, 2000; BTDA, 2001, p. 2; BTDA, 2002; BTDA, 2003; BTDA, 2004.

sales of completed programmes. However, the proportion of European sales is now much larger than it was in the 1980s, before the wide-scale introduction of commercial television. In 1982, for example, overseas receipts from Europe only accounted for 18 per cent of £33 million in overseas revenues, compared with almost 64 per cent of revenues attributable to sales in North America (see Schlesinger, 1986, p. 275).

In terms of the type of programming sold, there have been some significant shifts (see Table 2.4). Sales of largely completed television programmes still account for the largest share at 40 per cent of all sales in 2003. But the share taken by sales of television programmes has fallen steadily since 1998, when they accounted for 75 per cent of sales. However, total sales increased by almost 83 per cent between 1998 and 2003 to $921 million. This is due to increases in revenues from video (+396 per cent), co-productions (+165 per cent), formats (+530 per cent) and licensed merchandise (+417 per cent).

Revenues in 2003 from video/DVD (13.9 per cent), co-production (12.5 per cent), formats and local production (6.8 per cent) and licensing (25.9 per cent) are still significantly lower than revenues from sales of television programmes, but combined now account for over 59 per cent of overseas revenues. The shift in revenue sources supports the view that exporters are having to look to alternative strategies to access overseas markets, which reportedly saw a 20 per cent decline in prices for off-the-shelf product in the eighteen months up to 2000 (David Graham & Associates, 2000, p. 38). Sales from formats and local production are still modest, and likely to be based on a small number of hit shows such as the BBC's *Weakest Link* and Endemol UK's *Changing Rooms*, which were both sold to the US. But the figures are also likely to be underestimated because Celador, the creator of *Who Wants to Be a Millionaire?*, is not a member of the BTDA. Similarly, revenues from licensing are likely to be based on a small number of children's hits such as HIT Entertainment's *Bob the Builder* and *Teletubbies*, sold by the BBC outside the US. But again figures are likely to be underestimated, because Ragdoll, the producer of *Teletubbies*, which holds US rights to the series, only became a member of the BTDA in 2002. The steady growth in co-production revenues, largely from America (94 per cent of co-production revenues), bears testimony to the fact that expensive productions with overseas potential are increasingly funded from overseas sources because of pressures on domestic budgets.

Distributors also earn revenues from exploiting ancillary rights in the British market and from secondary sales of programming to British cable and satellite channels, and these can exceed overseas revenues. For example, BBC World-wide earned £338 million from publishing and new media in 2002–03 compared to £168.8 million from programme sales (including programme sales in Britain), representing 51.3 per cent and 25.6 per cent respectively of turnover of £658 million. Its revenues from Britain at £331.2 million (57 per cent) were also sig-nificantly higher than its overseas revenues at £228.8 million (39 per cent) (BBC Worldwide, 2003b).

Income from the exploitation of secondary rights in Britain was estimated to account for £276 million of revenues in 2001, broken down into video/DVD (£166 million), books (£80 million) and music (£30 million) (Channel Four, 2002a, p. 7). This figure does not include revenues from licensed merchandise. In 1999, secondary sales of programming to British channels were estimated to total £100 million (David Graham & Associates, 2000, p. 45). In 2000, BBC Worldwide earned £22 million from programme sales to its British joint venture channels, almost 16 per cent of its total television programme sales revenues of £138 million (BBC Worldwide, 2000, p. 10). These figures suggest that a com-bination of the secondary exploitation of programming overseas (£430 million in 2001) combined with the secondary exploitation of programming in the domestic market would have generated revenues in excess of £800 million in 2001, with approximately 45 per cent of revenues generated in Britain itself.

Future outlook

This chapter has provided an overview of the nature of programming trade and how the trade in programming functions in respect of markets, the role of buy-ers, the type of programmes sold and the different ways of raising revenues in overseas markets. It has explained the predominance of American suppliers in economic terms and examined the performance of British exporters from avail-able trade data. What becomes overwhelmingly clear is that the emphasis of the trade in programming is shifting from sales of off-the-shelf programming to co-productions, co-financing, formats and local production.

Co-production finance provides larger budgets for original and possibly pres-tigious programming, which can be claimed as original by each partner in the production. Formats, although still responsible for a small share of British export revenues, satisfy a growing demand for local production. The rise in income from video and licensed merchandise is an indication of the growing importance of programming brands, particularly in the children's and entertainment market.

At this point it is also worth mentioning what the future might hold for international distribution. In theory advances in technology might render international distribution redundant. Just as consumers download music from the Internet, it might be possible for consumers to compile their own schedules by directly downloading programming or bits of content from vast libraries of material, which have already been branded and adapted for different language markets (see Oliver, 2000; Tambini, 2000, p. 8). Growing consumer experience of paying directly for pay television, the popularity of computer games, and limited amounts of interactivity on some television programmes (Internet voting for example on *Big Brother*), suggests that consumers might be open to navigating their way towards desirable content and interactive experiences.

However, such a scenario ignores the added value brought by those involved in the international exploitation of programming, which goes beyond simply selling finished programmes. Trade data have already shown us that there has been a shift from sales of completed television programmes to other types of sales, which reflects the need to fund domestic productions from other sources. Direct consumer access works well for straightforward one-off decisions to purchase a video or a DVD. But media content needs to be originated, funded and marketed in an increasingly fragmented and complex marketplace. Licensing and video require the skills of brand management, which can extract the maximum promotional potential from a broadcast airing. Format sales and local production require production skills. And the ability to locate co-production finance and pre-sales requires a strong contact base and reputation for delivering programming. These skills will always be needed whatever technological advances are made, and with pressures on domestic funding their importance is likely to increase.

Notes

1. At NOS a centralised acquisitions department operates a claims system to prevent the broadcasting affiliates within NOS from competing against each other and driving prices up.
2. With the exception of footage from international news agencies.
3. The network terrestrial channels (BBC 1, BBC 2, ITV, Channel Four and Five) were estimated to be responsible for two-thirds of expenditure on programming in 2001, equivalent to £2.9 billion compared to £1.4 billion spent by the cable and satellite sector (ITC, 2002a, app. 1, pp. 4–5).

4. This includes situation comedies.

5. For example, according to the TBI Programme Prices Guide 2003, Dutch free-to-
   air television pays $4,000–10,000 per hour for documentaries compared to
   $25,000–80,000 in Germany, $1,000–5,500 in China and $500–3,000 in India (TBI,
   2002, pp. 482-4)

6. UK television export figures for 2003 reveal that 94 per cent of co-production
   revenues ($115 million) are sourced from the USA ($108 million) (BTOA, 2004).

7. This data omits Canada and Latin America, which are also significant exporters,
   and must therefore be viewed with some caution.

8. The Motion Picture Association reported that US sales to overseas broadcasters
   were down 5 per cent in 2001 at $3.6 billion. This was offset by an 8 per cent climb
   in pay television sales to $1.8 billion, giving a total of $5.4 billion (Anon., 2002a,
   p. 26).

9. In a survey undertaken in March 1998, Italy and Spain were shown to source 19
   per cent and 14 per cent of their fiction respectively from Latin America, compared
   to 8 per cent and 1 per cent respectively from Europe (Buonanno, 2000, p. 22).

3

Policy Interventions – Promoting British Exports

In 1999, the Department for Culture, Media and Sport (DCMS) published two reports on the export performance of British television. The reports formed part of the Labour government's broader concern with the export potential of the 'creative industries', but the emphasis on television exports was noteworthy, because television exports had never constituted a specific focus of government interest before. Previous administrations had 'merely regarded' television exports 'as commercial export fields' with export achievement occasionally recognised with a Queen's Award for Exports (Tunstall, 1977, p. 277). But traditionally, governments had always been more concerned with the regulation and performance of television in the domestic marketplace.

Moreover, as one sector of the creative industries, television programme exports were hardly significant. A government Mapping Document published in 2001 established that the creative industries in total generated £112.5 billion in revenues and £10.3 billion in export earnings. Television exports of £440 million in 1999 came some way behind the export performance of software and computer services (£2.76 billion), publishing (£1.65 billion), music (£1.3 billion), design (£1 billion), advertising (£774 million), film and video (£653 million), art and antiques (£629 million) and interactive leisure software (£503 million) (DCMS, 2001a; DCMS, 2001b).

If television exports had never featured strongly in broadcasting policy debates before, it is useful to explore why they appeared on the agenda after a Labour government was elected in 1997, and the implications of that debate not only for television exports, but also for broadcasting reform. The previous chapter considered how trade functions in practice. This chapter looks at how the export sector has been affected by government policy.

Television exports move onto the policy agenda
Cultural objectives and the desire to serve the needs of domestic audiences as citizens are not always compatible with the industrial goals associated with

international competitiveness, export markets and the 'supposed' interests of consumers and entrepreneurs (see McQuail, 1995, p. 161). This constitutes the core dilemma of policy approaches to television exports, a dilemma that became clearly evident in the Labour government's approach to the creative industries.

New Labour and the creative industries

The Labour government's interest in television programme exports stemmed directly from its concern with the creative industries. In turn the focus on the creative industries can be seen as one outcome of the long-term decline in manufacturing and the recognition of the communications sector as a significant source of jobs and export revenues (DCMS, 1998; Frith, 1999, p. 5). Alongside the economic post-industrial reasons for embracing the creative industries, Freedman detects political and symbolic motivations as well, including the desire to redefine and 're-brand' 'what it means to be British' in 'a world increasingly characterized by global flows of finance, information, and images' (Freedman, 2000, p. 312). However, Labour's embrace of the inevitability of globalisation and the potential benefits of maximising exports and attracting inward investment sits uneasily next to the idea of national culture and specifically British television serving British audiences with domestically originated content. Freedman suggests that Labour sought to tackle this contradiction between the global and the local by 're-branding' Britain as 'a creative, dynamic, forward-looking country that is built on a strong heritage', yet is also ready to 'commercialise and seek international markets' (Ibid., p. 324). As one sector of the creative industries, television would become part of this 're-branding' exercise.

Labour had been developing a strategy for the creative industries that acknowledged the significance of the creative economy as a core part of Britain's identity and future since the late 1980s (Labour Party, 1997). Tracing the roots of the creative industries agenda in Labour's first term of office, Blanchard argues that this approach not only provided a way of tackling what the Conservative government had left behind in terms of a privatised economy, it also offered a way of distinguishing 'New' Labour from what were perceived as the failed strategies of 'Old' Labour (Blanchard, 2001, pp. 3–4). The focus on creative industries, including IT and technology, allowed Labour to position itself as the champion of new, dynamic industries firmly ensconced in a competitive private sector, that emphasised entrepreneurialism and 'pragmatic market liberalism' rather than the communitarian values and interventionism of 'Old' Labour's 'cultural industries' initiatives of the 1980s (Ibid.). Under 'New' Labour there were limits to state intervention because it was believed that the minimum of regulation best served both national and commercial interests in a globalised media and communications economy (see Blair, 1996, p. 204; DTI/DCMS, 2002a, p. 3; Freedman, 2000, p. 329). This acceptance of a common-sense view of globalisation, propelled by technological change, has provided a useful commercial and ideological pretext for pushing through fundamental reform of domestic broadcasting media, opening up British television to global market forces.

So when New Labour came to power in 1997, its approach to the media was not radically different from the free market policies of the Conservative government that preceded it. For example in 1994, under the Conservatives, the BBC was encouraged to adopt a more commercial approach and evolve 'into an international multi-media enterprise, building on its present commercial services for audiences in this country and overseas' (DNH, 1994, p. 1). Under Labour, this corporatisation of the BBC continued. When a licence fee increase was awarded in February 2000, it was made contingent on the Corporation making £1.1 billion in savings by 2006–07 from increased efficiency and commercial activities, including partnerships and joint ventures (Smith, 2000).

Mapping television exports

To push forward the creative industries agenda the Labour government established the inter-departmental Creative Industries Task Force (CITF) in June 1997 under the leadership of the DCMS. The CITF's remit was to provide a forum for ministers and industry figures to discuss policy and identify ways of maximising the sector's economic potential (DCMS, 1999c, p. 6). The first outcome of these deliberations was the *Creative Industries Mapping Document*, an audit of the creative economy, published in November 1998 (DCMS, 1998). The notion of culture as an economic force was set out from the start, with a clear focus on global opportunities and the need to remove barriers to free trade and international competitiveness (Ibid., p. 10).

The Mapping Document looked at the economic performance of each of the creative industry sectors, but its audit of television imports and exports drew attention to a less than favourable balance of payments position, based on figures from the Office of National Statistics (ONS) (see Table 3.1). A small surplus of £24 million in 1985 had ballooned into a deficit of £282 million by 1996 (DCMS, 1998, p. 103). The deficit would rise to £403 million by 1999, largely fuelled by programmes acquired by cable and satellite channels (DCMS, 2001a).[1]

In a breakdown of revenues by territory for 1996 it was not surprising to see a deficit with North America (exports £49 million; imports £273 million), but Britain also appeared to be in deficit with Europe as well (exports £128 million; imports £190 million) (DCMS, 1998, p. 103). The overall picture of deficit is

Table 3.1: International transactions of British television companies 1985–2002

Year	Exports (£ million)	Imports (£ million)	Surplus/deficit
1985	110	86	+24
1987	117	130	-13
1990	128	207	-79
1993	181	268	-87
1994	255	317	-62
1995	245	400	-155
1996	234	516	-282
1997	313	606	-293
1998	444	692	-248
1999	440	843	-403
2000	551	767	-216
2001	673	1,007	-334
2002	684	1,237	-553

Source: DCMS, 1998, p. 103; DCMS, 2001a; ONS, 2002; ONS, 2003.

no doubt true, but the ONS figures need to be treated with some caution, for they include receipts and payments from other types of transactions, including the leasing of transmission rights and transponder and encryption costs (DCMS, 1999b, p. 7; ONS, 2002). The need for more reliable data, broken down into exports by type (television, video, co-production, formats, licensing) was one reason for instigating an annual survey of export revenues by the British Television Distributors' Association (BTDA) (see Chapter 2).[2] According to ONS data, by 2002 exports to the US had grown to £194 million, set against imports of £742 million. Imports from Europe totalled £428 million compared to exports of £350 million.[3] In 2002, exports of other services (including merchandising) were estimated at £425 million, with imports reaching £231 million (ONS, 2003).

The 1998 Mapping Document's survey of the television and radio sector concluded by drawing attention to a number of issues that needed to be considered in the light of further sector growth (DCMS 1998, p. 107). One of those issues was how to improve the export performance of the television sector. Another was how to ensure that channel expansion did not simply lead to an increase in imports and a widening trade gap. As we shall see the import side of the equation would not be examined, suggesting that another issue had higher priority. This was 'how to develop regulation to continue to protect the public interest while ensuring that it does not create unnecessary obstacles to the development of the industry' (Ibid., p. 107). The government wanted to maximise the international potential of television, but public policy on imports flew in the face of a commitment to free trade and international competitiveness. Any consideration of imports and the imposition of quotas would also have constituted a threat to the satellite sector, which is heavily reliant on imports and also to the development of digital television, which the government is keen to promote. BSkyB, part of Rupert Murdoch's News Corporation, has a substantial investment in both, and New Labour, which had nurtured the support of the Murdoch-owned media, was unlikely to risk undermining this relationship by tackling imports (Blanchard, 2001). Consequently imports were not addressed, but television exports were already conveniently on the agenda. Under the previous Conservative government, officials from the Department of National Heritage (DNH)[4] and Department of Trade and Industry (DTI) had already initiated discussions with industry about a study of export markets (Ibid., p. 7). This study began in October 1997 after Labour came to power.

'Building a global audience' and the 'wrong model' of television

Britain's trade deficit in television programmes provided a starting point for the first study of Britain's television export performance (DCMS, 1999a, p. 14). The research was carried out by David Graham & Associates and funded by eight exporters (including BBC Worldwide, Carlton, Granada and Pearson) with match funding from the DTI. A summary of the main findings, based on data collected between September 1996 and August 1997, was published by the DCMS as *Building a Global Audience: British Television in Overseas Markets* in April 1999 (DCMS, 1999a).

The report's central conclusion was that the industry was underperforming, because it was failing to sell programmes that foreign buyers, particularly in the commercial sector, actually wanted to buy. Although Britain came second after the US as a source of imports in many territories, the gap was large and it was pushed into third and fourth position in the major Western European territories of Germany (third), France (third) and Italy (fourth) (Ibid., p. 17). Drawing on interviews, primarily with buyers from Europe, British drama was found to be 'too dark; too slow; unattractive; too gritty or socio-political' (Ibid., p. 24) with 'distasteful characters', 'storylines' and downmarket lifestyles, reinforcing a negative image of Britain (Ibid., p. 25). British comedy was judged to have lost its appeal and ability to be 'funny', and its sustainability was affected by a lack of team-writing, which worked against the production of longer series (Ibid., p. 27).

Britain's failure to produce attractive programmes was compounded by practical issues such as the inability to produce sufficient numbers of episodes (a minimum of thirteen) for longer runs and a failure to produce enough ninety-minute television movies or sixty-minute series episodes that fitted available slots (Ibid., pp. 21–2). The report also concluded that British producers were not taking advantage of the benefits of co-production, particularly with partners in Europe, which would have enhanced access to international markets (Ibid., pp. 29–31).

The report suggested that it was possible to get 'international markets right' and keep 'your own cultural identity' (Ibid., p. 13), but its solution to what it perceived as a failure to meet the demands of a competitive international marketplace was radical. According to this analysis the failure to export was due to a public service-inspired regulatory culture, which prioritised the domestic audience, and therefore made the 'wrong' type of television for international consumption (Ibid., p. 32). If the British industry was to do better it would have to adopt a more commercial model to be found in the US, and increasingly across Europe too, where German producers were apparently reaping the rewards from investment in internationally attractive action-adventure series and television movies (Ibid., pp. 32–3).

Building a Global Audience argued that domestic regulation in Britain and export performance were 'in tension, if not in conflict' (Ibid., p. 40). It added that the government should 'consider the need for international competitiveness when framing policies for the domestic home market', because the industry's 'historic achievements and present virtues' were now looking 'out-of-date' (Ibid., p. 41). The ability of British broadcasters to fully fund production largely in the domestic marketplace had reduced the incentive to consider export potential, resulting in programming which was 'out of step with world markets' (Ibid., p. 38). On the free-to-air channels content rules that specified news, current affairs and regional coverage at peak time, combined with budgetary considerations that encouraged cheaper but less exportable daily domestic 'soaps', were highlighted as obstacles to growth in exports. These programmes that satisfied domestic audiences took up time that could have been used to develop 'locomotive' drama and entertainment for the international market (pp. 39–40).

The report made some additional recommendations about the need for better statistics, a stronger industry body, better communication between producers and distributors, a consideration and assessment of tax breaks and support mechanisms, and talent agreements, but the central assumption was the inadequacy of the domestic television environment for promoting exports. It was a clear example of prioritising international considerations over domestic ones, and although it did not represent the views of the government, the liberalising tone may well have reflected them.

But there were some significant omissions and contradictions. The report acknowledged the tendency of maturing local markets, particularly in Europe, to increase levels of domestic programming because these were more popular with local audiences (Ibid., p. 20). However, it did not consider how this tendency might affect all acquisitions, not just acquisitions from Britain. The focus of the research, backed up by selected quotations, seems to have been primarily about failure in Western Europe. However, there was less detail about the context in which acquired programming is selected and scheduled. The British share of imports by volume in Germany (3 per cent), France (8 per cent), Spain (3 per cent) and Italy (1 per cent) was deemed poor (Ibid., p. 17). Yet apart from the very wide gap with the US, the findings only show differences of 1 or 2 per cent with Australian, French and German exporters, and they rest on only one year's worth of data.

There was rather less analysis of Britain's largest export market, the USA, where Britain had a 35 per cent share of imported programmes by volume, and the importance of America as a source of co-production funding for British programmes. Nor was there much consideration of why the US enjoys dominance in the trade in television, and even of how US exports might be faring in a climate geared towards increases in local programming. The assumption of the report was that the regulatory environment of the free-to-air broadcasting market was at fault for export failure. Yet there was no examination of imports and the satellite sector's reliance on imports.

Given that fiction constitutes the most heavily traded genre internationally, it was not surprising that the report should focus on Britain's ability to export fiction. However, this left less space to consider factual programming and animation, where content is often less culturally specific, and therefore more exportable. To be fair, the report appeared before the success of the British quiz formats *Who Wants to Be a Millionaire?* and *The Weakest Link*. The emphasis at this point was firmly placed on the sale of taped programmes, rather than the ability to market ideas and formats and exploit ancillary rights. This constitutes a significant omission, because the sale of formats has less to do with 'the rejuvenation of the British "brand"' through the production of 'positive, glossy, mainstream drama series' (Ibid., p. 26) and rather more to do with adaptation to suit very distinct local preferences. In this case the notion of 'Britain' does not feature at all.

Rejecting the 'wrong model'
In the light of the damning conclusions of *Building a Global Audience*, the DCMS decided in April 1999 to form an inquiry panel to take forward its recommendations (DCMS, 1999d). The Creative Industries Task Force (CITF) inquiry's report was published by the DCMS on 26 November 1999 (DCMS, 1999b). With a membership drawn largely from commercial broadcasting and

the independent production sector, and including representatives from the BBC's commercial arm, BBC Worldwide, the inquiry was broken down into three sub-groups, each dealing with a separate aspect of the debate. These were Overseas Markets (trade figures and industry promotion), Investment (tax incentives, support schemes, merchandising and programme rights) and the Right Product Group, which looked at the nature of Britain's television product.

Many of the recommendations made by the inquiry centred on providing better information and practical support. These included a more effective and better-funded BTDA, the provision of better statistics and improvements in government support for television export initiatives (Ibid., p. 6). There were also recommendations about more flexible tax incentives, a rights fund to encourage animation, the relaxation of rules on programme-related merchandising for children's programmes, and the clearer separation and valuation of programme rights (Ibid., p. 17).

The most interesting findings, however, came from the Right Product Group, chaired by Rupert Gavin, Chief Executive of BBC Worldwide. Its conclusions, which garnered the most publicity, constituted a rejection of *Building a Global Audience*'s assertion of export underperformance and, more importantly still, they constituted a rejection of any need to radically alter the domestic marketplace.

The Right Product Group made a point of highlighting those findings that indicated anything but underperformance. Britain's 9 per cent share of the global export market by volume in 1996–7 not only outperformed its closest rivals (France and Australia 3 per cent each), but also exceeded Britain's 4.7 per cent share of global GDP (Ibid., p. 33). At peak time, the most valuable time period, Britain's 13 per cent share by volume was more than six times larger than its closest rivals, France (2 per cent) and Australia (2 per cent) (Ibid., p. 33). Furthermore, British exports grew at an average compound rate of 30 per cent between 1991 and 1997, compared to the 10 per cent compound annual growth in the world trade in television services (Ibid., p. 33). Britain might lag behind the US with its 68 per cent share of the market, but it still outperformed its nearest rivals, and was clearly not underperforming.

In terms of the market share of global trade by genre, Britain came a clear second to the US in factual programming (18 per cent), feature films (12 per cent), drama and comedy (8 per cent), TV movies (6 per cent) and entertainment (8 per cent).[5] In children's television Britain came fourth (4 per cent), behind Japan (6 per cent) and Canada (5 per cent) (Ibid., p. 34).

The rejection of underperformance was accompanied by a rejection of any drastic changes to the style, scheduling or commissioning of British programmes

(Ibid., p. 42). Any dramatic modification of programming to increase exports was not realistic, because British programmes, which are still predominantly funded in the domestic marketplace, had to serve British audiences first, and British audiences happened to prefer 'gritty' or 'realistic' drama (Ibid., p. 30). Longer series runs that fitted in with international requirements were desirable, but financially risky for advertising-funded broadcasters if a production failed to attract an audience (Ibid., p. 39; Willis, 1999). In this vein, the inquiry concluded: 'Developing the international business is important for the industry, but serving the UK audience is essential. Dramatic modification to the style of UK programming is not, therefore, a realistic aim' (Ibid., p. 39). The Right Product Group had not only placed successful performance at home above the demands of the international marketplace, it had also rejected the idea of export failure.

Successful, yet marginal – exports lose centre stage

A press release issued by the DCMS shortly after the publication of the inquiry's report concentrated largely on the findings of the Right Product Group. Fortuitously this appeared in the same week that Britain won six out of seven categories in the International Emmy awards in the USA. The DCMS response suggested that it was keen to play up the 'greater than expected success' of export performance, but also careful to insist that 'the UK could do still better' (DCMS, 1999e). More importantly, Chris Smith, the DCMS Secretary, appeared to accept the report's key finding of no change for the domestic sector, when he stated: 'We need to build on this success, but not at the expense of continuing to provide a high quality service to the domestic audience. The British viewer must come first' (Ibid.).

The argument about underperformance appeared to have been buried. If there was no evidence of export underperformance, there was no need to radically alter the domestic television industry and harness it to the export market. The government noted the 'healthy export position' and reiterated that improvements should not occur 'at the expense of the home broadcasting market' (DCMS, 2000a), but the rejection by the inquiry of any fundamental change to the domestic marketplace left the government little scope to take things forward.

The DCMS agreed to some minor changes, including the provision of better trade statistics, and the maintenance of a small amount of financial support for export promotion (Ibid.). Yet any recommendations with significant financial implications, such as the introduction of a more sympathetic tax incentive regime, were sidestepped. The CITF inquiry had after all indicated that the export position was healthy, and a government committed to the market and free trade could hardly be expected to subsidise what was by all accounts a profitable and growing sector. With no apparent problem, exports as a pressing issue moved to the margins. The balance of trade problem, of course, remained, fuelled largely by imports by the satellite sector. But a government committed to liberalisation and free trade was hardly likely to tackle the imports issue, and besides, although television trade was in deficit, the creative industries sector as a whole was in trade surplus by £3.4 billion (DCMS, 2001a).

Phase II of the CITF inquiry was announced in July 2000 and took the form of another report, *Out of the Box*, commissioned from David Graham & Associates (2000). The brief was to look at how the domestic programme supply market could best be adapted to realise British creative potential (DCMS, 2000b). It would focus on the economic relationships within the television industry, the impact of new content platforms (including international channels), prospects for original production, revenue streams, talent rights agreements and the allocation and retention of programme rights. The latter had been glossed over by the two previous reports, but was gradually attaining a higher level of significance, as the focus of attention switched back to the domestic context and the regulatory structures that were deemed to hold the television economy back.

In assessing export performance *Out of the Box* still contained an underlying sense of export failure attributable to a 'public service programming framework', which constrained drama content in prime-time schedules, reducing the potential for programming 'with real international potential' (David Graham & Associates 2000, p. 42). There were exhortations to improve in respect of drama co-productions with European partners (Ibid., p. 40), and observations about the slowness of British companies, other than the BBC, to exploit the opportunities presented by international channels (Ibid., p. 43). The CITF report on exports had advised against any radical changes to the domestic marketplace. But *Out of the Box*, like *Building a Global Audience* before it, had at its core reform of a domestic market that had been 'plumply cushioned against the full force of domestic and global competition' (Ibid., p. 117). The failure of British broadcasters to become global media companies was attributed to a domestic market that was insufficiently competitive, and inhibited 'a truly vigorous market for programme-related rights', the asset base of production and distribution (Ibid., p. 118).

Out of the Box underlined the lack of competition in the domestic production sector, where 80 per cent of the market was dominated by twelve companies, including the BBC, which alone had a 40 per cent share of the production market (Ibid., p. 9). The independent production sector was characterised as fragmented and undercapitalised because of its reliance on fully-funded commissions. Fully-funded deals meant that the commissioning broadcaster usually retained all rights to exploit programming in secondary and overseas markets, leaving independent producers unable to build capital assets from the intellectual property they had created. Yet the rewards from programme-making rest in being able to exploit programming assets across a range of windows at home and overseas, with the primary broadcast licence constituting just one part of the financial reward from production. However, to retain rights with licensed deals as opposed to fully-funded deals, independent producers had to risk funding some of the costs of production themselves.

Out of the Box concluded that a broadcaster should be entitled to 'compel' the use of its own distribution facilities if it had fully funded a production. But this should not apply if its own distribution arm funded a deficit, because investment by a distributor should be open to competition (Ibid., pp. 124–5). There was little suggestion at this stage that the BBC and Channel Four might be exploiting their position in the marketplace to secure excessive rights, and reference was made to the fact that the Office of Fair Trading had rejected producer association PACT's (Producers Alliance for Cinema and Television) 1999 complaint to this effect (Ibid., p. 36). This view would change as the issue of programming rights began to occupy a more central position in the debate about the future of British television.

Television exports – a policy cul-de-sac

The dialogue between exporters and government continued, but television exports as a specific focus was subsumed within a wider exports remit. In April 2002, the government established the Creative Exports Group (CEG), a platform for exchanges between the government and trade organisations, including the BTDA. With an emphasis on research, identifying issues, and lobbying, the CEG is also concerned with music, film, advertising, radio, computer services and the publishing industries (DCMS, 2002a).

In the meantime, the exports debate as it emerged during the course of 1999 needs to be viewed within the broader context of the consistent push since the 1980s towards a dismantling of rules on ownership and content and the move towards a more 'commercial' model of television. This had begun under the Conservative government, and the trend would continue under New Labour, culminating in the publication of the *Communications Bill* in November 2002 (DTI/DCMS, 2002b). The notion of export failure might have proved difficult to support on the basis of evidence, but domestic reform of broadcasting was an entirely different matter. In this respect the Right Product Group's earlier rejection of export failure and of any drastic change to domestic television to support exports proved to be only a temporary reprieve.

If anything, the government's subsequent actions, in the light of the industry's call for tax incentives, could be considered as extremely unhelpful to exporters. Introduced in 1997, sale and leaseback (so-called Section 48 tax relief) was a scheme whereby an investor purchases a production, writes off the acquisition against taxable income and then leases the production back to the production company over a period of up to fifteen years. The government abolished it for television productions in the 2002 budget. The use of sale and leaseback had contributed up to 10 per cent of production costs for qualifying productions. For producers suffering the effects of reduced domestic licence fees and a declining ability by distributors to provide deficit finance against international rights in a difficult economic climate, sale and leaseback had become very important, particularly for high-cost drama (BTDA, 2002, p. 4; Granada, 2002a, p. 21).

In 1999–2000, investors purchased £800 million of films and television programmes. Producers benefited to the tune of £65 million and television accounted for a third of this sum (BTDA, 2002, p. 4). For independent producers, the ability to offset a deficit gave greater scope to retain rights for international exploitation. However, the Treasury halted the scheme for television productions because some television companies were thought to be abusing it. Facing declining advertising revenues, some were using sale and leaseback to fund cheaper long-running serials and reality programmes, which would normally be funded in-house, rather than using it for high-budget dramas and factual programmes, where budget shortfalls are more common (Ibid.). The implications of the abolition were serious, and there were reports that some productions, including a Granada drama based on the life of Henry VIII starring Ray Winstone and Helena Bonham Carter (screened by ITV in 2003) had come close to cancellation (Clarke, 2002). For distributors, abolition was a threat to the sort of large-scale quality drama productions that help to drive a catalogue in overseas markets.

Exports as part of the bigger picture – broadcasting reform

The short-lived emphasis on exports was superseded by a larger project, the fundamental overhaul of the British communications sector. This began with the publication of a Green Paper in July 1998, followed by the Communications White Paper, *A New Future for Communications*, in December 2000 (DTI/DCMS, 1998; DTI/DCMS, 2000). Within this larger project, exports played only a small part. Echoing the findings of the CITF report, the White Paper stated that Britain continued to 'punch above its weight in international awards and exports' (DTI/DCMS, 2000, p. 48). It added, 'That success is not an accident. It is founded on the economic, democratic and cultural characteristics of our broadcasting' (Ibid., p. 49). However, in spite of any passing praise for the television programme export sector, the underlying imperative of international competitiveness and deregulation of the communications sector as a whole was at the heart of the government's project.

The government declared that it wanted to make Britain 'home to the most dynamic and competitive communications and media market in the world' (Ibid., p. 10) through a combination of 'lighter touch' regulation and 'tough protection of the genuine public interest' (Ibid., p. 3). This deregulatory stance was reiterated in a policy document accompanying publication of the Draft *Communications Bill* in May 2002:

> Today's world combines a fast changing consumer environment with an increasingly international and competitive market place. In this world it is essential that the UK reinforces its position as one of the most attractive places for communications companies to do business. Unnecessary regulations need to be removed wherever possible. By eliminating undue burdens on business we can drive innovation, increase investment, raise employment and bring better services to consumers. (DTI/DCMS, 2002a, p. 3)

Regulation was being reoriented away from securing the public interest to securing a business environment that gave business, including overseas investors, maximum scope for action. This reorientation of regulation away from the needs of viewers towards the needs of consumers and business interests was relevant to television exports in two specific areas. The first related to the relaxation of ownership rules for commercial free-to-air television to attract inward investment. The second area was linked to the domestic programme supply market and the allocation of rights for overseas exploitation.

Ownership

Restrictions on ownership were eased by the Conservatives in the 1996 Broadcasting Act in the hope that Britain's commercial free-to-air broadcasters would rise onto the global stage. A spate of mergers occurred among the ITV companies, but it is clear that Granada and Carlton, which emerged as the two dominant players within ITV, did not become significant transnational operators in the mould of European rivals like Bertelsmann. They also lagged behind the publicly funded BBC in respect of international activities and overseas income generation (see Chapter 4). Throughout the 1990s they were more interested in securing their position in the domestic market than on improving their standing on the international stage.

In the December White Paper, the government announced its intention of replacing the 15 per cent audience share limit in respect of domestic ownership of commercial free-to-air television as a precursor to promoting 'the international standing' of ITV as a unified company (DTI/DCMS, 2000, pp. 40–1). But it also announced its intention of retaining those rules that prevented non-European Union interests from acquiring a controlling interest in the commercial free-to-air services, ITV and Five (Ibid., p. 44). This stance on foreign ownership would change following the appointment of a new Culture Secretary, Tessa Jowell, in June 2001 and after consultation with industry.

In the *Consultation on Media Ownership Rules*, published by the DTI and DCMS in November 2001, the government stated, 'Our working assumption remains that we will keep the current prohibitions on non-EEA ownership of broadcasters' (DTI/DCMS, 2001a, p. 18). The wording implied that it was open to persuasion. It was keen that ownership rules should aim 'to create the most competitive market possible whilst ensuring plurality of voice and diversity of content' (Ibid., p. 14), but consolidation might help to create 'a more significant international presence' (Ibid., p. 7).

Most commercial industry respondents to the government's media ownership consultation exercise were content to see foreign ownership rules change, provided there was reciprocity from other countries, notably the US (DTI/DCMS, 2001b). Carlton, one of the ITV companies active in exports and a possible candidate for a US takeover, opposed the retention of the rules prohibiting non-EU-ownership, because they inhibited British companies from competing in international markets. It argued that their removal would not only open up opportunities for inward investment, but also opportunities for British-based companies to invest in and develop alliances internationally (Carlton Communications, 2002a, p. 2). The television regulator, the ITC (Independent Television Commission), no doubt influenced by the position of ITV companies like Carlton, was no longer opposed to a rule change as it had been earlier (ITC, 2000). Provided there was reciprocity from overseas partners the ITC now saw potential advantages 'both for inward investment into the UK media industry and from opportunities for UK players to showcase UK creative talent in major overseas markets' (2002b, p. 2).

Unsurprisingly given the wealth of industry support for the rule changes, the Draft Communications Bill published by the DTI and DCMS in May 2002 removed what were labelled as 'outdated', inflexible and 'inconsistent' restrictions on non-EU ownership of the ITV companies and Five. Change was justified on the grounds of the global character of communications 'with companies investing across continents as well as within countries' (DTI/DCMS, 2002a, p. 2). It was hoped that the removal of the rules would encourage inward investment, allowing Britain 'to benefit rapidly from new ideas and technological developments, aiding efficiency and productivity' (Ibid., p. 56). Content regulation to secure 'high quality, original programming' would guard against the dangers of increased consolidation, including presumably any increase in imports stemming from foreign ownership (Ibid.). The government's reasoning was that it was nonsense to allow European investment in British commercial free-to-air television (for example the RTL Group's control of Five), but not to allow US investment (Ibid., p. 4). The nationality of a company in this instance was less important than its ability to attract investment and its contribution to jobs.

What are the ramifications of such a change, and for television programme exports in particular? In theory bigger broadcasters will be able to make more expensive television, which will be more exportable. In its survey of the programme supply market the ITC saw potential benefits from overseas investment, including access to new management, expertise and talent, new approaches to commissioning (longer runs and pilots), and access to critical mass in distribution through affiliation with broadcasters overseas (ITC, 2002a, p. 16).

Others feared the change would lead to the swamping of domestic television culture with American programming and influence. The parliamentary Joint Committee on the Draft *Communications Bill*, chaired by Lord Puttnam, considered the *Communications Bill* in its entirety and published its findings in July 2002. It was not convinced by the government's reasoning, and it went on to recommend that any lifting of restrictions be delayed until after a review by the new communications regulatory body, Ofcom (Office of Communications), and the competition authorities (Joint Committee, 2002, p. 66). A decision could then be made on evidence rather than 'largely unproven expectations' (Ibid.). According to the Committee, US investors would have a stronger incentive than European investors to use pre-existing material on British channels on the grounds of language, but what was more likely to happen was

> a determined and sophisticated attempt, backed by enormous marketing expertise, to shift the balance of audience and regulatory expectations away from domestic content produced primarily with a British audience in mind, towards a more US or internationally focused product mix. The inescapable reality is that a US media company investing in the United Kingdom will be concerned every bit as much with enhancing the wider market value of its domestic content as with increasing its return on an investment in the British-based marketplace. (Ibid., para. 248, p. 65)

According to the BBC, with changes in ownership, there was 'a real risk that US companies, will buy, not to invest, but in order to increase their own profitability by selling more US programmes into the UK market' (BBC, 2002, p. 16). By this reckoning, if levels of US imports were to increase on commercial free-to-air television there would be a reduction in domestic production and a smaller pool of British programmes to export. However, others have argued that fears about increases in imports are groundless. This is because a combination of content regulation and audience preferences for local content at prime time militate against the 'dumping' of American imports on a mainstream channel like ITV (Clive Jones, cited in Joint Committee, 2002, para. 241; Granada, 2002a, p. 20; ITC, 2002a, p. 59).

Channel Four was concerned that overseas ownership and economic pressures might lead to the development of programmes and formats that had international sales potential at the expense of distinctive and diverse programming created specifically for British audiences (Channel Four, 2002b, pp. 7–8). It suggested that US owners, in the interests of economic efficiency, might close the commercial broadcasters' in-house distribution operations, incorporating British-originated product into a single worldwide sales house (Ibid., p. 7). Others added that the ability to maximise foreign sales opportunities might decline if specialists in the international marketing of British programming were replaced by generalist sales operations, working out of the US (Joint Committee, 2002, annex 4, pp. 126–7). This would leave Britain in a 'peripheral market position within a giant international production and distribution machine' (David Puttnam, cited in BBC, 2002, p. 16).

In spite of strong opposition within Parliament to the relaxation of the rules on foreign ownership, the government held firm to its original intentions with only minor amendments. In July 2003 it struck a deal with Lord Puttnam, who had organised opposition to the ownership clauses in the House of Lords (Rose, 2003, p. 1). The government agreed to include a clause forcing the new regulatory authority, Ofcom, to submit any broadcasting merger or acquisition to a public interest test. Ofcom will look at the bidder's share of the 'public voice' and decide whether the acquisition is against the public interest. The test could apply to an overseas takeover of a single ITV, but is more likely to be effective against a potential acquisition of Five by News Corporation, with its extensive cross-media interests in Britain.

The programme supply market

The *Communications Bill* had opened up discussions about the future of the British production sector. Rather than the narrow reviews of exports conducted in 1999, this was a wider perspective, linking rights exploitation and success in overseas markets more directly to the economic health of domestic production.

However, in the first instance the Draft *Communications Bill*, published in May 2002 took little account of production and the programme supply market, as opposed to broadcasting (David Graham & Associates, 2002; PACT, 2002a, p. 2).

The parliamentary Joint Committee on the Draft *Communications Bill*, called upon to scrutinise the bill, took on board these concerns, recommending a periodic review of the programme supply market with a view to determining whether the market operated in a 'fair, transparent and non-discriminatory manner' (2002, p. 84). In August 2002, the Culture Secretary, Tessa Jowell, belatedly announced a review to be undertaken by the outgoing television regulatory authority, the ITC. Included among the broader objectives of establishing an economic overview and market assessment, the review was also set the objective of identifying 'significant international markets and their impact on UK programmes' (DCMS, 2002b).

The issue of rights had been bubbling away throughout Labour's administration. *Out of the Box* had dealt with rights, but had not constituted a full investigation into how broadcasters might be abusing their position in the value chain to secure an excessive share of rights (David Graham & Associates, 2000). PACT, the producers' association, had repeatedly drawn attention to what it perceived as the plight of independent producers in a marketplace dominated by a small number of powerful broadcasters, which treated the 25 per cent independent production quota as a 'ceiling' rather than a 'floor' (1998; 2000; 2002a; 2002b). It saw restrictive practices by the broadcasters at the root of Britain's 'poor' competitive performance overseas. Although some independent producers had achieved notable foreign successes (*Teletubbies*, *Who Wants to Be a Millionaire?*), the sector had failed to reach its full commercial potential through domestic and overseas expansion, because independents were unable to build up assets based on the intellectual property they created (PACT, 2002b, p. 3).

The ITC *Review of the UK Programme Supply Market*
The ITC published its review in November 2002, drawing on thirty-nine submissions of evidence from broadcasters and predominantly larger producers. Alongside its investigation into the effectiveness of the 25 per cent quota for independent productions, the review placed intellectual property rights at the centre of policy debate for the first time. It established that the five terrestrial channels, foremost the BBC with a 40 per cent share, accounted for 90 per cent of expenditure on all independent commissions (ITC, 2002a, p. 29). This not only gave broadcasters bargaining power to squeeze prices on the purchase of primary broadcast rights, but also leverage to retain all secondary broadcast rights for exploitation at home and abroad and tertiary rights (from publishing and consumer products). As a consequence, the UK-based rights distribution market, worth £700 million per year, was highly concentrated, with the BBC's rights-owning vehicle, the Commercial Agency, and its commercial sales arm,

BBC Worldwide, estimated to handle over half of all intellectual property rights originated in Britain (Ibid., p. 29).

The review estimated that 64 per cent of independent commissions, mostly by the BBC and Channel Four, were fully funded by the broadcasters on a cost plus production fee basis (Ibid., p. 31). Consequently the broadcasters (and their distribution arms) retained most rights, with independent producers participating in a 'delayed' 30–50 per cent share of net profits from the exploitation of secondary rights after the deduction of royalties, distribution costs and the recoupment of any distribution advances (Ibid., app. 3, p. 12). The BBC defined fully-funded commissions as those where the BBC (either fully itself or with investment from BBC Worldwide or a third party distributor) funded the programme and provided 100 per cent of the cash flow (BBC, 2002, p. 47). The advantage for producers was that productions were cash-flowed with less financial risk. For those productions without significant potential on secondary channels and in international markets this was an ideal situation.

However, the cost plus system delivered low returns from production fees and back end share and no assets, making it difficult for independent producers to attract venture capital or develop alternative revenue streams from secondary exploitation that would allow them to grow, diversify and invest in further productions. According to the ITC review, this inability to grow on the basis of retained rights was reflected in the fragmentary and 'fragile' nature of the independent sector – with approximately fifty medium-sized companies accounting for a quarter of the production market by share of turnover and a further 500 companies representing 10 per cent of the market (ITC, 2002a, p. 5, pp. 27–8).

The inability to retain rights from commissions and a lack of scale from undercapitalisation means that very few independent production companies have an international presence. However, the few independent production companies that did retain rights derived their profits primarily from secondary rights exploitation rather than production, which delivers low profits (see ITC, 2002a, app. 3, p. 12; RDF Media, 2002a; Shed Productions, 2002; Wall to Wall Television, 2002).

Unlike fully-funded commissions, with licensed commissions the broadcaster pays a fee to cover some of the budgeted costs (60–90 per cent) in return for primary broadcast rights for a limited period with no interest in any secondary or tertiary rights. This means that the producer or their chosen distributor can exploit other rights. This was the system applied by the commercial ITV network under mandated terms of trade imposed by the Monopolies and Mergers Commission in 1993, and most licensed commissions were attributable to ITV. However, licensed commissions involve more risk as the producer has to fund development and any shortfalls in the budget from other sources such as pre-sales, co-production funding or distributor advances. If the programme has commercial value the risk is worthwhile, because the producer retains control of rights, which can be exploited across different outlets and overseas.

In their submissions to the ITC, independent producers complained that they were being pushed into accepting fully-funded commissions rather than licensed commissions because of restrictive trade practices and a weak bargaining position (ITC, 2002a, p. 43). The full brunt of criticism was levelled firmly at the BBC, which was criticised for being 'at best opaque, and slow, and at worst disingenuous and manipulative' in its treatment of independents (Ibid., app. 3, p. 7). Producers claimed that the BBC manipulated prices and 'bundled' rights to ensure that the fully-funded route was the only available option. This was achieved through the offer of low primary licence fees for licensed commissions, which made it unfeasible for producers to recoup a deficit from the exploitation of secondary and tertiary rights (Ibid., pp. 43–4; also Granada, 2002a, p. 22; Shed Productions, 2002).[6] BBC Worldwide, the BBC's in-house distributor, was accused of over-investing in rights to cover deficits and secure distribution of programmes that were then handled as fully-funded commissions (Granada, 2002a, p. 22; PACT, 2002b, p. 19). Advances are recouped ahead of any returns to the producer, but because the sums were so high producers claimed that they only saw negligible and delayed net receipts (see Hat Trick Productions, 2002, p. 5; Granada, 2002a, p. 22; Tiger Aspect Productions, 2002).

Convinced by the 'weight of perception' of unfair treatment, the ITC review recommended that all free-to-air broadcasters should develop new Codes of Practice for their dealings with independent producers to be approved and enforced by the new regulatory body, Ofcom (ITC, 2002a, p. 54–6). It also suggested a formal market investigation by the ITC and Ofcom with the objective of developing more detailed solutions to the competition concerns raised by the review. These included:

- The unbundling and separate pricing of primary broadcast rights from secondary and international rights, with broadcasters in the first instance only able to acquire primary rights to independent productions in line with current practice at the ITV network.
- A requirement that broadcasters publish indicative tariffs for primary rights so that independent producers are aware of the scale of funding available for different genres and slots.
- An insistence that negotiations with distributors (BBC Worldwide, Channel Four International) connected with broadcasters about secondary rights take place separately and at arms length from negotiations with the commissioning broadcaster about primary broadcast rights.

The ITC review rejected claims that a shift towards broadcasters paying for primary broadcast rights would affect the commissioning of programmes with no secondary value in the marketplace. Instead it argued that if broadcasters wanted these programmes 'with the most PSB [public service broadcasting] value', they would have to pay the costs of producing them (ITC, 2002a, p. 57). It also rejected claims that the move towards paying for primary rights would raise the costs of highly sought after commercial content, resulting in less expenditure on public service content. It pointed out that broadcasters might actually end up paying less for the most commercial programmes, if producers were free to locate deficit funding elsewhere (Ibid.). Finally it rejected any possible disadvantage to BBC Worldwide. If Worldwide was truly 'the most efficient distributor' as it claimed, it would continue to secure the distribution of independent productions (Ibid.).

The review suggested that Ofcom should consider how the proposals might 'adversely affect the capabilities of the BBC Worldwide and Channel 4 International to compete effectively as international distributors', but it held back from recommending a separation of BBC Worldwide from the BBC to create a more level playing field (Ibid., p. 13). It observed that any change would require an assessment of the international success of Worldwide and the value it returned to the BBC and ultimately to licence-fee payers (Ibid.). More ominously the review suggested that separation might be considered by Ofcom as part of its ongoing investigation of the market. A 49 per cent sell-off of BBC Worldwide had already been recommended in 1999 in a DCMS-commissioned report on the future funding of the BBC, but had been rejected by the government (DCMS, 1999f). However, constant criticism of the corporation's commercial activities suggests that the option of selling off BBC Worldwide is likely to become a prominent issue as the BBC heads towards the renewal of its Charter in 2006 (Elliott, 2003). Indeed in June 2004, the BBC launched a comprehensive review of its commercial activies to report by the end of 2004, amid rumours that BBC Worldwide or parts of it may be sold off.

On 15 January 2003, the government responded to the ITC's recommendations, agreeing to implement all but two of the proposals in the *Communications Bill* (DCMS, 2003). Alongside several amendments aimed at strengthening the 25 per cent quota for independent productions, the government also agreed that the free-to-air channels should be subject to binding codes of practice in their dealings with independent producers, subject to approval and enforcement by Ofcom. The broadcasters were asked to submit codes of practice to the ITC by June 2003. Ofcom approved these new codes of practice drawn up by free-to-air broadcasters for commissioning programmes from independent producers in January 2004.

The implications of the Review of the UK Programme Supply Market

The new codes of practice could have profound implications for in-house distributors. Channel Four International is entirely dependent on independent productions and some of BBC Worldwide's most successful international brands, particularly in children's programming, have come from the independent sector (*Teletubbies, Tweenies, Fimbles*). In their evidence to the review both organisations referred to the global scale of their international operations and the importance of adopting an integrated approach, which recognised the importance of rights consolidation to extract the maximum return from overseas markets (BBC Worldwide, 2002b, p. 34; Channel Four, 2002a, p. 26). BBC Worldwide warned against the fragmentation of rights across a number of independent producers, because smaller players would be less able to take on the financial risk associated with investing in high-quality domestic productions to the detriment of the British production base (BBC Worldwide, 2002b, p. 35). For Channel Four it was

> important to stress that it is effective *exploitation* of these rights that generates value, rather than ownership of the rights per se. Control of programme rights by either broadcaster or producer is of no value if there is no effective means to exploit the rights in a way that generates a commercial return. (Channel Four, 2002a, p. 16)

It also stressed the added value that broadcasters brought to the table in terms of development, marketing and promotion, which benefited secondary exploitation (Ibid., p. 17). Independent producers do not just sell their programmes, but supply them to channels, which provide creative input consistent with a channel's brand and audience.

Larger independent producers, on the other hand, with a regular supply of broadcasting work, perceive changes in the way rights are handled as an incentive to invest in programming and take risks. They now see a greater chance of growing their businesses on the back of retained rights, which could attract external investment. According to leading independent RDF Media:

> The BBC will argue that it is only through maintaining in-house production that programmes of the scale and ambition of *Blue Planet* get made. But in our view RDF could develop a *Blue Planet* just as effectively if ours was a better capitalised business. Indeed we'd probably develop more programmes like *Blue Planet* than the BBC because our incentive would be so much greater than that offered to any in-house producer. (2002a, p. 9)

In theory the codes of practice will provide scope for greater competition with independent producers exercising their right to choose a distributor after the sale of primary rights to the broadcaster. However, the benefits of rights retention at the cost of fully-funded commissions might not benefit the vast majority of smaller producers whose programmes may have little value in secondary and international markets. Much will depend on how much is paid for primary rights and the size of any deficits that need to be covered from overseas sales. For programmes without commercial value a producer will still need to secure as much money as possible from a broadcaster.

Smaller, more specialised distributors may benefit from an increase in licensed commissions, but the small number of independent distributors in Britain (see Chapter 4) and the inability of most independent producers to fund or distribute their own productions will probably result in broadcaster-distributors remaining the distributor of choice for many. Some producers may establish in-house distribution arms, but this is labour-intensive, costly and demands expertise. One commentator noted that some independent producers were often very good at securing funding in the US, France and Germany. However, they might find it more challenging to pursue 'huge swathes of the world that buy programmes for $300 an hour' rather than the ten markets capable of paying more than $10,000 an hour (R. Dilnott-Cooper, cited in Marlow, 2003a, p. 23). Moreover, if producers sell their programming to the top three markets to make up any budget shortfall, they might find it difficult to find distributors willing to risk offering advances for the right to sell in less profitable parts of the world (Ibid.).

The prospective changes do, however, seem to have awakened renewed interest from city investors (Cassy, 2003, p. 4; Roy, 2003, p. 14). In May 2003, it was revealed that the Chrysalis TV Group, since renamed All3Media, the production company responsible for the ITV drama *Midsomer Murders*, was in talks with buyers backed by the venture capital group Bridgepoint to sell the company for a reputed £45 million, a sale that was concluded in the summer of 2003. In July 2003 Kleinwort Capital Trust acquired 45 per cent of Hat Trick Productions, the producer of internationally successful branded comedy formats *Have I Got News for You* and *The Kumars at No. 42*. Growing investor interest constitutes one step towards the creation of larger production companies capable of securing larger commissions with retained rights. However, the test of the changes to rights allocation will depend on how quickly the new codes of practice are implemented and the extent to which the new regulatory body, Ofcom, is prepared to use its powers of enforcement.

Review

In one sense the debate about exports had been a bit of a red herring. The Labour government nurtured the idea of the 'creative industries' on the premise that Britain was not only defined by its cultural industries, but that these were also the platform for Britain to engage competitively with global markets 'as a showcase for Britishness and British life' (Tambini, 2000, p. 8). Within this context television programme exports were used as an example of Britain needing to do better. Britain was first found to be failing as an exporter of television, requiring a 're-branding' of domestic television to satisfy international markets. But little attention was given to high levels of imports by cable and satellite channels because this conflicted with a commitment to free trade. Then it was argued that Britain was not failing as an exporter at all, and that there was no need to restructure British television to produce the 'right' type of programmes for international consumption. The domestic audience came first.

Yet this assessment masked other concerns, voiced most vehemently by the independent production sector, that there were indeed fundamental faults in domestic television. These concerns related to the programme supply market and the perception that free-to-air broadcasters, foremost the BBC, had excessive market power, which reduced Britain's capacity to be an effective exporter and inhibited the growth and potential of the independent production sector.

The Labour government's strategy for raising the international presence of British television has been to relax foreign ownership rules for the free-to-air commercial channels, ITV and Five, and to accept changes in the trading relationship between broadcasters and independent producers. These changes may make the commercial broadcasters and independent producers more attractive to outside investors, allowing British companies to consolidate and work more effectively in international markets. This is in keeping with the government's view of sustaining an environment favourable to investment and trade in a globalised economy. But the desire to attract inward investment that will enable British television to engage more effectively internationally sits uneasily next to a free-to-air broadcasting system that has always prioritised domestic content targeted at domestic audiences.

There are fears, yet to be realised that overseas investors, particularly from the US, will change the priorities of British television production in favour of what best serves the commercial interests of American owners and the broader international market.

Changes in the way programme rights are allocated promise a range of outcomes. A pessimistic view holds that the fragmentation of rights among independent producers will reduce the ability to secure funding in overseas markets for high-cost programming. A more optimistic view holds that *some* independent producers will have a greater incentive to explore international markets and build a more sustainable business on the basis of retained rights. BBC Worldwide will still, of course, have privileged access to BBC in-house productions, but it will have to compete much harder to retain the right to market the best independent productions and also deliver value to the licence fee-funded core.

What had started as a debate about the failure to export had been turned around to examine who really exercised market power in the domestic market. The original goals of British policy, stretching back to the Conservative government, had been to create national champions through the encouragement of the BBC's commercial activities and of ITV's desire to consolidate as one company. However, the ITC review served to sow doubt about whether such large broadcasting organisations are always best qualified to raise Britain's international standing in television. The ITV companies after all have not had a strong international strategy or presence (see Chapter 4), and the ITC review demonstrated that the BBC's global commercial ambitions were often at odds with the interests of independent producers. The wings of the BBC and Channel Four have been clipped with respect to ownership of programme rights. ITV and Five may become part of large American conglomerates, with uncertain yet potentially profound implications for domestic production. Whether independent producers also emerge as significant global players has yet to be seen. But it is likely that if this does happen, they will emerge from the small circle of larger companies that have already established an international presence. Bearing this in mind it is appropriate at this point to examine some of the key players involved in the export of programmes and formats.

Notes

1. Oliver argues that Britain is not in deficit in the trade in television programmes (exports £323 million; imports £307 million in 1997) if one ignores feature films shown on television (Oliver, 2000).

2. The BTDA statistics, which only deal with exports, calculated revenues of £430 million in 2001 compared with £673 million estimated by the Office of National Statistics (ONS). The BTDA does not represent all exporters, but it does represent all the large players (BBC Worldwide, Granada, Carlton, Channel Four). The discrepancy may be attributable to the inclusion of the leasing of transmission rights and transponder and encryption costs, but the ONS figures exclude other transactions in services, which are calculated separately and include merchandising revenues and sales commission earned as agents.

3. In Europe, Britain was in deficit in 2002 with France (exports £27 million, imports

£57 million) and the Netherlands (exports £30 million, imports £112 million). The ONS is unable to give specific explanations because of the confidentiality of the data. Dutch programmes are hardly present at all on mainstream British television, but substantial imports from the Netherlands are likely to be attributable to pornography imports by subscription cable and satellite channels (ONS, 2003).

4. Now known as the Department for Culture, Media and Sport.

5. The report only refers to the shares of the US, UK, France, Australia, Canada, Germany, Italy and Japan. South American exporters of *telenovelas*, including Mexico and Brazil, seem to be notable omissions, and it would be interesting to see how Britain's position would change if these were included. The report noted (p. 33) that Britain was only the third source of imports for Spain, Italy and France. For Spain and Italy certainly, it is likely that Britain would have been displaced by South American imports (Buonanno, 2000, p. 22; De Bens and de Smaele, 2001, p. 65).

6. According to PACT, 9 per cent of BBC 2 commissions were licensed in 2002, compared to none for BBC 1. However, the BBC's budget contribution averaged only 26.6 per cent compared to 94.4 per cent by the ITV network, 73.7 per cent by Channel Four and 70 per cent by other channels (PACT, 2002b, p. 20). According to PACT, only 4 per cent of Channel Four commissions were licensed deals (Ibid., p. 23).

4

British Players in the International Marketplace

In Britain the market for the exploitation of secondary rights is highly concentrated. Compared to over 500 production companies, belonging to producers' association PACT (Producers Alliance for Cinema and Television), membership of the distributors' trade body, the British Television Distributors' Association (BDTA) is limited to just under forty companies (Table 4.1).

The BTDA was established on a formal basis in 1999 as a platform for improving communications between producers and distributors and as a forum to represent the sector's interests. Some of its members are foreign-owned (DLT from the US, Southern Star from Australia), but are members by dint of having British-based operations. More importantly, membership does not include the British-based operations of the US studios. Since 1998 the BTDA has published an annual survey of export performance by genre and territory (see Chapter 2). The BTDA represents companies responsible for about 80 per cent of British exports, but there are some significant omissions – including Celador (*Who Wants to Be a Millionaire?*) and RDF Media (the creator of the *Scrapheap Challenge* and *Faking It* formats).

In spite of its small membership the BTDA represents a change from the earliest days of distribution in the 1960s, when international activity was confined almost exclusively to the distribution of in-house productions by the sales arms of the broadcasters. The increase in the number of distribution outfits can be traced back to the growth of the independent production sector following the creation of Channel Four in 1982 as a publisher-broadcaster. As fully-funded commissions, much of the new programming was distributed by Channel Four's own distribution arm, Channel Four International. However, for a small proportion of programming, demand was created for distribution by companies other than the broadcaster-distributors. The sector also benefited from the 1990 Broadcasting Act, which required ITV and BBC to take 25 per cent of qualifying productions (excluding news, sport) from the independent sector. Again this benefit was of course only partial, in that most independent productions were

Table 4.1: Membership of the British Television Distributors' Association

3DD Entertainment	MercuryMedia International
BBC Worldwide	Minotaur International
Beckmann International	Optomen Television
Beyond Distribution	PACT
Carlton International Media	Parthenon Entertainment Ltd
Channel Four International/4 Rights	Portman Film and Television
Chatsworth Television Distributors	Ragdoll
Chorion PLC	S4C International
Chrysalis Distribution	Screentime Partners Ltd
Cineflix International UK Ltd	September International
Cumulus Distribution Ltd	Southern Star
DLT Entertainment UK Ltd	Target
Eagle Vision	The Television Corporation
Entertainment Rights	TVF International
Explore International	TV-Loonland
Fremantle International Distribution	VCI Group
Granada International	Wall to Wall
High Point Film & TV Ltd	Zeal TV
Hit Entertainment	Zig Zag Productions
London Films	

Source: BTDA website June 2004, <www.btda.org>.

distributed by broadcaster-distributors, because most were fully funded with broadcasters retaining all rights. The number of producer-distributors and non-aligned distributors has always been limited by the ability to gain access to product. The networking arrangements for the ITV Network Centre gave some extra scope, because ITV only acquires primary broadcast rights, leaving producers to make their own arrangements for distribution.

Following the recommendations of the ITC's review of the programme supply market in 2002, the situation has changed, resulting in greater opportunities for independent producers to retain rights for overseas exploitation. Changes in the terms of trade will allow some producers (but clearly not all) to build assets and become international players in their own right.

What follows is a brief historical background and breakdown of the distribution business with selected case studies of some of the key players. This includes the broadcaster-distributors, BBC Worldwide, Carlton International Media, Granada International and Channel Four International, which account for the bulk of British trade, and three case studies of independent producers (RDF Media, Wall to Wall Television, HIT Entertainment), which have built international businesses by retaining rights. The list is by no means exhaustive, but serves to identify the activities, strategies and performance of some of the most active companies.

Breaking down the distribution sector

Players involved in the international exploitation of television programming can be categorised into three types – broadcaster-distributors, producer-distributors and non-aligned distributors.

Broadcaster-distributors

Broadcaster-distributors, the in-house sales arms of the broadcasters, are the largest operators in the marketplace. They include BBC Worldwide, Channel Four International, Carlton International Media (the sales arm of ITV franchise-holder Carlton Communications), Granada International (the sales arm of ITV franchise-holder Granada) and S4C International (the sales arm of Welsh public broadcaster S4C).[1] Carlton International Media and Granada International merged at the start of 2004 to form Granada International. The strength of BBC Worldwide and the ITV sales houses rests on a considerable back catalogue and access to in-house productions, which together accounted for 38 per cent of total qualifying programmes on the network terrestrial channels in 2001 (excluding news, sport) (ITC, 2002a, app. 1, p. 13).

They also handle material from other sources, including independent productions fully funded by the parent broadcaster. It has been estimated that BBC Worldwide and Channel Four International distributed approximately three-quarters of the independent productions commissioned by their parent organisations in 2000 (Ibid., app. 1, p. 32). However, as we saw in Chapter 3, moves to split primary broadcast rights from secondary and international rights in the commissioning process give independent producers greater scope to select alternative distributors. At the ITV network, for example, where independent commissions are licensed for primary transmission only, just 30 per cent of programmes from independent producers were distributed by broadcaster-distributors in 2000 (Ibid., p. 33). Yet this has to be set against the ability of Carlton and Granada to secure the lion's share of commissions from the ITV Network Centre, a situation which may endure after Carlton and Granada's merger in 2003 to form 'one ITV'. Granada, for example, produced 56 per cent of ITV's commissioned programme hours in 2002 (Granada, 2002b, p. 3).

Not surprisingly, therefore, it is broadcaster-distributors that account for the lion's share of international exploitation. According to a survey commissioned by PACT in 2002, the market for programme distribution breaks down as follows (PACT, 2002b, p. 10): BBC Worldwide 49 per cent; Carlton International 19 per cent; Granada 13 per cent; Channel Four International 16 per cent; others 3 per cent.[2]

Another way of gauging the size of the market is to set stated income from the individual sales houses against revenues earned overseas (see Table 4.2). Interestingly what this demonstrates is that a large proportion of revenues ranging from approximately one-third to almost two-thirds are in fact generated in the British market – from secondary sales to other British-based channels and from publishing and licensed products. Overseas revenues are small, particularly in comparison to group turnover, undermining the claims of Carlton and Granada, for example, to be global operations. The data also confirms the strong position of BBC Worldwide, whose overseas revenues (excluding income from

Table 4.2: Broadcaster-distributor revenues (£ million)

	Turnover	Overseas Revenues	Group Turnover
BBC Worldwide[1]	578.2 (2002)	252.6 (2002)	3,383 (2002)
	578.5 (2003)	228.8 (2003)	3,532 (2003)
Carlton International[2]	89.5 (2002)	46.3 (2002)	965 (2002)
Granada International	63.0 (2002)	21.0 (2002)	1,408 (2002)
	80.0 (2003)		1,411 (2003)
Channel Four	36.9 (2002)		774 (2002)
International[3]/4Rights	33.3 (2003)		779 (2003)

Source: Annual Reports.
Notes:
1. Turnover excludes revenues from joint ventures.
2. The overseas revenues of the sales subsidiaries are not broken down separately, but one has to assume that most of the overseas revenues by destination of the parent companies Granada and Carlton are attributable to the international sales houses.
3. In 2002, Channel Four International was combined with the Consumer Products division as 4Rights, and generated revenues of £36.9 million on group turnover of £774 million, but this figure has not been broken down according to geographic destination.

joint venture channels) far exceed those of rival broadcaster-distributors and account for more than half of the BTDA's estimate of $666 million (£426 million) in export revenues in 2002. BBC Worldwide itself claims to have a 54 per cent share of Britain's total television export revenues, based on BTDA data (BBC Worldwide, 2003a). Together with Fremantle (formerly Pearson), BBC Worldwide, Granada, and Carlton were estimated to account for more than 70 per cent of total sales in 2000 (David Graham & Associates, 2000, p. 38).

Broadcaster-distributors such as BBC Worldwide and Channel Four argue that it is the large scale of their operations that breeds success. This allows them to risk substantial investment in marketing, geographic coverage and programme advances, reinforcing their ability to leverage content and brands to create markets (BBC Worldwide, 2002b, p. 3; Channel Four, 2002a, p. 16). Some independent producers, however, would argue that their needs are not best served by broadcaster-distributors, as it is the producer who has the greatest incentive to maximise revenues from their properties either through in-house distribution or by appointing an independent distributor (RDF Media, 2002a; Wall to Wall Television, 2002).

Table 4.3: Top independent production companies with in-house distribution capability by turnover, 2003 (£ millions)

Company	Turnover	Key exports
HIT Entertainment	169	*Bob the Builder, Barney, Angelina Ballerina, Pingu, Kipper*
TalkbackTHAMES	131	*Pop Idol, The Bill, How Clean is Your House?*
All3Media (formerly Chrysalis TV Group)	93	*Midsomer Murders, Ultimate Force*
Endemol Entertainment UK	90	*Ground Force, Changing Rooms, Ready Steady Cook*
TWI	72.5	*The British Empire in Colour*
The Television Corporation	68.3	*Robot Wars, Britain's Worst, Paradise Hotel*
RDF Media	45.3	*Faking It, Scrapheap Challenge, Perfect Match, Banzai, Wife Swap*
Celador	42.95	*Who Wants to Be a Millionaire?, Britain's Brainiest Kid*

Source: Broadcast Supplement, 19 March 2004, pp. 4–5.

Producer-distributors

At the second level there are independent production companies with their own distribution arms such as the Chrysalis TV Group, renamed as All3Media in December 2003 (*Midsomer Murders*), HIT Entertainment (*Bob the Builder*), RDF Media (*Faking It, Scrapheap Challenge*) and the Television Corporation (*Robot Wars, Britain's Worst*). Producer-distributors are companies that have retained rights for overseas and secondary exploitation. Few specialise in international exploitation of drama, because the high costs and risk involved make these largely a preserve of broadcaster-distributors. While the profit margins for production in Britain are low, the secondary exploitation of properties allows some independent companies to raise their profitability significantly. It is for example significant that some of Britain's top production companies, also operate their own distribution arms (see Table 4.3).

The ability of producer-distributors to secure secondary rights has depended on one or a combination of the following:

- Securing a commission from the ITV Network Centre, which only acquires primary rights for a set period, leaving secondary rights with the producer.
- Brokering deals for entertainment and drama with talent attached, allowing leverage to secure more lucrative terms in negotiations with broadcasters, for example for the retention of formats.
- Bringing money to the table for production in the form of co-production finance, pre-sales or in very rare cases funding raised from stockmarket launches.

The most successful companies have built assets by focusing on key brands rather than relying on the smaller returns from exploiting back catalogue, and the fortunes of smaller companies can be transformed by one international hit, particularly in America. Examples include children's television specialists HIT Entertainment (*Bob the Builder*) and Ragdoll Productions (*Teletubbies*), whose success can be traced back to profits from merchandising, rather than production, where licence fees from programme sales rarely cover production costs (see Chapter 2). Celador's experience with the quiz show *Who Wants to Be a Millionaire?* is also illustrative, because most of its profits are generated from secondary exploitation rather than production in Britain. In the year ending September 2002 Celador International, the international sales arm, generated turnover of £29.4 million and trading profits after tax of £5.8 million. In the same period, Celador Productions, engaged primarily in British production, generated turnover of £20.9 million and profits after tax of only £1.7 million (Celador International, 2002; Celador Productions 2002). The lower financial risk associated with factual and entertainment programming and the retention of format rights has given others, such as RDF

Media (*Scrapheap Challenge*, *Faking It*), Wall to Wall (*Frontier House*) and the Television Corporation (*Robot Wars*), the opportunity to build a production and format business in the American market (see Chapter 5).

However, the vast majority of independent production companies are domestically focused and do not operate their own distribution operations. Furthermore, not all programmes have an international value. Rights in themselves have no value unless they are effectively exploited, and most independent producers do not have the resources to market their own programmes internationally. The effects of fully-funded commissions have tied most to distribution by broadcaster-distributors. The implementation of codes of practice by the broadcasters, allowing for the separation of primary broadcast rights from secondary rights in the negotiation process, will alter this situation. With more opportunity to retain rights, some producers may opt to invest in their own distribution operations or appoint alternative distributors. For those who decide to retain rights, one difficulty will be in finding non-aligned distributors. In all probability the proposed changes will benefit those few independent production companies that have already started to make their presence felt in the key territories of America and Western Europe with internationally attractive programming and formats.

Non-aligned distributors

Finally there are those distributors who concentrate on representing the programmes of a range of producers and format holders. These constitute a very small sector of the market – by PACT estimates only 3 per cent. A difficult business climate resulted in consolidation and closures in the late 1990s, reducing the pool of smaller independent distributors from which independent producers could select (Keighron, 2001, p. 38). First, there was the problem of locating properties, because broadcaster-distributors retained rights to most independent productions. The situation was compounded by competitive pressures, which resulted in production deficits that were too large for smaller distribution companies to support (Ibid., p. 40). Advances are non-returnable and a distributor is at risk if the programme is cancelled or does not sell well to recoup costs. Second, the most successful independent producers have tended to incorporate distribution within their own companies.

To create a business, independent distributors have had to find alternative strategies rather than simply selling finished product. One way is to act as a broker securing co-production funding and pre-sales in return for distribution rights and possibly a share of back end. Some, like Entertainment Rights, the children's specialist, have acquired properties to create an asset base (*Basil Brush*, *Postman Pat*), invest in production and transform themselves into brand managers, along the lines of HIT Entertainment (see later). Target has built a business by focusing not only on independent producers in Britain, but also on producers and format owners in other English-speaking countries. For example, it sold the reality talent format *Popstars* based on an idea originally developed in New Zealand. It has also developed relationships with producers such as Shed Productions, which retained rights to its ITV drama series, *Bad Girls* and *Footballers Wives*, allowing it to appoint Target as a distributor.

Transnational ownership

British distribution has largely been characterised by the distribution of British programmes by British companies. However, as we saw in Chapter 3, the changes brought about by the 2003 Communications Act allow American companies to acquire ITV companies Carlton and Granada (who merged in 2002), and Five, including their in-house distribution operations. Second, the potential opportunities for independent producers to retain secondary rights to their productions promises to make some of these producers more attractive to overseas investors.

Changing ownership patterns and consolidation within the industry suggest that there will come a point when the international exploitation of British programming is undertaken increasingly by non-British companies. For example, FremantleMedia (formerly Pearson Television until October 2001) is the production arm of the European conglomerate the RTL Group, which owns a 65 per cent share in Five, as well as television interests in nine European countries.[3] Pearson, its predecessor, had already become internationally active, acquiring Australian production company Grundy (*Neighbours, Sons and Daughters*) and US television movie distributor ACI in 1995, followed by US entertainment and game-show producer All American in 1997 (*The Price is Right, Family Feud, Baywatch*). Alongside its production activities in thirty-nine countries including North America, FremantleMedia operates a distribution arm, Fremantle International Distribution. This markets British programming and formats from Fremantle's British production entity TalkbackTHAMES, as well as programming from other labels within the production group, including Grundy (*Neighbours* Australia), Ufa (*Hinter Gittern/Behind Bars* Germany) and FremantleMedia Productions North America (*Baywatch*).

Similarly, Endemol Entertainment UK (formerly Bazal), the producer of the British version of the Dutch format *Big Brother*, and the originator of home makeover format *Changing Rooms*, is part of a larger European enterprise owned by the Spanish-based telecoms and media giant Telefónica. The emergence of European-based transnational groupings such as RTL Group and Telefónica contrasts with the largely British-based operations of British exporters.

Case study – BBC Worldwide

BBC Worldwide Ltd is a wholly owned commercial subsidiary of the BBC, and its principle commercial arm. It was established in 1994, replacing BBC Enterprises. Its role is to develop and undertake the BBC's commercial activities, exploiting rights associated with BBC programmes and the BBC brand, for programme sales, the operation of commercial television channels, video and DVD, events, publishing, product licensing, the Internet and interactive media. The range and scale of its activities are unmatched by other distributors.

Worldwide exists to maximise the value of the BBC's assets for the benefit of the licence-fee payer and its profits are reinvested into the BBC's licence fee-funded programming. In 2002–03, cash-flow returned to the BBC totalled £123 million on turnover of £658 million (BBC Worldwide, 2003a, 2003b). However, Worldwide's investment in programming needs to be placed in context and compared to the BBC's total investment in original production of £1.2 billion in 2001–02 (BBC, 2002, p. 4). In 1997 Worldwide was set the target of delivering £210 million to the Corporation on turnover of £1 billion by 2007. Table 4.4 shows the growth in BBC Worldwide's revenues and its financial contribution to the BBC between 1997 and 2003.

Although Worldwide is a commercial business, it is not like other commercial distribution outfits, because it is accountable to its publicly funded parent, the BBC, rather than shareholders. This relationship with the BBC renders it subject to restrictions that do not apply to its competitors. It must not contravene

Table 4.4: BBC Worldwide revenue growth 1997–2003 including cash-flow return to the BBC (£ million)

	1997–8	1998–9	1999–00	2000–01	2001–02	2002–03
Turnover	422	446	514	587	660	658
Group turnover[1]	409	420	464	520	578	578
Cash flow to BBC	75	81	82	96	106	123
Including investment in BBC programmes[2]	50	58	79	76	81	N/A

Source: BBC Worldwide Annual Reviews; BBC Worldwide Report and Financial Statements, 2003; BBC Worldwide, 2002b, pp. 19–23.

Notes:

1. This excludes the BBC's share of income from commercial joint ventures.

2. This includes investment by Worldwide and its commercial partners.

European state-aid rules by subsidising commercial activities from licence-fee income. It is also required to abide by the BBC's Fair Trading Commitment, an obligation stemming from the BBC Charter and Agreement. This stipulates that it must only engage in commercial activities that are consistent with and support the BBC's role as a public service broadcaster (BBC Worldwide, 2002a, p. 30). As a commercial subsidiary, it must not risk licence-fee payers' funds, and it is required to pay for the commercial rights to BBC programmes at 'fair' rates (Ibid.).

BBC Worldwide negotiates terms with the BBC's Commercial Agency (formerly Rights Agency). Established in 1997 and originally co-funded by the BBC and Worldwide, the agency became fully funded by the BBC in 2001 to reinforce the 'arm's-length' relationship (Elliott, 2003, p. 21). The Commercial Agency manages all of the BBC's commercial relationships for the exploitation of programming on behalf of BBC production departments. BBC in-house productions are offered first to Worldwide as the BBC's 'preferred distribution partner' for investment consideration rather than other distributors, after the BBC has declared the amount of funding it is prepared to put into a production (BBC, 2002, pp. 48–50).

Previously if budget deficits on independent productions were covered by investment from BBC Worldwide (or third party distributors), and if the production was cash-flowed by the BBC, the programme was treated as fully funded and all rights with the exception of format rights owned or created by the producer resided with the BBC (Ibid., p. 47). However, as we saw in Chapter 2 this process became subject to criticism, with accusations that Worldwide overbid for rights, resulting in low returns for independent producers after Worldwide had recouped its investment and distribution fee. With greater leeway now to bring in alternative distributors, some producers believe their share of back end profits will be larger. The prospect of independent producers retaining more rights to their productions with the introduction of new codes of practice is likely to affect Worldwide's ability to secure rights to the most attractive independent productions, which in certain cases (*Tweenies*, *The Fimbles*, *Teletubbies*) have been its best-selling properties.

More seriously for the BBC, the ITC Programme Supply Review reopened the debate for Worldwide to be sold off amid growing concerns that the BBC's commercial activities are in conflict with its public service obligations. In addition to independent producers who accuse the BBC and Worldwide of manipulating trading terms to secure secondary rights, commercial channel operators resent Worldwide's expansion into new services, including jointly owned commercial channels, which benefit from BBC programming. For example, the UKTV joint venture with Flextech Television (see later), benefits from a fifteen-year programme supply deal with BBC Worldwide, signed in 1997, which gives it a first look at BBC content (Holmwood, 2003, p. 13).

However, disquiet about the Corporation's commercial activities conveniently ignores the fact that successive governments have encouraged these activities. The drive to maximise commercial revenues has its roots in the Conservative government's 1994 White Paper on the BBC, which encouraged the evolution of the Corporation 'into an international multi-media enterprise, building on its present commercial services for audiences in this country and overseas' (DNH, 1994, p. 1). The Corporation had always been involved in commercial activities on a small scale, but it was the 1996 Royal Charter that endorsed commercial activities as core objectives of the BBC, giving it a public duty to commercially exploit its assets (DNH, 1996). This was the price demanded by government for maintaining the status quo on the licence fee as the principle source of funding and for sanctioning new licence fee-funded digital services.

The 1996 Charter allowed the BBC to develop and pursue new markets at home and abroad through commercial joint ventures without recourse to the public purse. These have found expression in a global partnership with the American company Discovery Communications Inc., for factual co-productions and the launch of joint-venture international channels, and with Flextech Television, the content division of Telewest Communications, for the supply of commercial subscription channels under the UKTV brand in Britain.

The Labour government has continued the push to make the BBC more commercially aware. The last licence fee increase of £200 million per year until 2006 was linked to the Corporation making £1.1billion in savings by 2006–07 from increased efficiency and commercial activities, including joint ventures and public-private partnerships (Smith, 2000). Encouraged by the government, the BBC has promoted itself as Britain's national champion in global markets, 'bringing the best of British culture, both classic and contemporary, and the highest standards of journalistic integrity and authority to audiences all over the world' (BBC, 2000, p. 30).

Commercial activities

In 2002, Worldwide sold 40,000 hours of programming to over 550 broadcasters in sixty-nine countries, underlining its position as Europe's largest exporter of television programmes (BBC Worldwide, 2002a, p. 4). Programme sales are just one part of its wide-ranging activities and accounted for approximately 26 per cent of turnover in 2002 and 2003 (see Table 4.5). More than half of its income derives from publishing and new media – including licensed products.

Table 4.5: BBC Worldwide revenues by activity (£ million)

	1997–8	1998–9	1999–00	2000–01	2001–02	2002–03
Television sales	126.0	127.6	138.4	150.0	172.3	168.8
Publishing/new media	256.6	255.9	277.0	300.2	331.7	338.0
Channels	26.3	36.8	48.4	67.3	71.8	53.2
Share of joint ventures		26.0	50.0	67.6	81.6	79.5
Discontinued activities		–	–	2.1	2.4	18.5[1]
Total	408.9	446.3	513.8	587.2	659.8	658.0

Source: BBC Worldwide annual reviews/BBC Worldwide reports and financial statements.
Notes:
1. Includes BBC World and Beeb.com.

Table 4.6: BBC Worldwide revenues by geographic origin (£ million)

	1997–8	1998–9	1999–00	2000–01	2001–02	2002–03
UK	273.2	267.4	282.0	299.3	323.2	331.2
Americas	43.9	53.4	63.0	84.3	108.8	105.8
Rest of world	91.8	99.5	118.8	133.9	143.8	123.0
Discontinued activities				2.1	2.4	18.5
Total group turnover*	408.9	420.3	463.8	519.6	578.2	578.5

Source: BBC Worldwide Annual Reviews/BBC Worldwide reports and financial statements.
* Excludes BBC income from joint ventures.
Note:
1. In 2003/04 BBC Worldwide reported sales of £657 million, returning £141 million to the BBC. This was
an increase of £17 million on sales of £640 million in 2002/03 (excluding £18.5 million generated by the
discontinued BBC Worldwide activities of BBC World, now incorporated into the Global News Division
and Beeb.com).

However, although programme sales account for only about a quarter of revenues, they form the core of Worldwide's global brand strategy, providing a platform for further business in publishing, video and consumer products. Revenues from Britain accounted for over half of group turnover in 2002 and 2003, based largely on income from publishing, video/DVD and consumer products, but represent a decline from 1997–8 when Britain accounted for more than two-thirds of revenues (see Table 4.6).

Global brands

The development of global brands on a multi-territory, multimedia basis has been a central part of Worldwide's strategy since 1997, and these brands were estimated to account for 23 per cent of turnover in 2000–01 compared to 15 per cent in 1999 (BBC Worldwide, 2001).

Factual brands include the natural history series *The Blue Planet* and the *Walking with . . .* franchise, both products of Worldwide's joint venture with Discovery Communications Inc. The creation of brands requires substantial investment, and Worldwide's co-production partnership with Discovery, concluded in 1997, has been key in the drive to develop factually based 'landmark' programming. BBC Worldwide and its commercial partners invested:

- £4.4 million in *The Blue Planet* (8 x 50 mins) (56 per cent of budget)
- £5.7 million in *Walking with Beasts* (6 x 30 mins) (75 per cent of budget)
- £3.6 million in *Walking with Dinosaurs* (6 x 30 mins) (75 per cent of budget) (BBC Worldwide, 2002b, p. 4).

Branded formats include the quiz show *The Weakest Link* and the long-running popular music show *Top of the Pops*. *Top of the Pops* can be seen in 110 countries and is recreated locally in many others, including France (France 2), Italy (Raidue), Germany (RTL), Belgium (Jim TV) and the Netherlands (BNN/N2). Format sales of *The Weakest Link*, which has aired in over eighty countries, contributed £10 million in sales in 2001–02 (BBC Worldwide, 2002a, p. 6). Worldwide's focus on formats as global brands began in the late 1990s with Worldwide investing more than £300,000 a year (£60,000 per show) into pilots developed by BBC Entertainment, including *The Weakest Link*, *Friends Like These* and *Dog Eat Dog* (Fry 2002b; Waller, 2000). Worldwide had always been involved in the format business (*Noel's House Party, Ready, Steady, Cook, Pets Win Prizes*), but the business was mainly confined to Europe and it was not involved in the production of overseas adaptations of its formats. This changed with the development of *The Weakest Link*. To maintain control of the brand, Worldwide has sought to co-produce the show in the major territories, working with local producers, but contracting directly with broadcasters (Jarvis, 2001). In this way it not only benefits from the sale of the format, but can also benefit financially from production.

Children's properties are a major source of brand exploitation, because of opportunities in consumer products, publishing and video, and with global sales of £70 million in 2000 are BBC Worldwide's leading brands (BBC Worldwide, 2000). The business has been built on the development of long-running series for younger children including *Teletubbies* (1997), *Tweenies* (1999) and *The Fim-*

bles (2002), made by independent production companies Ragdoll, Tell-Tale Productions and Novel Entertainment respectively. *Tweenies* was financed with £4.6 million from BBC Worldwide, and *The Fimbles* was funded with a £3.5 million contribution (BBC Worldwide, 2002b, p. 6). *Teletubbies* had sold to 120 countries including China by 2002 (BBC Worldwide, 2002a, p. 16), generating £116 million in sales for BBC Worldwide since its launch and an estimated £1 billion at retail (BBC Worldwide, 2003c). *Tweenies*, launched in 1999, had sold to more than thirty countries by 2001 (BBC Worldwide, 2001, p.13), generating £93 million in sales for BBC Worldwide by 2003 (BBC Worldwide, 2003c).

Drama, unlike other genres, is too culturally specific to be branded on a global scale, but Worldwide's participation is important for key programmes. *The Lost World* (2 x 75 mins), based on Sir Arthur Conan Doyle's dinosaur adventure, was produced with £1.4 million of investment from Worldwide and its commercial partners, Arts and Entertainment in America in association with RTL Television in Germany, equivalent to more than half the total budget. It sold to thirty-eight countries and generated more than £6.9 million in revenues (BBC Worldwide, 2002b, p. 6).

To reinforce the BBC corporate brand and counter the marginalisation of acquisitions in overseas schedules, Worldwide has also developed BBC-branded blocks to slot into foreign television schedules. These have the benefit of accommodating shorter-run sitcoms and one-off documentaries, and can also be used to introduce more 'stretching' programmes (Homewood, 2001). Branded blocks include BBC Wild, BBC Britcom, BBC Learning Zone and BBC Exclusiv, the latter available on the commercial channel Vox in Germany.

Channels

To counter the decline in sales of completed programmes, BBC Worldwide has also invested in new platforms for British programming with a network of wholly owned and joint-venture commercial channels at home and abroad unmatched by any other British player (see Tables 4.7, 4.8 and 4.9). These aim to generate revenues from programme sales and subscriptions and provide additional outlets for British programming and talent. While the wholly owned channels raise awareness of the BBC brand, the commercial joint ventures build equity. By 1999–2000 BBC joint-venture channels accounted for 33 per cent of Worldwide's revenues of £138 million from television sales (BBC Worldwide, 2000).

Of the wholly owned channels (Table 4.7), BBC America, available in 34.5 million US homes in 2003, has proved successful as a showcase for British programming (see Chapter 6). BBC Prime was established in 1995 as a means of exploiting BBC Worldwide's catalogue in the pan-European market. Broadcast in English with no localisation of content, its impact is marginal, because it is

Table 4.7: BBC Worldwide wholly owned channels

Channel	Area of operation	Households 2003 (million)
BBC World[1]	Global	253.6 – launched 1995
BBC Prime	Europe, Middle East, Africa	11.5 – launched 1995
BBC America	America	34.5 – launched 1998
BBC Food	South Africa, Scandinavia	0.8 – launched 2002

Source: BBC Worldwide Annual Review 2002–03.
Note:
1. In 2002, BBC World was incorporated as a separate commercial company, as part of the BBC's global news division. BBC World replaced World Service Television, established in 1991.

Table 4.8: BBC Worldwide joint venture with Flextech in Britain

Channel	Households 2003 (million)
UK Horizons	8.3
UK Style	8.4
UK Drama	7.9
UK Gold	8.9
UK Gold 2	7.9
UK Food	7.9
UK History	9.3 – launched 2002
UK Bright Ideas	8.6 – launched 2002

Source: BBC Worldwide Annual Review 2002–03.

Table 4.9: BBC Worldwide joint ventures outside Britain

With Discovery Communications (DCI)		Households 2003 (million)
Channel	Area of operation	
People and Arts	Latin America	13.5
Animal Planet	Asia	80.1
Animal Planet	Latin America	10.8
Animal Planet	Europe	13.5
Animal Planet	US	81.4
With DCI and NetStar		
Animal Planet	Canada	0.9 – launched 2001
With DCI and Jupiter Programming		
Animal Planet	Japan	1.7
With Foxtel and FremantleMedia		
UKTV	Australia	1.2
With Alliance Atlantis Communications Inc.		
BBC Canada	Canada	0.6 – launched 2001
BBC Kids	Canada	0.9 – launched 2001

Source: BBC Worldwide Annual Review 2002–03.

only available in 11.5 million households. Alongside BBC World, BBC World-wide's global twenty-four-hour English-language news service, BBC Prime, barely covers its operating costs and does not have the resources to localise (see Chalaby, 2002, p. 198). BBC World was launched in 1995 as a response to CNN, and uses the BBC's existing network of international correspondents and news bureaux. Available in 253 million homes in 2003, it targets the top 5 per cent of households including the international business community like its American rivals, CNBC and CNN (Ibid., p. 191). BBC Food was launched in 2002 in South Africa and Scandinavia.

As part of its joint venture with Discovery Communications Inc., BBC World-wide operates jointly owned commercial factual channels, Animal Planet (in Asia, Latin America, Europe, the US, Canada and Japan) and People and Arts (in Latin America), alongside a range of joint-venture channels with commercial partner, Flextech, in Britain (see Tables 4.8 and 4.9). Mirroring BBC America, BBC Worldwide has also established joint-venture channels in its other English-speaking markets of Canada (BBC Kids, BBC Canada) and Australia (UKTV). Although BBC Worldwide has equity in the joint-venture channels, it has no liability to fund any losses.

Case study – Granada International and Carlton International Media

Granada International and Carlton International Media were the remnants of the individual distribution outfits that used to represent the various ITV broadcaster-producers, which have since disappeared as each company acquired its rivals.[4] In October 2002 Granada and Carlton Communications announced their intention to merge following amendments proposed in the *Communications Bill*, subject to approval by the Competition Commission, which came in October 2003. Their international operations merged at the start of 2004, creating a single distribution outfit for ITV broadcasters for the first time, with over 33,000 hours of programming and 1,800 feature films. The creation of a single ITV represents the long-awaited outcome of many years of lobbying by Granada and Carlton to be allowed to create the scale thought necessary to participate on the global stage and create one of the leading commercial broadcasters in Europe (Carlton Communications, 2002b).

Although BBC Worldwide represents over half of British exports by value, his-torically it was the ITV companies that were more successful overseas, particularly in North America. ITC, whose catalogue was acquired by Carlton, produced and exported action-adventure spy series (*The Prisoner, The Saint, Secret Agent*) to the US in the 1960s. Thames Television, which lost its franchise in 1993, was suc-cessful in the 1970s and 1980s in the US syndication market with the comedy series *The Benny Hill Show* and with sitcom formats such as *Man about the House*, which became *Three's Company* on the American ABC network (see Chapter 5). In 1983 British overseas earnings from television programme sales were tenta-tively estimated to total £60 million with two-thirds attributable to ITV (Schlesinger, 1986, p. 277). Thames generated roughly half of ITV's overseas income with estimated revenues of £18 million in 1983 (Ibid., p. 278).[5]

There was a strong incentive for the ITV companies to maximise foreign pro-gramme sales in the 1980s, because until 1986, the 1981 Broadcasting Act levied an excess profits tax of 66.7 per cent on domestic profits exceeding £650,000 or 2.8 per cent of advertising revenues. The levy did not apply to overseas profits. The ITV companies therefore sought to shift revenues to overseas sales and to allocate costs to domestic production of expensive drama (Alvarado, 2000; Collins, 1986; Collins, Garnham and Locksley, 1988). In 1986, the gov-ernment decided to reduce the levy to 45 per cent on British profits in excess of £800,000 and apply a 22.5 per cent levy on overseas profits, thus reducing the incentive to export.

The levy was a contributory factor in ITV's reputation for exporting quality drama during this period. Between 1982 and 1986, Granada vigorously pursued a strategy of producing high-budget literary-based drama for sale overseas – such as *Brideshead Revisited* and *Jewel in the Crown*, a thirteen-part series, which was shot on location in 1983 over six months in India (Alvarado, 2000, p. 311). Alvarado argues that this series and others were not made for altruistic reasons, but for financial reasons to avoid tax, but 'by dropping the Levy and introduc-ing a franchise bidding system [with the 1990 Broadcasting Act], the British government has simultaneously been both blindly greedy and destroyed the incentive for such high-level investment' (Ibid.). The 1990 Broadcasting Act required the ITV companies to blind bid for their franchises, and pay an annual percentage of their revenues to the government for their licences. Some paid too much, and this spelt the end of costly dramas, which were fêted abroad but less efficient in securing the necessary advertising revenues to pay off the gov-ernment. After the phasing out of the levy and the introduction of the franchise-bidding system, ITV became more closely attuned to its role as a mass-appeal broadcaster, concentrating on domestic series and serials that appealed to domestic audiences and advertisers rather than buyers overseas. The shift towards more episodes of daily serials (*Coronation Street*, *Emmerdale*) left less space in a crowded schedule for drama with international appeal.

Carlton International Media

Until its merger with Granada International, Carlton International Media was part of Carlton Communications' Content Division and generated revenues of £89.5 million in 2002 (£81.1 million in 2001).[6] These were actually greater than the group's production revenues of £75.5 million in 2002 (£100.6 million in 2001) (Carlton Communications, 2002b, pp. 18–19). Overseas revenues for Carlton Communications plc totalled £46.3 million in 2002 (£78 million in 2001) compared to £918.3 million in British revenues, primarily from advertis-ing. Although this is not specified one has to assume that the vast majority of these overseas revenues accrue to the activities of Carlton International (Ibid., p. 53).

Carlton International was established in the wake of Carlton taking over the London weekday franchise from Thames in 1993. Associated with the smaller of the ITV in-house production houses, responsible for 30 per cent of ITV's drama output (Carlton Communications, 2002b), it always had to contend with a shortage of internationally appealing material to feed its international catalogue comprising over 18,000 hours of programming.[7] As a consequence it had to look to other sources of programming to sustain its business.[8]

First, unlike most other British distributors, Carlton built a business based on the exploitation of over 2,000 feature film titles, marketed as the Carlton Film Collection. It owned the Rank, Rohauer, Korda and Romulus collections of classic British films, including *The Thirty-Nine Steps* and *Brief Encounter*. Rank Films was purchased in 1997 and includes the popular British *Carry On* comedy films. In 1999, Carlton acquired the ITC (Independent Television Corporation) catalogue of more than 300 films and 5,000 predominantly British television titles from Universal Studios for $150 million (Methven, 1999). This increased its library by 50 per cent to 15,000 hours. The ITC library includes the 1960s cult television series *The Prisoner* and *The Saint*, which are popular on video/DVD, as well as feature films such as *On Golden Pond*, *Sophie's Choice* and *The Eagle Has Landed*. The ITC purchase also provided access to the 1960s supermarionation series *Thunderbirds*, *Captain Scarlet* and *Joe 90*, which formed the core properties of a consumer products division, with plans for new series. The 'classic' archive programming was sold alongside Carlton's contemporary ITV dramas, including the detective series *Inspector Morse* (sold in more than 200 countries) and more recent contemporary productions such as *Bertie and Elizabeth* and *Bob and Rose*, which both sold to forty-five territories in 2002 (Marlow, 2003b, p. 6).

Second, the distributor sought to source product in the American market. Carlton's American outpost, the Los Angeles-based Carlton America, was a specialist in the acquisition and production of American television movies. Carlton acquired the remaining 50 per cent of Hamdon Entertainment, a US co-producer and financier of television movies in October 1999. Rebranded as Carlton America, this US-based production entity supplied Carlton International with up to sixteen American television movies a year. Made for the US networks these sell well in Asia and Europe, where demand for American television movies is high. In 2001, Carlton established a factual production outpost in America, Carlton Production LLC to develop factual programming and build on its existing relationships with *Newsweek* and the Public Broadcasting System (PBS) (Carlton Communications, 2002b, p. 19). The PBS relationship was cemented in 2001 with the establishment of a joint $20 million production fund to develop American drama and documentaries, which Carlton distributes internationally (Marlow, 2002, p. 23). As part of the merger agreement with Granada, Carlton America merged with Granada's US production entity, Granada Entertainment USA, to form Granada America at the end of 2003.

Game-show formats were represented by a separate wholly owned British subsidiary, Action Time, which owned or represented more than sixty-five formats. It was acquired by Carlton in 1997. In 2002 it concluded format deals with the American network Fox for *Naughtiest Blunders* and with CBS for *King of the Castle* (Carlton Communications, 2002b). Action Time lost its separate identity in 2004 following the merger with Granada.

Granada International

Granada International, part of Granada plc, was established in 1998 as the result of a rebranding exercise to replace its predecessor BRITE, the jointly owned international sales arm of the Granada Media Group and Yorkshire Television. In 2000, Granada reported that its international distribution business generated revenues of £58 million on group turnover of £1,087 million (Granada, 2000, p. 33). By 2003, revenues from international distribution and production had risen by 27 per cent from £63 million in 2002 to £80 million on group turnover of £1,411 million, fuelled largely by format sales in the US (Granada/Carlton, 2003, p. 52). Revenues from the international production of formats grew from £18 million in 2002 to £32 million in 2003, with catalogue sales growing by only £4 million to £45 million (Ibid., p. 55).

As Granada acquired other ITV franchises, including Yorkshire Television, the catalogues of each purchase were incorporated into Granada International. The last significant acquisition occurred in 2000 when Granada acquired United News and Media (UNM). In addition to the incorporation of the Anglia and Meridian broadcasting franchises (HTV was sold to Carlton), the purchase was meant to offer a stronger proposition in the international marketplace because of UNM's strength in wildlife (with the *Survival* catalogue), drama (including the historical epic *Hornblower*) and animation (with Cosgrove Hall). UNM's distribution business, ITEL, was integrated into Granada International to create a library of over 17,000 hours of programming. After the merger with UNM there was a rationalisation of Granada's production business. The children's operation was streamlined in 2001 as a result of a drop in commissions from the ITV network (Anon., 2001a). With the closure of *Survival*'s Norwich production base and a shift of production to Bristol in 2001, the UNM *Survival* and *Partridge* wildlife brands were dropped in favour of the *Granada Wild* brand.

The focus of Granada International differed from Carlton because it had access to a much larger domestic production base totalling 6,500 hours in 2002 for both ITV and other broadcasters, including 56 per cent of the ITV network's commissioned hours (Granada, 2002b). As a result, programming produced in Britain for the ITV network formed the core of its international activities. This comprises long-running serials such as *Coronation Street*, *Emmerdale Farm* and *Heartbeat*, contemporary dramas such as *Cold Feet*, detective series *Poirot* and *A Touch of Frost* and literary-based, co-produced period drama such as *The Forsyte Saga* and *Dr Zhivago* (Granada, 2002b). Top international sellers include *Coronation Street*, *Poirot* and *The Forsyte Saga*, which each generated £2 million in overseas sales in 2002 (Ibid., p. 7).

Like Carlton, Granada sought to transplant its production expertise internationally. The Hothouse (formerly Greenhouse), a department specialising in the development of entertainment formats for international exploitation, was set up in 1999. Successful format sales include *Boot Camp* to the American Fox network in 2001, and *I'm a Celebrity . . . Get Me Out of Here!*, which was sold to and produced by Granada for the American network ABC in 2002.

Granada's international operations include the US production outpost, Granada Entertainment USA (renamed Granada America in 2003 following its merger with Carlton America), in Los Angeles, which has produced television movies, local versions of some of Granada's most popular domestic dramas (*Cracker*, *Cold Feet*) and entertainment formats for American broadcasters (see Chapter 5). Granada's German production outfit, Granada Produktion für Film und Fernsehen, delivered twenty-two hours to German television in 2002 (Granada, 2002b, p. 5). In Australia Granada has a 10.03 per cent shareholding in commercial broadcaster Channel Seven. It also runs an Australian production arm, Granada Media Australia, which not only produces for Australian broadcasters, but also functions as a local production house for Granada productions filmed in Australia, including the American and British versions of the reality game show *I'm a Celebrity . . . Get Me Out of Here!*. However, set against the scale of its domestic production activities, and of those of its rivals such as FremantleMedia, which has production operations in thirty-nine countries, Granada still has some way to go before it can call itself a truly global player.

Case study – Channel Four International

Channel Four International Ltd is the international sales and co-production arm of publicly owned and commercially funded Channel Four. In 2001, it was incorporated as part of 4 Ventures, Channel Four's grouping of commercial businesses, where it generated revenues of £25.3 million on group turnover of £734 million in 2001 (Channel Four, 2002c). If revenues from the Consumer

Products division (publishing, video, music and licensed product) are added, this rises to £34.5 million. By 2002, the combined revenues from programme sales and consumer products had risen to £36.9 million on group turnover of £774 million, with Channel Four International contributing £30.7 million from programme sales (Channel Four, 2003).

According to Channel Four International's own accounts, 36 per cent of its revenues came from Britain in 2002, followed by the US with a further 33 per cent. European sales trailed with an 11 per cent share (Channel Four International, 2003). British sales are largely attributable to Channel Four's digital channel E4, with whom Channel Four International has a guaranteed output deal and to sales to other British channels in the secondary market place (Channel Four, 2002a, p. 17; Morris, 2002).

Unlike BBC Worldwide, Carlton International Media or Granada International, Channel Four International does not have access to an in-house production infrastructure to feed its catalogue. It is almost entirely dependent on access to independent productions commissioned by Channel Four. Channel Four International's strategy has therefore focused on building 'creative and commercial' partnerships with independent producers 'from the creative development of the idea between producer and commissioning editor, through to its exploitation in secondary markets by 4Ventures' (Channel Four, 2002a, p. 14). In addition to providing advances to fill funding gaps on internationally attractive programming, its skill has been in locating funding, particularly for factual programming, through longstanding partnerships with the PBS, the Discovery Channel, National Geographic and the History Channel in the US, the ABC in Australia and ZDF in Germany. According to Mike Morris, Channel Four International's Marketing Director, these relationships are mutually beneficial in both creative and financial terms:

> We have a range of long-running co-production arrangements with the broadcasters, whereby we will take a certain number of projects into the relationship, and they will bring a certain number of projects into the relationship. So we don't have to go out individually each time and try and do a co-production. ... So suppose the channel decides they want to make a programme on the *Mayflower*, for example. We know they want to make the programme, we develop a treatment with the producer and with the Channel about that programme. We'll take it to WGBH [in the US] and we will secure whatever we can in terms of co-production funding. ... We don't take any commission on that. We put that money straight into the programme budget. Then we get international rights for the rest of the world. That's the reason why we do it. We do it to provide a service for the channel. (Morris, 2002)

Constituting the vast majority of its export efforts is factual programming including cookery programmes (*Nigella Bites*), historical series (*The Six Wives of Henry VIII*), and one-off documentaries such as *How the Towers Fell Down*, which sold to nineteen countries in 2002 (Marlow, 2003b, p. 6). But sales of one-off programmes are costly in terms of marketing and contracts. Hour for hour, more revenues can be generated from sales of drama (Morris, 2002). Notable successes include the format sale to the American premium channel Showtime of gay drama *Queer as Folk*, which has since aired as three series. Other drama successes include *Shackleton*, an epic adventure story about polar exploration, starring Kenneth Branagh. Co-produced with partners in America (A&E) and Australia (ABC), it sold in twenty countries in 2002 (Marlow, 2003b, p. 6).

The implications of codes of practice for the allocation of programme rights and the prospect of separating primary broadcast rights from secondary rights, allowing independent producers greater leeway to choose alternative distributors, poses particular challenges to Channel Four International's business. Some of its most important suppliers (Wall to Wall, RDF Media) are already adept at securing funding in the US marketplace, and a freeing up of the market may well encourage others to follow their lead.

Case study – HIT Entertainment plc

As a specialist in the production and distribution of television properties for young children, HIT Entertainment's international strategy is quite unlike other British companies, demonstrating the special nature of children's television, which more than any other type of programming offers extensive opportunities for ancillary rights exploitation in video/DVD and consumer products. Since it was established in 1989 as an independent distributor of programming owned by third parties, the company has undergone a transformation, based on ownership of all rights in enduring character-based children's properties. It is now a multimedia, rights-owning group with its own animation and live action studios and a thriving international business.

Recognising that the sale of programmes owned by others offered only limited potential for growth, and that budgets for the acquisition of children's television programmes were declining worldwide, it became a specialist in brand management (Caminada, 2001). This was achieved through the funding and development of its own productions (*Bob the Builder*, *Angelina Ballerina*, *Rubbadubbers*) and strategic acquisitions of established properties (*Barney*, *Thomas the Tank Engine*, *Pingu*) with licensing potential in the US, Japanese and Western European markets.

Children's entertainment has been used as a platform for the development of an ancillary rights business, based on internationally attractive brands, that now

Table 4.10: HIT Entertainment plc turnover by destination, class and origin of business (£ Million)

	2000	2001	2002	2003
Turnover	20.6	52.3	121.0	168.9
Turnover by Destination				
USA	5.6	32.0	87.2	108.6
UK	9.0	12.6	19.2	27.8
Rest of World	2.7	3.7	10.0	21.0
Europe	3.3	4.0	4.6	11.5
Turnover by Class of Business				
Home entertainment	2.1	19.9	61.3	75.5
Consumer products	5.0	20.3	47.3	72.1
Television	13.5	9.9	8.6	12.2
Stage show	–	2.2	3.7	9.1
Turnover by Origin				
USA	–	28.0	91.1	112.6
UK	20.6	24.3	29.9	53.0
Rest of World	–	–	–	3.2
Pre-tax profits	4.9	7.5	27.3	39.7

Source: HIT Entertainment plc annual reports and accounts 2000–03.

outperforms television programme sales (see Table 4.10). While television sales accounted for two-thirds of turnover in 2000, they accounted for only 7 per cent of revenues by 2003, with the vast majority of revenues attributable to consumer products (licensing) and home entertainment (video and DVD). In this context, television sales are the motor that drives profits in other areas. Sales in America of *Bob the Builder* to Nickelodeon's pre-school outlet, Nick Junior, and of *Angelina Ballerina* to PBS have driven sales of video and consumer products. By 2003 HIT accounted for 12 per cent of the American children's non-theatrical home entertainment market making it the fourth largest children's video distributor. In Britain it is the largest pre-school video/DVD distributor with a 34 per cent market share (HIT Entertainment, 2003, p. 12).

The transformation of the company began in July 1996 with a launch on the Alternative Investment Market, which raised £2.7 million in funds (HIT Entertainment, 1996). A full stock market listing in August 1997 raised a further £8.1 million (HIT Entertainment, 1997, p. 17). A further rights issue in October 1998 raised £14.1 million (HIT Entertainment, 1998, p. 4) and an additional £7.6 million was raised in July 1999 (HIT Entertainment, 1999, p.14).

This allowed the company to fully fund its own productions and establish its own animation facility, HOT Animation, in Manchester in 1997 for the production of the stop-frame animation series *Bob the Builder*, which had been licensed to nearly 200 broadcasters by 2003 (HIT Entertainment, 2003, p. 14). The company established a video division in 1997 and a consumer products division in 1998. Focusing on HIT's core brands, the consumer products division manages licensing deals with leading toy manufacturers (Hasbro, Mattel/Fisher-Price, Lego and Brio) and publishers (Scholastic, Penguin, Simon & Schuster, and Random House) (HIT Entertainment, 2001, p. 5).

The risk is that the properties funded by stock market rights issues may not fulfil expectations, particularly in a market that became flooded in the late 1990s with pre-school programming that was chasing too few slots and too little money. However, the potential benefits from a hit like *Bob the Builder* are substantial as HIT has demonstrated in North America and key European markets.

However, to continue its growth HIT needed to show that its performance was based on more than one successful property, namely *Bob the Builder*. In 2001 it acquired the Lyrick Corporation in the US for £189 million (Ibid., p. 2). Lyrick produce *Barney*, an enduringly successful live action pre-school property about a dinosaur, which has aired on the PBS network in the US since 1992, building a considerable presence in licensed products. The acquisition not only added production facilities in the US, but also provided better access to the US video and licensing market, allowing HIT to benefit from Lyrick's existing relationships with key US retailers (HIT Entertainment, 2001, p. 4). The incorporation of Lyrick fundamentally changed the focus of the company. First, revenues from the US now dominate accounting for two-thirds of turnover in 2003 by origin (see Table 4.10). Second, the thrust of the company was pushed even further towards the exploitation of ancillary rights, which accounted for 93 per cent of revenues in 2003.

HIT's growth has been fuelled by further acquisitions, reducing reliance on its first big hit, *Bob the Builder*. In 2001, the company acquired all rights to *Pingu* for £15.9 million, a stop-frame property with significant licensing potential and popularity in Europe and especially Japan, where it generated £2 million from consumer product royalties in 2001 (Ibid., pp. 2–3). In 2002, it acquired British rival Gullane Entertainment, owner of the pre-school property *Thomas the Tank Engine* and the *Guinness World Records* (HIT Entertainment, 2002, p. 5), for £137 million. The key to HIT's growth has been the ownership and development of brands with long-term value, that are driven by television exposure and work across different markets in home entertainment (video/DVD) and consumer products. Of all British-based players involved in the international circulation of British programmes, it is the only company to have shifted the geographic focus of its operations from Britain to the US. In 2004, HIT announced plans to launch a children's pre-school channel in the US following a deal with the US-based Jim Henson Company to distribute its 440 hour family classics including *Fraggle Rock* and *The Hoobs*.

Case study – RDF Media

RDF Media was founded in 1993. As one of Britain's largest independent producers, specialising mainly in factual and entertainment programming, its hit shows include *Scrapheap Challenge*, *Faking It*, *Wife Swap*, *Shipwrecked*, *Banzai* and *Perfect Match*.

RDF's most notable export accomplishments have been format and production sales to US broadcasters. A US production office was established in Los Angeles in 2001 on the back of an order by Discovery's TLC channel for a US version of RDF's Channel Four series *Scrapheap Challenge*, in which teams compete against the clock to build machines from scrap. This has been re-versioned and produced by RDF in Los Angeles as several series of *Junkyard Wars*. TLC followed this up in 2002 with an order for a US version of RDF's Channel Four series *Faking It*, in which individuals are challenged to excel in a profession at odds with their experience. This too was produced in Los Angeles. *Banzai*, a spoof gambling show, originally shown on Channel Four, was re-versioned for the Fox Network's autumn 2003 schedule. In 2002, the ABC network ordered a pilot based on RDF's format for the Channel Four reality show *Wife Swap*. And sister network ABC Family ordered thirteen episodes of *Perfect Match*, a dating format, also originally broadcast on Channel Four, in which contestants allow their friends to pick a perfect partner. The US operation, which now includes a New York office, was reported to have generated £11 million in 2002, equivalent to a third of RDF's total turnover (Hughes, 2003, p. 20). RDF expects its US revenues to account for 50 per cent of its turnover by 2004, as the company continues to establish itself as a US producer (Waller, 2003a).

Capitalising on its expertise in producing the original versions in Britain, local production allows RDF to benefit from 'the ideal dream ticket' of selling the format and earning production revenues from the US market (Frank, 2001). With a foothold in the US and with opportunities for original commissions from American broadcasters, RDF is looking to create a 'virtuous circle' with RDF's London office bringing shows to the US and RDF's LA office bringing shows to Britain (Hughes, 2003, p. 20). The ambition is to create a company that can be sold or floated, based on the retention of format rights and long-running, returning series in America and Britain (Lambert, cited in Wells, 2002, p. 6).

It is this ability to retain rights in its productions and formats that has generated profits, rather than production activities in Britain (Frank, 2001). For example, RDF funded the development of *Scrapheap Challenge*, which was fully funded by Channel Four. RDF retained distribution rights. As such it not only benefited from a 30 per cent share of back end receipts alongside Channel Four's 70 per cent share, but also from a 30 per cent commission from its activities as the distributor of the programme (Frank, 2001; Bruneau, 2001).

In the year ending 31 January 2003, RDF Media generated post-tax profits of £609,270 (2002: £360,898) on turnover of £33.3 million (£24.5 million in 2002) (RDF Media, 2003, p. 8). In its submission to the ITC *Review of the UK Programme Supply Market*, it pointed out that its profits came almost entirely from the exploitation of secondary rights, with its production division generating no profit at all (RDF Media, 2002a). Turnover was projected to reach £35 million in 2002 with pre-tax profits of £1.2 million (Ibid.). RDF argued that such low returns made it difficult to attract the external investment necessary to take creative risks necessary for growth. Like other independents it attributed its low returns from production to a lack of competition among British broadcasters for content and unfair terms of trade which favoured broadcasters and kept production budgets and production fees low (Ibid.).

As a key supplier to Channel Four, RDF has managed to negotiate better terms for the retention of rights, and a larger back end share on its projects (Frank, 2001). To develop the profitability of its business it has concentrated on returning series (*Scrapheap Challenge, Faking It, Perfect Match*) and formats, which can be exploited overseas in addition to one-offs that are less profitable, but satisfy creative impulses within the company (Ibid.). It has also sought to avoid programmes with high clearance costs for music and archive material or programmes that are presenter-led (Ibid.). Other strategies employed by RDF to grow its international business include an Independent Producers Fund, worth over £1 million, launched in 2001 after an injection of £3.2 million in capital by venture capitalist Sagitta Private Equity for an estimated 20 per cent stake (Frank, 2001; Waller, 2003g). The fund is used to secure distribution rights and a share in back end receipts by funding programme development, budget deficits, and providing sales advances to producers. By accessing the fund, independent producers can negotiate a better back end share (50–60 per cent rather than 30 per cent) for their productions with broadcasters, because they are bringing money to the table. RDF's goal for the fund is to acquire and invest in higher-quality properties, which can be sold to free-to-air broadcasters worldwide, rather than lower-paying channels in the cable and satellite sector (Frank, 2001).

Case study – Wall to Wall Television

Wall to Wall Television established its own in-house distribution arm in 2003. Prior to this it had built an international business by retaining rights to the programmes it makes, and provides a good example of the opportunities open to independent producers with internationally appealing factual programming suitable for the American market. In its evidence to the ITC *Review of the UK Programme Supply Market* its success was attributed to three factors:

> First, we have been able to control rights. Secondly, we've been able to choose our own international distributor. Thirdly we've been able to price rights packages separately and negotiate according to the value of these rights in individual territories and media. (Wall to Wall Television, 2002, p. 5)

Wall to Wall began in 1987 by producing fully-funded programmes for Channel Four. Production fees of 10 per cent provided little scope for meaningful profit margins, and overseas exploitation remained under the control of Channel Four, with producers receiving a minority share (30 per cent) of any net profits generated from exploitation (Wall to Wall Television, 2002, p. 3). By 1993, Wall to Wall was producing 150 hours of programming a year, but it had no asset base or additional revenue streams (Ibid., p. 4). This situation changed when it brought American co-production funding to the table, allowing the company greater scope to control its intellectual properties and brands. By the end of 2002, Wall to Wall was working for seven broadcasters in the United States and claimed to be generating 50 per cent of its revenue from outside Britain (Ibid. p. 4). In 2003, its turnover was £16.86 million (2002: £14 million), with £5.8 million attributable to overseas income (Wall to Wall (Holdings), 2003).

The first strand in its overseas strategy centres on co-productions with US broadcasters of high-end programmes with budgets in excess of £300,000 an hour with the US contributing between 30 and 40 per cent of the budget (Shell, 2001). For example, *Ancient Egyptians*, a four-part dramatised documentary series budgeted at £6 million, was funded with a 30 per cent contribution from TLC in the US, 30 per cent from Channel Four, and pre-sales undertaken by Granada in Western Europe (Ibid.). This series made its US debut on TLC in December 2003 in a two-hour slot at 8pm. For its first co-production in 1993, *Baby It's You*, a series about child development, Wall to Wall found a distributor, ITEL, and brought in TLC as a co-producer. This series aired as *Babies' World* in the US. To secure the deal the company deferred its production fee and made the programme at cost in order to build a direct relationship with TLC (Shell, 2001; Wall to Wall Television, 2002, p. 4). When the programme became a hit, it generated more revenue than all previous Wall to Wall programmes put together (Ibid.). Importantly it helped to cement Wall to Wall's relationship with TLC and others in the Discovery family. Similar programmes followed, drawing on the brand and filming technique, including *A Cat's World*, *A Dog's World* and *A Horse's World*.

A second strand in building a US business is based on Wall to Wall's *House* franchise originally devised and broadcast on Channel Four as the living history experiment *The 1900 House* and since extended to include *1940s House* and *Edwardian Country House*. *The 1900 House* was developed as a domestic series and should have been fully funded with distribution going automatically to Channel Four International. However, an oversight at C4I allowed Wall to Wall and its distributor ITEL to market the programme overseas (Wall to Wall Television, 2002, p. 4). It was sold to PBS in the US, where its success led to an agreement with public service affiliate WNET in New York to develop a US version, *Frontier House*, a Wall to Wall/WNET co-production. Filmed in Montana, this followed the experiences of families reliving the experiences of nineteenth-century settlers in America. PBS have also acquired the British series *1940s House* and *Edwardian Country House*, with further US projects (*Colonial House*) in the pipe line (Ibid.).

The third strand in building a US business involves the production of lower budget ($40,000–150,000 an hour), high-volume, fully-funded work directly for American outlets such as TLC (*Paleo World*) and Discovery Health (*House Arrest*). This provides the company with cash flow, but as work for hire it retains no rights (Shell, 2001). According to Chief Executive Alex Graham, the distinction is that the high-end co-productions trade on a specific Britishness, but the volume portion of the business reinforces its strength on both sides of the Atlantic (cited in Shelton, 2001, p.15).

In its first forays into the US market, Wall to Wall used the distributor ITEL, since incorporated into Granada International. However, having established direct relationships with US broadcasters, it now secures US funding on its own account.

Notes

1. Channel 5 International was closed at the end of 2002.

2. The same survey broke down the share of programme production as follows: BBC 38 per cent; Carlton Productions 6 per cent; Granada 20 per cent; Sky 3 per cent; other broadcasters 9 per cent; independents 25 per cent (PACT, 2002b, p.10).

3. In July 2000, Pearson Television merged with the Luxembourg-based CLT-Ufa to form the RTL Group. The production division, including Pearson's production subsidiaries, was renamed FremantleMedia. The RTL Group is 90 per cent owned by Bertelsmann.

4. In 1982, ITV programmes were marketed internationally by ITC Ltd (representing ATV), Thames Television International (representing Thames Television Ltd), Richard Price (representing LWT), Trident Television (representing Yorkshire Television) and Granada Television International (representing Granada Television) (Guback and Varis, 1982, p. 32).

5. Collins, Garnham and Locksley attributed £17.4 million of foreign programme sales to BBC Enterprises in 1984 (£12.4 million in 1983). In 1983, the ITV companies earned £59.5 million from export sales, with 70.9 per cent (£42.2 million) of revenues attributable to North America (1988, pp. 64–5).

6. A separate Directors' Report and Accounts lodged for Carlton International Media Ltd for the year ended 30 September 2001 and submitted in September 2002 gives a much lower turnover of £39 million in 2001 (£24.4 million in 2000) with £28 million attributed to overseas sales (£18 million in 2000) (Carlton International Media, 2002).

7. According to a PACT survey Carlton Productions was responsible for 6 per cent of British programme production, compared to 20 per cent by Granada (PACT, 2002b, p. 10).

8. This represents a continuation of the strategy undertaken by Carlton International's predecessor, CTE (Central Television Enterprises), which was absorbed following Carlton's acquisition of Central, the Midlands franchise in the mid-1990s. As a new broadcaster, CTE also found itself bereft of content to sell when it took over the Midlands franchise from ATV in 1983.

5

Collaboration and Emulation – The American Connection

There's domestic television and there's American television. In every territory in the world that is how it divides. (Root, 2001)

The story of British television and American culture, then, is a story of assimilation without final control, a story in which difference matters as it helps de- and reconstruct the familiar. It is a story in which the reception of artifacts from one nation by another shifts from moments of dominance to moments of liberation and back again in an unpredictable ebb and flow. ... It is, finally, a story in which meanings constructed 'here' speak about, with, and to meanings from 'there' – and vice versa – and in which nothing, inevitably, is completely different. (Miller, 2000, pp. 182–3)

Between these comments we get a sense of the different perceptions about the impact of British television in the United States, Britain's largest single market – accounting for 43 per cent of British television exports by value in 2003 and 35 per cent of US television imports by volume in 1997 (BTDA, 2004; DCMS, 1999a, p. 17). On the one hand this impact is marginal because of the largely self-sufficient nature of the American marketplace, with European programming accounting for less than 2 per cent of US transmissions (EC, 1999, p. 7). On the other hand the impact goes beyond actual volume, involving the assimilation of British ideas, genres and forms to create new forms of American programming with a 'quality' previously associated only with the imports (Miller, 2000, p. 166). Miller, for example, argues that American family-based miniseries such as *Rich Man, Poor Man* (ABC, 1975), *Roots* (ABC, 1977) and even the serial *Dallas* (CBS) owe a debt to *The Forsyte Saga*, a family-based serialised drama from Britain which aired on American public television in 1969 (2000, pp. 165–7; Lealand, 1984, p. 58). As we will see, a more direct impact became apparent in the 1990s when American versions of British dramas, game shows, reality and lifestyle formats were used as a means of rejuvenating American schedules in a more competitive multi-channel environment.

Generally, however, the British presence on American screens has been characterised by peaks and troughs, punctuated by occasional excitement that Britain has finally 'cracked' this notoriously difficult yet lucrative territory. The cycle invariably involves the initial acceptance of programmes and formats deemed innovative and different, and the gradual incorporation of these features into American programming, removing the need for imports, and necessitating further innovation. With the growing importance of international revenues, British exporters have tried to break out of this cycle, allowing a shift from the margins of American television to a more central position – ideally on the more financially rewarding free-to-air networks rather than public television and cable. However, as we have seen (Chapter 3), the belief that British companies could break the cycle on their own and emerge as significant global players seems to have largely evaporated in respect of British government policy. The 2003 Communications Act opens up British commercial broadcasting to US ownership in the belief that harnessing British ideas and content to American finance and distribution muscle will finally help the British production sector to break out of the protected confines of the domestic market. Success in America is equated with Britain emerging as a more prominent actor on the global stage with global revenues feeding into domestic production.

This chapter starts with a brief overview of the American television market, before considering the historical presence of British programmes on American screens. It continues with an examination of gatekeeper perceptions of British programmes in the key areas of drama, factual programming, children's programming and entertainment formats, and the strategies employed by British exporters to break into the market. The analysis draws largely on interviews undertaken between June 2001 and September 2002 with American and British executives. It seeks to establish what type of programming is attractive and why, the factors that have encouraged US gatekeepers to invest in British programming, how this programming is promoted and used in schedules, and emerging trends in the market which affect that presence. It concludes with an assessment of BBC America, an attempt to build an alternative British-owned channel for showcasing British content.

Market overview

The American television market can be broken down into the following outlets, starting with the national networks, which constitute the core of American television.

The networks

These include the free-to-air commercial broadcasters ABC, CBS and NBC, which were joined in 1986 by Fox and in the 1990s by UPN, WB and Pax. With the exception of formats acquired since the late 1990s (*Who Wants to Be a Millionaire?* on ABC, *The Weakest Link* on NBC), the networks have not been a significant outlet for British programming since the 1960s. The networks accounted for 54 per cent of prime-time viewing in the 2001–02 season, and the emphasis is on domestic entertainment and fiction (Nielsen Media Research, cited in TBI, 2002, p. 293).

The syndication market

The syndication market comprises station groups in local markets who license first-run programming developed specifically for syndication (game shows, talk shows, court shows and some fiction), and sitcoms (*Friends*, *Frasier*) and series (*ER*) which have aired on the networks (reruns) (Hazleton, 2000a, p. 15). In the case of over 1,500 stations 'owned and operated' by the networks or affiliated by contract to them, syndicated programming is aired in off-network time periods outside prime time. Cable networks also compete for the top reruns. Syndication is where large budget deficits from network production can be recouped once there are sufficient episodes (sixty-five) to meet the demands of daily stripped syndication. This demand for long-running programming, which can be stripped across the week, excludes most British programmes. However, the success of game-show formats *Who Wants to Be a Millionaire?* and *The Weakest Link* has resulted in original syndicated versions for prime-time access, extending the runs that began in prime time on the networks. However, without the right product and with distribution dominated by the studios, most British distributors tend to concentrate their efforts on placing first-run programming on cable and public television (PBS).

Cable and satellite channels

With limited circulation of British programming on network television and in syndication, there is a stronger presence on cable channels available in over 69 per cent of US homes in 2001 (Nielsen Media Research, cited in MPAA, 2001). This presence is confined mostly to basic cable services rather than premium pay cable outlets such as HBO (Home Box Office) and Showtime, whose reputations rest on high-profile domestic production. Important outlets for British programmes on basic cable include generalist outlets A&E, Bravo and the USA Network; the factual channels of Discovery Networks, National Geographic and the History Channel; and the children's channel, Nickelodeon. Opportunities for off-the-shelf programming sales are also opening up in the digital market, and on BBC America, the satellite channel owned and operated by BBC Worldwide.

PBS (Public Broadcasting System)

Established in 1969 to provide a national network for America's numerous non-profit educational stations, PBS represents a significant outlet for British drama, factual programming, factual formats (*Antiques Roadshow*, *Frontier House*) and pre-school programming (*Teletubbies*). In the 1980s, PBS saw its strengths in factual programming, high-quality drama imports and pre-school programming colonised by commercial cable channels, and found itself having to compete for British programming. Chronically under-funded since its inception, it is subject to intense political scrutiny and heavily reliant on corporate sponsorship and financial pledges from its viewers. PBS stations WGBH (Boston) and WNET (New York) are important co-production partners for British players.

Public broadcasting syndication

This provides an outlet for older British sitcoms including *Are You Being Served?*, *As Time Goes By* and *Keeping up Appearances*, primarily from the BBC, which are acquired by local PBS stations. In 1999–2000, BBC Worldwide sold sitcoms to 110 separate public service licensees (BBC Worldwide, 2000).

'Survival of the biggest'

This division of the marketplace into many outlets obscures high levels of consolidation where American broadcasters are just one part of larger vertically integrated corporations (Holt, 2003). The trend towards consolidation was hastened by the repeal of the Fin-Syn (Financial Interest and Syndication) rules in 1995 by the Federal Communications Commission (FCC). From the early 1970s these rules barred the networks from owning the programmes they broadcast and from participating in the domestic syndication business. Following repeal of the rules, the Walt Disney Company purchased the ABC network in 1995; Viacom acquired CBS in 1999 and AOL and Time Warner merged in 2000. American television distribution and television production is now dominated by five vertically integrated groups with network access (Viacom, Disney, News Corporation, Time Warner[1] and NBC/General Electric)[2] and one with a strong hold over the factual television sector, Liberty Media (See Table 5.1). These corporations also have wide-ranging interests in publishing, music, new media, retail operations, theme parks, international channels and international production as part of their integrated global image business.

   Their aim is to capitalise on synergies within the vertical structures of production and distribution and horizontally across different media and consumer

Table 5.1: Television station ownership in the US

Time Warner (until 2003 AOL Time Warner) (<www.aoltimewarner.com>)
<u>Key assets</u>: *Network television* – The WB Television Network; *Pay cable channels* – HBO; *Cable/satellite channels* – CNN, Court TV (with Liberty Media), TBS Superstation, TNT (Turner Network Television), Cartoon Network, TCM (Turner Classic Movies); *Production and distribution* – Warner Bros., Warner Bros. Studios, Warner Bros. Television (production), Warner Bros. Television Animation, Hanna-Barbera Cartoons.
General Electric (<www.ge.com>)
<u>Key assets</u>: *Network television* – NBC, Pax; *Cable and satellite channels* – CNBC (with Dow Jones), MSNBC (with Microsoft), A&E (25% with Disney and Hearst), the History Channel (25%), Rainbow Media Holdings (with Cablevision – includes American Movie Classics and Bravo), National Geographic (25% with Fox and National Geographic); *Local television* – Paxson-owned stations. Note: In October 2003, General Electric and the French company Vivendi Universal agreed to merge NBC and Vivendi Universal Entertainment to form NBC Universal.
Liberty Media Corporation (<www.libertymedia.com>)
<u>Key assets</u>: *Cable and satellite channels* – Discovery Communications Inc. (49% – with Cox and New Channels Corp. Includes The Discovery Channel, TLC, Animal Planet, Travel Channel, Discovery Health, Discovery Civilization, Discovery Home & Leisure, Discovery Kids, Discovery Science, Discovery Wings), QVC (home shopping 42%), Starz Encore Group (various entertainment/fiction services), Court TV (50%).
Viacom (<www.viacom.com>)
<u>Key assets</u>: *Network television* – CBS, UPN; *Pay cable/satellite channels* – Showtime Networks, the Movie Channel; *Basic cable channels* – Nickelodeon, Noggin (with Sesame Workshop), MTV, the Paramount Channel, VH1, Comedy Central, BET (Black Entertainment Television), TNN (the National Network); *Local broadcasters* – UPN stations, CBS stations; *Production and distribution* – Paramount Pictures, Paramount Television, Viacom Productions, MTV Productions, Nickelodeon Studios, Spelling Entertainment Group, Worldvision Enterprises, King World Productions (first-run syndication).
The Walt Disney Company (<www.disney.com>)
<u>Key assets</u>: *Network television* – ABC; *Cable/satellite channels* – ABC Family, the Disney Channel, Toon Disney, Soapnet, ESPN (80%), Classic Sports Network, A&E Television (37.5% with Hearst and GE), the History Channel (37.5%), Lifetime Television (50% with Hearst), E! Entertainment (with Comcast and Liberty Media); *Local broadcasters* – ABC-owned and –operated stations; *Television production and distribution* – Buena Vista Television, Touchstone Television, Walt Disney Television, Walt Disney Television Animation.

Source: 'Who Owns What', *Columbia Journalism Review* at <www.cjr.org> (20 May 2003).

products in a scenario where broadcast exposure is used to build brands, and value is realised in secondary markets (see Aksoy and Robins, 1992; Segal, 2002, p. 14; Sinclair, 1996, p. 37). This makes access for outsiders, including British exporters, more difficult, as corporations aim for self-sufficiency and seek to retain control and ownership over all aspects of their business, across different windows, and increasingly on a global scale (Segal, 2002, p. 14; Sofley, 2000a). For example, in 1991 CBS acquired 17 per cent of its prime-time programming from its in-house production arm. By 2001, this had risen to 70 per cent (Channel Four, 2002a, p. 19). In 2002–03 twenty-six out of ABC's twenty-nine pilots were produced or co-produced by Touchstone Productions, also a Disney subsidiary (Ibid.). In the 2002 season, twenty-seven out of thirty-two new prime-time network series were produced by companies with connections to the host network either via an in-house production arm or through co-ownership between the network and the producing studio (Seguin, 2002, p. 28).

Historical background

In his historical survey of British television in America, Miller describes a multi-linear, multivocal relationship between Britain and America, involving assimilation, dialogue, the negotiation of meaning by American audiences and further redefinition by the specific social, political and cultural circumstances of the time (2000, pp. 9–12). He suggests, for instance, that the portrayal of a strong independent female secret agent, Emma Peel, in the British series *The Avengers* offered young American middle-class women a different role model in the 1960s when women's lives were changing, and American television offered nothing comparable (Ibid., p. 74). British programmes were perceived as similar yet different from what was on offer in the American marketplace, and provided a source of innovation that could be used to reinvigorate American productions. *The Avengers* provided American television producers with a model for a female crime fighter they would then incorporate into their own spy and police shows, albeit attuned to American sensibilities (Ibid., p. 73).

What is also clear is that American interest in British programming has always been cyclical. Imports of British films and some television series (*The Adventures of Robin Hood*, *The Adventures of Lancelot*) went on throughout the 1950s. But the earliest peak occurred in the 1960s. Replicating the conventions of American television series, British producer Lew Grade's ATV exported action-adventure and secret agent series aimed at prime-time network television to fund further production at home (Tunstall, 1977, p. 101). The most successful were *The Saint* (NBC, 1967–9), *Secret Agent* (CBS, 1964–6) and *The Prisoner* (CBS, 1968). According to Miller it was not Grade's 'mid-atlantic' formula that contributed to their success, but the reflection of contemporary cold war themes, and the connection with another British export, 1960s spy hero James Bond (2000, pp. 26–9). The era ended when ABC cancelled ABC-UK's *The Avengers* in 1969 after three years. American producers had started to produce their own espionage series, drawing on similar themes and duplicating James Bond on American terms (Miller, 2000, p. 42).

When opportunities for selling British programmes dried up on network television in the late 1960s, new opportunities emerged with the creation of PBS in 1969. PBS was influenced by British public service broadcasting, and similarities in ethos combined with a lack of funding to produce its own fiction opened up opportunities for the BBC's 'prestige' period drama (Tunstall and Machin, 1999, p. 94). The first major purchase was the BBC's *The Forsyte Saga* in 1969, a family serial based on John Galsworthy's novels, whose literary provenance provided a point of difference to the daily soap operas circulating on American television at the time (Miller, 2000, p. 80). The success of the *Forsyte Saga* led to the establishment of *Masterpiece Theatre* in 1971, a weekly strand of British drama, run by the PBS station, WGBH, in Boston, and sponsored by Mobil Oil (now ExxonMobil). This relationship was extended in 1980 when Mobil agreed to sponsor WGBH's *Mystery!* strand of British thrillers and detective series. Mobil hoped that the association would improve the company's tarnished corporate image with what was perceived as an elite, educated and therefore influential audience (Jarvik, 1997, p. 238; Smith, 2002, pp.180–1). For PBS, British drama underlined its commitment to 'quality', but some have argued that the cheapness of British imports stopped public television from developing as a force for the production of more challenging American contemporary fiction (Smith, 2002, pp. 181–2).

Throughout the 1970s, British television programmes were mostly confined to PBS, appealing to an older, educated elite in terms of drama, or a younger, educated elite for cult hits in syndication, such as *Monty Python's Flying Circus*. British television only broke the barrier to appeal to a mass audience when its 'Britishness' was disguised. This occurred with the network adaptation of British sitcom formats in the 1970s. Foremost among these were *All in the Family* (based on the BBC's *Till Death Us Do Part*, CBS, 1971–5), *Sanford and Son* (based on the BBC's *Steptoe and Son*, NBC, 1972–7) and *Three's Company* (based on Thames' *Man About the House*, ABC, 1977–84) (Collins, Garnham and Locksley, 1988, p. 72). These were reshaped to suit American notions about race, women and class. For example, Steptoe's rag and bone yard was relocated from London to a black neighbourhood in Los Angeles, thereby extending the series' demographic appeal across racial lines (Miller, 2000, p. 151). However, attempts to tempt the networks with original British programming were less successful. In the early 1970s, Granada offered its most successful long-running serial 'soap', *Coronation Street*, set in a working-class district of Manchester, free to any US network that would take it, but the offer failed to find any takers (Hoskins and Mirus, 1988, p. 509).

In the 1980s, American demand for British programming grew as cable became established. Like PBS before it, some cable channels used British programming to differentiate themselves from their rivals and fill gaps in their schedules at low cost. British programming fitted the bill, because it had a reputation for 'quality', and could therefore be used to attract more upscale and wealthier audiences. In 1983–4, for example, the BBC sold 200 hours to the fledgling American cable channel Arts and Entertainment (A&E) for $15,000 an hour (Schlesinger, 1986, p. 275). By the 1990s, the cable market began to change as channels started to concentrate on strengthening their brands and differentiating themselves from rivals. Rather than relying on domestic reruns and acquisitions, they began to formulate strategies for original programming targeted to fit those brands (Hazleton, 2002a, p. 41). This strategy limited opportunities for the sale of completed programming, but it did open up opportunities for co-funding more expensive and therefore risky fiction and factual programming, which no cable channel could afford to finance on its own.

At this juncture it is worth noting the resistance of the American market to overseas programming. Those who commission and buy programmes assume that audiences are intolerant and this colours their decisions. Besides, why buy a foreign drama, even an English-language import from Britain, when there are plenty of long-running home-grown productions that have already proved successful in the domestic market? All imports to the US, including British imports, suffer from high levels of cultural discount because it is assumed that American viewers will fail to identify with the cultural substance of the material. While PBS and some cable outlets may be happy to accept programming which is recognisably British, those seeking to define their own brand and appeal to a particular target audience are less accommodating. One BBC Worldwide executive claimed, 'Quite frankly I think they are looking for things that can be made American. . . . They're not looking for British programmes, they're looking for programmes that can be Americanised' (Carlisle, 2001). These views are echoed by others, who point to the growing popularity of formats rather than off-the-shelf programming and the cyclical nature of any American interest (Root, 2001). However, programming that obscures its origins does not build audience expectations for more British product or create a platform for significant cross-cultural exchange (see Cunningham and Jacka 1996, p. 170). This poses a dilemma for British companies seeking investment in British programmes, and the problem is particularly acute for British drama.

Drama – at the margins of 'the slightly less mainstream'

> There are two very clear end-users of British drama – A&E and WGBH. So often it's either one or the other. (Paul Sowerbutts, Managing Director, Channel Four International, cited in Keighron, 2002a, p. 23)

Historical and literary-based British drama, which was regarded as innovative on PBS and even potentially influential in the 1970s, is no longer perceived as sufficiently different, and has proved vulnerable to attempts by American channels to create distinctiveness on their own terms through original production. Instead, pay television, specifically HBO, emerged in the 1990s as a critically acclaimed originator of contemporary long-running dramas, including *Sex in the City*, *The Sopranos* and *Six Feet Under*. As we will see later, the current cycle suggests that the innovation, energy and ideas that were once associated with British drama have shifted to other areas – notably factual programming and formats. However, in spite of the difficulties of selling British drama, America remains crucially important in providing the funding necessary to create high-end British drama in the first place. Without US co-funding, many high-profile, public service-imbued British dramas would fail to get off the ground.

In terms of volume, but not necessarily price, the most important co-funding partnership is with WGBH in Boston, which has run the anthology series *Masterpiece Theatre* on behalf of PBS for over thirty years. Originally based on literary adaptations acquired from the BBC, the strand now draws from a broader range of period and contemporary serials and one-offs. The BBC remains WGBH's most important partner, and WGBH is usually involved in the BBC's annual big budget literary adaptation. In 2003, it was George Eliot's *Daniel Deronda*. In 2002, it was Anthony Trollope's *The Way we Live Now*, preceded in 2001 by Elizabeth Gaskell's *Wives and Daughters*.[3] Other partners include Granada (*Jewel in the Crown* 1984–5, *Prime Suspect* 1995, *The Forsyte Saga* 2002), Channel Four (*White Teeth* 2003, *Anna Karenina* 2002) and Carlton Productions (*Bertie and Elizabeth* 2002). Screened every Sunday at 9pm, the *Masterpiece* strand acquires between twenty-five and thirty hours of new programming a year, mostly from Britain. Over half of these are co-funded productions. However, in December 2002, a question mark was placed over the survival of the strand, when ExxonMobil, its sponsor since 1971, announced that it would end its sponsorship in 2004, leaving PBS to locate $7 million a year to maintain acquisitions (Stewart, 2003a).

WGBH's *Mystery!* strand caters for period and contemporary detective series. Examples include literary adaptations such as Agatha Christie's *Poirot* (LWT/Granada), Peter Lovesey's *Dead Gorgeous* (Carlton), the Elizabeth

George *Inspector Lynley Mysteries* (BBC) and Colin Dexter's *Inspector Morse* (Carlton). In 1993, ExxonMobil dropped its sponsorship, and in 2001 *Mystery!* became a summer strand, reflecting a desire within PBS to free up the schedule to show more American drama (Eaton, 2002; Torrance, 2001). According to PBS President Pat Mitchell, research had shown that audiences were increasingly confused about where to find British drama because cable channels (BBC America, A&E and Bravo) were also screening British programmes. As a consequence, 'we were seeing some erosion of our identity as a broadcaster. More to the point, however, we were hearing a need for some more home-grown material' that would keep the key over-fifties demographic, but also attract new over-fifties, who were not making the migration to PBS once they hit the age band (cited in Marlow, 2001, p. 8).

However, the economics of a move towards more home-grown production are complicated because PBS does not have the funds to match Hollywood or HBO. This suggests that there will continue to be a need for productions from Britain. The desire to increase levels of American origination has, however, led to other forms of co-operation with British partners. In 2001, Carlton International established a $20 million production fund with PBS and the Corporation for Public Broadcasting to develop American drama and documentaries, which Carlton would distribute internationally. The first project, *Skinwalkers*, broadcast in November 2002 as part of the *American Mystery!* strand, was executive produced by Robert Redford and produced in the US by Granada's subsidiary, Granada Entertainment USA (Marlow, 2002, p. 23).

The second key relationship is with cable channel A&E. More than PBS, A&E has seen a shift towards original production. Having purchased more than 50 per cent of its schedule from Britain in the 1980s, maturity in the late 1990s led to the development of US movies and series to 'broaden our palette and get an American presence in our drama' (Delia Fine, cited in Hazleton, 2000b, p. 11). The new strands did not exclude British participation, and the American court drama series *100 Center Street* (since cancelled) and the detective series *The Nero Wolfe Mysteries* were co-productions with FremantleMedia and distributed worldwide by Fremantle International Distribution.[4] By 2002, the shift towards American production had reduced involvement with British programming to five to ten short co-produced 'signature' pieces. This is programming that not only transcends cultural barriers, but can be heavily promoted to raise the visibility of the channel (Fine, 2002; Schwalbe, 2002; Torrance, 2001). Examples include the period adventure series *Hornblower* (LWT/Granada), based on the C. S. Forester Napoleonic novels, and period literary adaptations (*Longitude*, Granada for Channel Four; *Vanity Fair*, BBC; *Pride and Prejudice*, BBC; *The Mayor of Casterbridge,* Sally Head Productions for ITV). Major event series include the historical drama *Shackleton* (Channel Four), about the Arctic explorer, and an adaptation of Sir Arthur Conan Doyle's *The Lost World* (BBC), starring the US actor Peter Falk. Co-productions and acquisitions of British mysteries and detective series (*Dalziel and Pascoe*, *Silent Witness*, *Midsomer Murders*) for regular peak-time slots had been scaled back by 2002 because they attracted an audience that was considered too old (over fifty-four) and too female to attract advertisers (Fine, 2002).

Fiction is sometimes co-produced with the premium pay channels, HBO or Showtime, but this is infrequent, because of their emphasis on 'marquee' domestic drama. Recent collaborations between HBO and the BBC have focused instead on minority financial investment by the BBC in projects with British casts, such as the Churchill biopic *The Gathering Storm* (2002), starring Albert Finney and Vanessa Redgrave, and *Conspiracy* (2001), about Nazi plans for the 'final solution', starring Kenneth Branagh. Infrequent sales to other channels, such as Bravo (*Cold Feet* from Granada, *Nicholas Nickleby* from Channel Four, *Crime and Punishment* from the BBC), Comedy Central (*Absolutely Fabulous* with the BBC) and the Sci-Fi Channel (*The Prisoner*), are usually straight acquisitions, rather than co-productions.

The importance of co-productions

British relationships with WGBH and A&E are essentially co-funding relationships, where financial risk is shared in the expectation of a higher-quality production. With the arrival of A&E in the 1980s, WGBH found itself having to commit at an earlier stage for the material it really wanted (Eaton, 2002). With A&E's reduced reliance on British material, PBS has once again found itself in a strong negotiating position because it buys more British fiction than any other American outlet. However, the continuation of *Masterpiece Theatre* depends on British companies maintaining their commitment to high-profile drama. Yet financial pressures in Britain, arising from diminishing domestic licence fees and the withdrawal of the sale and leaseback tax break in 2002, have placed a question mark over the future viability of large-scale drama production, particularly at ITV (Clarke, 2002). For British broadcasters, the disadvantage of a PBS sale is that PBS never commits more than 25 per cent of a budget (Eaton, 2002), which means that budget shortfalls need to be recouped elsewhere in an international market which is not overly fond of British period drama (see Chapter 6).

The financial risk associated with drama means that A&E and WGBH collaborate mainly with the major broadcasters (BBC, Carlton, Granada, Channel Four) or broadcasters working with established independents (Company Pictures, Carnival Films, Tiger Aspect) to ensure the auspices of projects and the likelihood of their completion. Neither A&E nor WGBH is a passive partner. But A&E, as a commercial channel with no particular commitment to British drama per se, appears to be more insistent on a high level of consultation that matches the perceived preferences of its target audience and advertisers. According to Delia Fine, A&E's Vice President of Film, Drama and Performing Arts Programming:

> You can't just like the project or the idea. You and your partners really need to have a shared goal. . . . For example in the first draft, if the treatment is wildly different for our audience or what I would find satisfying it's going to be really difficult if the producers are really really happy with it. You're probably not going to have a good partnership, because you're never going to be trying to get the same thing out of it. So it's really important that both sides of the equation speak very candidly and very purposefully on how they see the project and on how they think it will shape and on the casting, virtually every aspect, including visual style. If you don't have a relationship going in to a project, then you are just opening yourself up to major problems down the road. So I think it's really important to have that kind of candour up front. (Fine, 2002)

With the growing importance of American financial contributions, Fine had detected a shift in attitude, which made British producers more receptive to a 'real creative partnership' rather than simply a financial one:

> At the beginning, everybody just wanted our money, and didn't want to hear anything from us and were somewhat resentful when they did. As time goes by though I find that most of the producers who I talk with are very open and very willing to think about collaboration and very more receptive to the fact that it is a partnership and needs to be a partnership. (Fine, 2002)

The degree of partnership depends not surprisingly on the level of financial input. With a lower financial commitment, WGBH's involvement ranged from consultation to mutual approvals. This included the selection of creative teams (writer, director, major cast) and input to the script. In one example Rebecca Eaton, the Executive Producer of *Masterpiece Theatre* and *Mystery!* argued that the final scene in Jane Austen's *Persuasion* (BBC, 1995), in which misunderstood affection is resolved, should end in a kiss between the protagonists. According to Eaton, there was no kiss in the book and in Jane Austen's time people would not have kissed in public, but through dialogue with the writer and director she made a convincing case, and the kiss was retained for the British version as well. However, while some producers valued such creative input and 'the eyes and ears of a partner who has a distance from the project and clearly knows the material and knows the genre', some paid 'lip service' (Eaton, 2002). According to Eaton, direct influence by *Masterpiece Theatre*'s sponsor, Exxon-Mobil, was not an issue but there is

> a very broad understanding of what kind of programming they're buying into. And we're very respectful of what we know they're buying into. So we don't take the train lightly off the rails, but within that there is a tremendous amount of latitude. (Ibid.)

A&E's financial contribution varies between 7 and 50 per cent of the budget, and there is an insistence on a high degree of creative involvement. Contracts contain a detailed list of approvals for the scripts, the director, the cast, rough cuts and final cuts (Fine, 2002; Torrance, 2001). Like WGBH, A&E sometimes edits programmes down to suit different slot lengths. However, at A&E this also served to hook audiences at the start of a programme. Fine explained this in terms of the more competitive nature of the American marketplace:

> In general we need a story to get going faster. We need a story to be faster-paced from the beginning. . . . Typically speaking I think the UK audience is much more patient sitting around for the first twenty minutes if need be for something to take off. I think that's changing, but here if you haven't got them hooked in the first couple of minutes you're toast. (Fine, 2002)

Shackleton (2 x 120 mins, 2002), commissioned by Channel Four, is a good example of the type of co-production favoured by A&E (Fine, 2002; Keighron, 2002a). It was written and directed by Charles Sturridge, who had also been involved with another A&E/Channel Four co-production, *Longitude*. With its focus on a charismatic polar explorer, it had international appeal. The casting of Kenneth Branagh in the lead meant that A&E had a name to drive promotion. A&E contributed 33 per cent of the £10 million budget, which also paid for a *Making of Shackleton* documentary to be used for promotional purposes. In return, A&E secured a high level of editorial involvement and a western hemisphere rights package.

Over the years, the literary-based event drama and mysteries acquired by A&E and WGBH have led to a range of expectations which are understood and accepted by American and British partners. Contemporary co-produced drama is a more difficult proposition demanding a greater degree of attunement to American sensibilities. *My Beautiful Son*, a two-hour co-production between Granada and Showtime, starring Paul Reiser, known from the American sitcom *Mad About You*, and British actor Julie Walters, was broadcast on ITV in 2001.

This was an unusual project as it incorporated both British and American locations and cast. American involvement, in this instance, necessitated a degree of compromise to heighten the programme's appeal for a more mainstream American audience. According to Caroline Torrance, Head of International Drama at Granada International, this is because the priorities of premium cable are very different from basic cable and PBS:

> Other broadcasters like Showtime, HBO, and Turner are absolutely one hundred per cent co-producers and they'll be very demanding editorially. You have to put American actors in, usually at least two well-known American actors. The story will have to have some American elements. It will have to open in America, because they reckon their audience will give them about twenty seconds before they flip channels and if the drama doesn't open in a familiar setting then the audience will flick onto another channel. If you notice in *My Beautiful Son*, it opens in America, it has to open in America. The first actor that you see has got to be an American actor. It can't open in Liverpool with Julie Walters, even though she's quite well-known. (Torrance, 2001)

HBO and Showtime can afford this leverage, because they are already successful initiators of drama in their own right, and there is less financial pressure to get involved in co-productions in the first place.

While *Masterpiece Theatre* functions as a showcase for British drama on PBS, British producers face competition for event drama on other outlets. A&E has broadened its range of collaborators, working with the French production company GMT on the mini-series *Napoleon* (2003), and with the Italian producer De Angelis on *The Magnificent Ambersons* (2003), and *The Benedict Arnold Story* (2003) about the US revolutionary war general. Delia Fine speculated that the difference was that European producers were looking specifically at an international market, shooting in English and incorporating internationally known casts, whereas British television 'is still commissioning and thinking specifically about what's going to serve your domestic audience' (2002).

The appeal of British drama

Differences between the ethos of WGBH/PBS and A&E are signalled in the motivations for co-production and the choice of programmes. At WGBH, the naming of the strand as *Masterpiece Theatre* (note the British spelling) suggests certain expectations about 'quality'. Recognisable literary provenance comes high as a determining factor and is linked to a particular type of audience with a high degree of cultural, educational and financial capital (Miller, 2000, p. 178). According to Rebecca Eaton:

If it's an adaptation of a period book then that goes right up to the front of the class for our consideration because that is the meat and drink of the series. That's what the *Masterpiece Theatre* audience looks to us for, and we try to keep a pretty steady diet of that. So one of the things that would get my attention is the title, the recognisability of the title, the pre-sold nature of something or the rough story outline. The next would be the script, or who they are thinking of to adapt. ... Primarily you would find that these are fairly literate scripts, these are high end thoughtful pieces, intelligently written material and then there's the production values and the cast, the acting quality follows. So you know to name yourself *Masterpiece Theatre* you set yourself up to have some pretty high standards. (Eaton, 2002)

Not all programmes fit the traditional expectations of *Masterpiece Theatre* because of their uncompromisingly British contemporary settings, but are sometimes still selected, because of a wider social and cultural significance which fits public broadcasting's mission. Eaton outlined two examples, which she felt had cross-cultural appeal in spite of their inherent 'Britishness'. The first dealt with institutional racism; the second offered a contemporary perspective on Shakespeare:

For instance this year [2002], we did two unusual things. We co-produced *Othello* [with Granada] and we acquired *The Murder of Stephen Lawrence* [from Granada]. Now I would say they were each *Masterpiece Theatres* in their own definitions. *The Murder of Stephen Lawrence* to me was just a stupendous way of using drama to illustrate a non-fiction event. I thought it was spectacularly done, very British, but universally important because the thing that happened to Stephen Lawrence happens in this country too. And I thought the creative use of television was remarkable. And *Othello* was contemporary and Shakespeare and the best way to redo Shakespeare the way that Andrew Davies [the writer] and LWT did it. (Eaton, 2002)

At WGBH, 'Britishness' is a selling point and the connection with a longstanding literary tradition is part of the appeal, in terms of its 'integrity' and 'authenticity' (Eaton, 2002). PBS audiences were deemed to be familiar with British fiction programming and patient about its slower pace, because 'our audiences are not typically American, they're pretty Anglophilic' (Ibid.). Regular exposure to British actors over thirty years made WGBH 'quite happy for all the cast to be British, because that type of production appeals to the particular audience they're aiming for' (Torrance, 2001). However, as British television adopts a more American-type model of television, there was concern that this distinctiveness might be lost (Eaton, 2002).

At A&E, the priority is to fulfil commercial objectives and there is no specific commitment to British drama. As previously noted, there has been a shift away from British detective series and a stronger focus on big-budget event drama, which can attract larger, younger audiences. Contemporary British drama was not thought to have 'that big event feeling' and even if it was 'beautifully written and wonderfully cast, they may not have that marquee glitter to them' (Fine, 2002). By contrast, titles known from literature or stories that did not unfold primarily in Britain (*Shackleton*, *The Lost World*) could be heavily promoted as 'a kind of British that's very accessible to an American audience' (Ibid.). The inclusion of these type of event series served a clear commercial purpose: 'One of the reasons we do these is to draw new viewers into the tent to sample the network' (Ibid.).

Drama formats and local production

The American market for British drama is important for co-production funding, but clearly limited. An alternative strategy has been to sell scripted formats allowing drama to be crafted, which 'to all intents and purposes becomes American and ceases to become something English' (Root, 2001), offering American producers savings on development on projects which have already worked in Britain.

Granada Entertainment USA,[5] established in Los Angeles in 1997, has been at the forefront in securing pilot deals for Granada formats (see Table 5.2). Access to the networks has been facilitated through the American talent agency William Morris, Granada's exclusive packaging agents for prime-time network drama (Ibid.). Agents are used for their relationships. Without them access to the networks is virtually impossible, because these are not straightforward rights sales, but production sales, and to pitch a production sale requires credibility and access to producers and talent, which a talent agency can supply through its relationships (Dilnott-Cooper, 2001; Morris, 2002; Schiff, 2001).

Acting as a rights holder and executive producer rather than as a deficit financier, Granada has produced pilots and series with Hollywood studio partners including Touchstone Television and Twentieth Century Television. With the studios providing deficit finance of up to $600,000 an hour, Granada avoids financial risk, but does not benefit from syndication and international revenues. Instead it gets its return from executive producer and format fees (Hazleton, 2001, p. 68; Hazleton, 2002b, p. 16; Root, 2001). British players are simply too small to risk the large deficits required for series production in the American market. Moreover, like all producers in the increasingly vertically integrated American system, British players need to collaborate closely with the production arms of the networks to secure deals, which limits their scope for manoeuvre.

Table 5.2: Selected British scripted formats in the US

Title (US title)	Genre	Year	Channel	Owner	Duration
Men Behaving Badly	Sitcom	1996-7	NBC	Pearson/Hartswood Films	2 series/35 eps
Cracker (Fitz)	Drama	1997-8	ABC	Granada	1 series/16 eps
Holding the Baby	Sitcom	1998	Fox	Granada	Aug–Dec 1998
Fawlty Towers (Payne)	Sitcom	1999	CBS	BBC	Mar–April 1999
Ballykissangel (Hope Island)	Drama	1999	PAX	BBC/Canada	Sep 1999–Apr 2000
Cold Feet	Drama	1999	NBC	Granada	1 season
Queer as Folk	Drama	2000	Showtime	Channel Four	3 series 2000–03
The Royle Family (The Kennedys)	Sitcom	2001	CBS	Granada	Pilot
Blind Men	Sitcom	2001	CBS	Granada	Pilot
The Young Person's Guide to Being a Rockstar	Drama	2001	WB	Channel Four	
The Grimleys (The Grubbs)	Drama	2002	Fox	Granada	8 episodes
My Wonderful Life	Sitcom	2002	ABC	Granada	Pilot
As If	Drama	2002	UPN	Granada	7 episodes
Touching Evil	Drama	2003	USA	Granada	Pilot
Cutting It	Drama	2003	ABC	Granada/BBC/GBTV	Pilot
The Kumars (Ortegas)	Comedy	2003	Fox	Hat Trick Productions	Pilot/Series
Coupling	Sitcom	2003	NBC	Hartswood Films	Oct 2003

Sources: *Broadcast*, C21, *Television Business International*.

Yet the impact of British formats has been mixed, with most shows dropped at the pilot stage or axed mid-run (see Table 5.2). *Fitz*, based on the psychological thriller *Cracker*, was dropped by ABC after sixteen episodes in 1998. An American version of Granada's contemporary relationship drama *Cold Feet* was cancelled by NBC soon after launch because it failed to secure a sufficiently large audience, in an environment where 'it's utterly a numbers and demographics game' (Root, 2001). *The Grubbs*, based on Granada's comedy series *The Grimleys*, was cancelled even before its launch in 2002. In October 2003, NBC dropped its remake of Hartswood Films' BBC 2 sitcom *Coupling* after just six episodes. A BBC/Granada joint venture, GBTV, launched in Los Angeles in 1999 to market drama formats, had not made a significant impact by 2002. The one sustained success has been Channel Four's gay drama *Queer as Folk*, which secured a third season on pay television outlet Showtime in 2003. By the summer of 2003, Granada Entertainment USA's main focus had shifted to reality formats in line with growing network demand.

However, failure to achieve enduring success with scripted formats has to be seen in the context of an abundant supply of domestically originated ideas. According to Antony Root, President at Granada Entertainment, this limited what British exporters could place:

> We're not going to sell a doctors' show here or a cop show here that is an American version of a British show. Because the Americans can come up with that material themselves, unless there's something stunningly original about the central character, which there was in *Cracker/Fitz*. (Root, 2001)

The situation also needs to be seen within the context of how network programming is commissioned. Failure is an accepted part of the annual cycle. In any year there may be 5,000 pitches in the pilot season, for pilots to be produced in January and February and decisions taken in May. Five thousand pitches might become 500 scripts, which end up as fifty pilots, and five series after heavy testing (Root, 2001; Hoskins and Mirus, 1988, p. 505). Samie Kim, Director of Current Programming at Fox, confirmed the high failure rate, adding:

> It's nothing specific to UK scripted shows. ... It's just that any show in the US – no matter where it originally came from – has an exceptional high chance of failure. Perhaps 85% of pilots never make it to series. ... It's not enough to be a great show – the stars must align for it to be a hit. The marketing has to be just right, the scheduling. ... For every show from the UK that fails in the US, there are 25 of our own shows that fail. (Cited in Waller, 2002a)

However, the rewards from formats are potentially substantial because of access to more lucrative prime-time slots on mainstream or premium outlets. According to Mike Morris, Marketing Director at Channel Four International, talking about Channel Four's sale of the format *Queer as Folk* to pay channel Showtime:

The reason we do formats is that it enables you to access nearer prime time and therefore bigger licence fees. ... If you made the thing [in the UK] and sold it to the US, you'd obviously make more money than selling it as a format. But the thing, that you make in the UK, wouldn't be something that you could sell for those sort of licence fees. (Morris, 2002)

Another alternative to selling British-originated drama is to produce locally for American networks – a strategy employed by a small number of companies including Granada, Carlton and FremantleMedia. This proved particularly apt for television movies (TVMs) with 'star' casts, which are in demand internationally and where the risk of deficit funding one-off productions is lower than for series production (Davis, 2001). According to one British distributor, a US television movie can generate $1.25 million from international sales in its first sales cycle over five years, which compares favourably with British drama where the deficits may be larger, but the prospects for international sales to recoup deficits are less promising (Dilnott-Cooper, 2001). US television movies had average budgets of $3.7–4 million in 2001, and US network broadcasters typically contributed between 50 and 80 per cent of funding, with shortfalls coming from distribution advances or less commonly from co-production and pre-sales (Davis, 2001; Root, 2001).

For example, in 2001 Carlton America, the Los Angeles-based operation of Carlton International, was acquiring or producing about sixteen television movies a year for the networks and cable (Davis, 2001). This provided Carlton International with a library of around 130 American titles for international distribution, producing revenues of $10–12 million a year (Hazleton, 2002b, p. 16). Granada Entertainment is also involved in the production of US television movies including *The Great Gatsby* (2000) for A&E and the BBC, and *Skinwalkers* (2002) for PBS/WGBH (Hazleton, 2001, p. 70; Root, 2001).

However, a decline in American and international demand had made this strategy more challenging by 2001 (Davis, 2001; Fuller, 2002; Root, 2001). In the late 1990s, each US network was estimated to be commissioning thirty to forty television movies a year with premium networks such as HBO, Showtime and Starz Encore producing, co-producing or acquiring sixty-five to seventy original productions a year (Fry, 2001, p. 52; Root, 2001). Television movies are expensive compared with some of the reality and entertainment formats that became more prominent in peak-time schedules from 1999. Unlike sitcoms or long-running serials, they do not build regular 'appointment to view' audiences. Moreover, international demand had declined because of the trend towards local programming, a situation exacerbated in 2002 by the collapse of the Kirch empire in Germany, a major buyer (Fuller, 2002; Root, 2001).

The challenge of producing fiction in the US for American outlets is exemplified by the experience of FremantleMedia (formerly Pearson Television). It developed an international strategy in the mid-1990s that focused on establishing a local presence in key markets (Elliott, 2001, p. 8). In the US, Pearson acquired the television movie producer ACI in 1995 and All American, the producer of the *Baywatch* series and game shows such as *The Price is Right* and *Family Feud* in 1997. These acquisitions provided opportunities to produce US movies and series, for which there was demand internationally, and the company used to distribute or co-produce eight to ten television movies and one long-running drama a year (Kuzmyk, 2002). However, in 2001 following a decline in demand for English-language drama, particularly in Europe, FremantleMedia announced a move away from deficit-funding American drama in favour of drama and entertainment formats that could be exploited by its local production operations (Hazleton, 2001; Hazleton, 2002b, p. 17; Kuzmyk, 2002; Winstone, 2002).

Factual television

In terms of volume, British factual programming surpasses the performance of fiction, because it is cheaper, less risky and there are easier ways to 'Americanise' it. This expanded market for factual programming is relatively recent and can be traced back to the growth of cable from the 1980s and in particular to the establishment of the Discovery Channel in 1985. Prior to this, factual programming was rarely screened on the networks, because of low ratings and disinterest from sponsors and advertisers (see Curtin, 1995). As a consequence British exporters were largely reliant on PBS for sales.

Discovery not only increased competition, but also altered industry perceptions about non-fiction programming by establishing a viable business aimed at discrete audience segments (Chris, 2002). However, the non-fiction programming that emerged on cable in the 1990s was very different from earlier forms, which although scarce had been characterised by in-depth research and attention to social and political issues. Discovery strategically cultivated the entertainment, story-led value of non-fiction and the creation of ageless 'uncontroversial' programmes such as natural history that could be re-aired on its outlets in global markets. According to Chris, cable's involvement in non-fiction has resulted in programmes that 'emphasize sensationalism, promote the entertainment industry itself, or offer content of dubious historic or scientific value' featuring natural disasters, unexplained phenomena, surgical procedures and the lives of 'ordinary' people, celebrities and animals (Chris, 2002, p. 11).

Discovery Communications

Discovery Communications Inc. (DCI) is the dominant player in factual programming, with a raft of expanding non-fiction sub-niches, which are promoted as distinct global brands. They include the flagship network the Discovery Channel (TDC), available in 85 million American homes in 2002, which focuses on exploration, adventure, nature, science, ancient civilisations and contemporary history. TLC is the second flagship network, with some crossover with TDC for event programmes, but with a stronger focus on reality and lifestyle formats such as *Trading Spaces*, based on Endemol Entertainment UK's home makeover show, *Changing Rooms*. Other significant DCI channels include Animal Planet, Discovery Health, Travel Channel and Discovery Kids. Since 1997 the channel portfolio has been extended to include a suite of digital networks – the Science Channel, Discovery Civilisation, Discovery Home and Leisure, Discovery Wings and Discovery en Español.

Although Discovery works with a range of British companies, its key relationship is with BBC Worldwide, with whom it has had a joint-venture partnership since July 1997. This was extended for a further ten years in 2002, securing the supply of BBC programming, and preventing the Corporation from entering similar agreements with competitors like National Geographic (Keighron, 2002b, p. 15). The agreement acknowledged that the BBC could not 'go it alone' on a global scale and was best placed to exploit its strengths and commercial ambitions in non-fiction with a commercial partner (Tunstall and Machin, 1999, pp.181–2).

At the first level the agreement gives Discovery a first look at BBC proposals for factual co-productions, such as *Walking with Dinosaurs*, *The Human Face* and *Blue Planet*. According to the BBC the co-production agreement generated $175 million in production investment in its first five years (BBC, 2002, p. 20; Keighron, 2002b, p. 15). Thus a large proportion of funding is secured in North America, reducing the necessity to chase pre-sales in other territories. In return Discovery gets North American rights and, depending on the level of financial involvement, a share of international rights. The BBC Sales Company, created in 1998 as a joint venture between BBC Worldwide and DCI licenses, co-produces and distributes factual programming on behalf of the BBC and DCI in the Americas. A second level involves joint ownership of international channels (Animal Planet in Latin America, Asia, Europe, Canada and Japan, and People and Arts in Latin America), and a 20 per cent share in Animal Planet in the US. A third level encompasses the distribution and marketing by DCI of BBC America, BBC Worldwide's wholly owned US channel.

Financial risk for the BBC is minimised because it does not share in any losses arising out of the partnership, but participates in the profits from channel revenues and programme sales to the joint-venture channels. The risk comes from the temptation to make programmes that meet the needs of the American marketplace rather than the needs of domestic audiences. This potential conflict of aims between commercial priorities and public service goals was highlighted by Paul Hamann, former BBC Head of Documentaries and History:

> Discovery is a fantastic brand in celebrating the world around you and that's an important part of the role that the BBC has to play to its viewers. But another important part is having programmes challenging politicians, investigating the world and the government around us. I don't see many of those programmes on American television as a whole. (Cited in Keighron, 2002b, p. 15)

Other outlets

A range of acquisitions and co-productions are undertaken with other channels including PBS, the History Channel (part of A&E Networks) and National Geographic.

At PBS most British factual co-productions are channelled through the PBS affiliates WGBH in Boston and WNET in New York. The key outlets are WGBH's science and technology series, *Nova*, WNET's *Nature* and WGBH's *Frontline* current affairs strand. Jarvik describes *Nova* as a 'British series housed at WGBH' (1997, p. 207). The strand was established in 1974 by Michael Ambrosino, a WGBH executive, who worked for the BBC's Horizon unit in 1973. However, the amount of programming undertaken with the BBC has declined since 1997 because of the BBC's relationship with Discovery. Of the eighteen to twenty new programmes commissioned by *Nova* each year, approximately 60 per cent are co-produced or acquired, with Channel Four International emerging as the main co-production partner in 2002 (Marlow, 2002, pp. 22–3; Willis, 2002). WGBH functions as a complementary outlet to Discovery because its interest in current affairs, science, business and religion are not part of Discovery's agenda (Willis, 2002).

The History Channel co-produces or acquires approximately thirty to thirty-five hours of programming from Britain a year, including about fifteen hours of co-productions (Maday, 2002). Co-productions include episodes from the BBC history strand *Timewatch*, Channel Four's history strand *The Real . . .* and the BBC series *Simon Schama's History of Britain* (Ibid.). However, acquisitions have declined as the channel has moved towards commissioning more original programming. Court TV, a channel focusing on trial coverage during the day, and investigative crime documentaries in prime time, intermittently acquires programmes (about ten a year) that suit its particular investigative style (Fichandler, 2002).

Opportunities for independent production companies

The increase in non-fiction channels and the relationship between BBC Worldwide and DCI forced other outlets to look at alternative suppliers. These include a small but growing number of independent British producers, such as Tiger Tigress Productions, Lion Television, Wall to Wall Television, TransAtlantic Films, RDF Media, Darlow Smithson Productions, Atlantic Productions and Windfall Films. Some, including Lion Television, RDF Media and Tiger Tigress, established offices in America to keep in closer touch with developments and key players. However, among buyers there was some scepticism about how many more British independents would risk doing business in America on their own account, because there was little incentive to do so when fully-funded commissions were available in Britain.

The lower financial risk associated with one-off programmes or short series, and the growing trade in formats, has opened up opportunities to break into the American market independently of broadcaster-distributors. For example, Wall to Wall built a business in the US based on a range of strategies including the raising of co-production finance (*Babies' World*, *Ancient Egyptians* for TLC), the local production of formats (*Frontier House* for WNET) and fully-funded production work (see Chapter 4).

The importance of co-productions

Co-production is used for costly 'landmark' programming with international appeal, which is too expensive for one broadcaster to shoulder alone – natural history, science, archaeology, history. With maturity in the late 1990s, cable channels underwent a shift away from acquisitions towards original production, including international co-productions, in order to achieve higher visibility in the marketplace (Fichandler, 2002; Hazleton, 2000b, p. 12). Executives at TLC and Discovery Health estimated that original production (commissions and co-productions) accounted for approximately 80 per cent of transmissions in 2002. Although off-the-shelf acquisitions offer a way of filling schedules cheaply, co-production allows channels to claim a commitment to original programming that marks them out from their competitors. It also provides opportunities to shape a project according to the specific commercial needs of that channel, something which is not possible with acquisitions.

In the competitive American marketplace, early participation in co-productions becomes especially important if certain types of programming are in short supply. For example, there are several outlets for natural history programmes (National Geographic, Discovery Channel, Animal Planet, PBS), but only one significant outlet for history – the History Channel. The History Channel tends to concentrate on American subjects and is consequently under less pressure to commit to programming early on, preferring to fully fund up to 95 per cent of its original production rather than co-produce with international partners (Maday, 2002). International co-productions tend to be limited to a small number of productions with budgets in excess of $500,000 an hour (Maday, 2002; Hazleton, 2000b, p. 12). At Discovery Networks, by contrast, there is even a degree of internal competition for the best co-productions, although TDC and TLC usually win out against the smaller specialist networks like Discovery Health (Egger, 2002).

British producers' ability to secure other sources of funding from European pre-sales was seen as an advantage by American buyers. Typically a US co-producer will contribute 25–40 per cent of a typical $300,000 budget for a fifty-two-minute programme in return for US rights over a set licence period. Budgets in excess of $250,000 apply to higher-profile flagship channels such as Discovery, TLC and the History Channel. Budgets for other channels (Discovery Health, the Travel Channel, Court TV) are lower, ranging between $130,000 and $300,000. With a 30–40 per cent contribution from the US and 30–40 per cent from a British broadcaster, the remainder is secured from pre-sales in the major European markets.

In return for their investment, American co-producers expect a high level of editorial input comparable to that expected for commissions. Whoever takes the lead financially 'gets to drive the editorial' (Egger, 2002). At DCI and Court TV editorial input is undertaken by in-house executive producers who oversee a number of productions and 'negotiate the editorial vision' with the co-producer. This is a continuous process and according to one DCI executive involves a significant degree of negotiation:

> It starts with a treatment. … and after we greenlight it, the producer will talk to our executive producer. … And our executive producer will have discussed it with the development people and the General Manager of our network, to make sure we're all on the same page with what we expect from the programme. … Our executive producers want to keep an eye on what we expect all the way through it, and nurture it through. So they'll sit down and meet, conference call of course if it's British. It depends on the size of the project. If it's a very large project, it's more face to face. It becomes a much bigger thing, and they'll talk to them about where the direction should go, all kinds of editorial comments. And the producer then usually goes to the other co-production partner [in Britain] and talks to them. And if there's a conflict of interest, we just have to work it out and so you get through that first stage and the treatment is written. Both our executive producer and whoever for the co-production partner will read the treatment again, give their editorial comments to the producer and then it's up to the producer to balance it. And if there's something that's not solvable get the partners on the line and try to solve it. (Executive, DCI, 2002)

The appeal of British programmes

> Many mid-budget natural history series are very Anglo-American in conception and
> finance. But the American preference is usually for British series filmed in more
> exotic places than Britain. The BBC natural history producers have become
> accustomed to obtaining about a quarter or a third of their budgets from the USA;
> together with foreign funding (from Australia, Japan, Germany, Canada, and
> elsewhere) this US funding has become a key ingredient of British 'quality' in
> factual programming. (Tunstall and Machin, 1999, p. 95)

As Tunstall and Machin indicate, there is demand for a certain type of British
programming that has little to do with contemporary British life. Accordingly
sales of the cheaper docusoaps and 'reality'-based programmes that filled British
screens in the 1990s are rare, although this does not necessarily apply to the formats on which these are based. However, the initial interest from buyers like
DCI was in high-profile natural history series like *The Blue Planet* and CGI-laden
epics like *Walking with Dinosaurs*, which could be heavily promoted and used as
events in the schedule.

The English language is one factor underpinning the appeal of British programming. At one level this is about face-to-face contact between executives
negotiating in a common language. In terms of programming, presenters or onscreen dialogue in languages other than English present a number of difficulties
for American buyers:

> It's much harder to strip off. You have talking heads, and when they're in a
> different language Americans don't like to read subtitles, so it makes that very
> difficult. If it's a foreign language it puts off American viewers because they have to
> read the subtitles or it has to be dubbed over. And they want their television to be
> easy. (Executive, DCI, 2002)

There are some exceptions. The History Channel, for example, works closely
with German broadcaster ZDF on co-funded documentaries dealing with the
Second World War (*Hitler's Holocaust, Hitler's Henchmen*) that appeal to its target male demographic (Maday, 2002).

However, a common language with Britain does not extend to a willingness
to incorporate British content, British narration or acknowledge British input
on screen. According to Sally Shell, Commercial Director at Wall to Wall:

> Basically they're buying an international programme. It's not a British programme.
> And they will get very upset if you say 'why do you want these British programmes',

because they are their programmes and that's the type of relationship we have with them. . . . They're getting high-quality programmes that work in their market. And they're paying a fraction of the price for what they would have to pay if they were making it themselves. (Shell, 2001)

This need to mould a programme to match the channel's brand and target audience was confirmed by a DCI executive:

Nothing against British programming, because we use it so much, but if we went around promoting it as British, it may get grouped in with the *Masterpiece Theatre* [PBS] type of programming and that's not the appeal of our channel. (Executive, DCI, 2002)

Most American viewers would not recognise a factual programme as a British production. In fact, American executives at both PBS stations and commercial cable channels are keen to incorporate a US story or angle as an integral part of a co-produced programme. Understandably this is about connecting with the domestic audience and in the case of cable about commercial priorities. At DCI, for example:

We're always looking to see if there's an American story. . . . We look to see if you can incorporate an American or an American expert or story of somebody in America. If we do a show on haunted houses, which we get a lot of proposals for from British producers, because of the legacy of the haunted house in Britain. And they'll come to us with ideas, it's all about haunted houses in Britain. And that just isn't going to go very well with American audiences, even though there's a sort of aura or mystique about it. They'll want to see something that's in their own country, and it's not so much that they wouldn't watch it. You're just not going to get as many people watching it . . . (Executive, DCI, 2002)

In the first instance programmes are Americanised with the addition of American narration. In the case of co-productions, scripts are sometimes rewritten and new material added to reflect American interests, although additional filming is rare because it adds to costs. In the case of WGBH's science and technology strand, *Nova*, programmes are front-loaded with a prologue to draw attention to key themes, but this also serves to fit material to PBS slots and overcome the shorter lengths of some British programming. According to John Willis, WGBH's Vice President of National Programming, this approach reflected PBS' difference in style and slower pacing (Willis, 2002). At TLC, Discovery Health and the History Channel, programmes are more likely to be adapted to accommodate advertising breaks, but also to enhance opening sequences and quicken the pace. According to Toni Egger, Vice President, Development, Discovery Health:

> Most of the time the work needs to be done in the top of the show to hook people because there's a slower pace to British programming than there is to US programming. So I would say we work to front end that. . . . If there is an American character or an American expert, we might try and move them up front to make the audience feel comfortable and then we think it's probably easier for them to accept characters. . . . We don't take British presenters with rare exception. (Egger, 2002)

However, intervention to promote an American angle was not always effective. Charles Maday, Senior Vice President of Historical Programming at the History Channel, recalled what happened with *The Ship* (2002), a co-produced series with the BBC, which challenged a multinational crew to follow in the steps of Captain Cook's epic eighteenth-century voyage to circumnavigate the globe:

> Before we produced *The Ship* we asked them as part of the co-production deal to include Americans as part of the crew and we versioned it slightly not terribly, but slightly to bring out the Americans. . . . And the Australians would do a little edit to bring out the Australians in the crew. . . . But it's limited because if you look at it some of the best characters, they aren't the American characters, they're the British characters. It's not black and white. It's more like who are the most interesting people on the ship. (Maday, 2002)

Longstanding British experience of factual programming was a further factor in using British material. In some cases there was direct influence. For example, WGBH's *Nova* was inspired by the BBC's *Horizon* science strand. Buyers often referred to quality as a factor, but the British presence also appears to be an out-come of the relative 'newness' of 'non-fiction' on US cable channels. With a public service background that demanded factual output, British producers had more experience of producing factual programming for mainstream television, and more opportunities to test it, without, in the case of the BBC, having to worry about advertisers and sponsors.

However, as the cable market has matured, although there is still demand for 'landmark' event programming on flagship channels like TLC and Discovery, the market for more traditional one-off documentaries which can be slotted into strands appears to be diminishing. On some channels, notably TLC and Dis-covery Health, this trend has been accelerated by larger amounts of domestically produced 'reality' and lifestyle formats, which offer the benefit of long-running serialisation at lower cost than one-off origination.

Discovery Health – the shift towards local origination

This tendency towards greater domestic origination is clearly visible at Discovery Health. Commissioned hours more than doubled between 2001 and 2003 (see Table 5.3), with British producers maintaining a consistent volume but declining share as Discovery Health commissioned more programming from American producers. Similarly there has been an expansion of co-produced hours, with British producers maintaining a consistent volume but declining share, because of a greater volume of co-productions undertaken with US producers who hope to recoup deficits from overseas sales (Egger, 2002).

According to Toni Egger, Vice President of Development at Discovery Health, higher levels of American content were dictated by the perceived needs of its largely female audience, which was not attracted to 'the very objective programme, with that kind of voice of god narration' typical of British one-off documentaries. Rather than 'straight' documentary formats that focused on the science of robotic surgery for example, Discovery Health looked for programming with 'dramatic integrity' and 'really strong stories about the surgeons that are being trained on these things and the patient', rather than the machines (Egger, 2002). However, the shift towards personal stories has drawbacks for British exporters because 'when we start telling personal stories we're better off telling US stories', and this favours US-based producers.

Factual formats

The shift towards domestic production may be affecting direct imports from Britain, but the shift has also sparked interest in factual formats, which can be adapted for the American market. Buyers saw Britain as a source of innovation and a testing ground for new ideas, which reduced risk:

> The advantage of looking to Britain for that is that generally it's caught on quicker. They've started doing it there before we had. But the advantage we get is that we

Table 5.3: Commissioning and co-production trends at Discovery Health

Year	Total commissioned hours	% from British producers	Total co-produced hours	% from British producers
2001	102	11.7 (12 hours)	45.5	24.7 (11 hours)
2002	128	12.5 (16 hours)	162	10.5 (17 hours)
2003	220	5.4 (12 hours)	133.5	12.7 (17 hours)

Source: Mullin, 2002.

can look at programmes and we can see a finished programme rather than just going off a proposal, so it's much easier to make a decision. You can see if it's going to work for American audiences, if you can see what's on the screen as opposed to what's on paper. (Executive, DCI, 2002)

TLC has become the most active buyer of British factual formats, turning Endemol Entertainment UK's home makeover format *Changing Rooms* into *Trading Spaces* in November 2000. This purchase was inspired by the screening of the British original on BBC America (Lee, 2002). Scheduled during the week at 4pm in 2002, *Trading Spaces* lifted TLC's slot average by 180 per cent, becoming 'appointment to view programming', and justifying a prime-time slot on Saturdays at 8pm (Waller, 2002b). In May 2002, it became the highest-rating show in TLC's history with an audience of 6 million (Ibid.).

'Reality' non-fiction formats based on CCTV footage of crime, such as *Americas's Most Wanted* (Fox), or *America's Funniest Home Videos* (ABC), had been circulating in prime time on the networks since the 1980s. However, lifestyle formats focusing on the home, garden and cookery and factual reality-based entertainment formats had been restricted largely to American daytime schedules, and the mainstream networks never broadcast shows that took place in 'ordinary' homes. The British experience showed American executives that factual entertainment could succeed in prime time with a mainstream audience, and a raft of further commissions followed in 2002 and 2003. Seriality, entertainment value, the allure of original production and cheapness compared to more traditional one-off documentaries added to the attraction (Egger, 2002; Fine, 2002).

In 2002, British producer RDF Media secured a format and production deal with TLC for its Channel Four hit, *Faking It*, in which individuals are challenged to 'fake' it in professions at odds with their own experience. This premiered in a 10pm slot in March 2003 (Waller, 2003a). In December 2002, ABC ordered a pilot based on RDF's Channel Four series *Wife Swap*, featuring a new-age mixed-race family swapping with a white, working-class family. The US version includes a host to introduce the format and mediate the discussion between the wives at the end, because 'Viewer tolerance for extremes is lower in the US', particularly on network prime time (Cathy Rogers, RDF LA President, cited in Hughes, 2003, p. 20). A thirteen-part series of RDF's dating format *Perfect Match*, originally broadcast on BBC 2, was ordered by the ABC Family Channel in 2002 (Waller, 2002c). What sets these deals apart from *Trading Spaces*, which is made by the US producer Banyan Productions, is that RDF is producing the US versions of its programmes itself through its Los Angeles outpost, and it therefore benefits financially from a format sale and a production fee (see Chapter 4).

Other factual format deals in 2002 included a BBC/TLC co-production of BBC 2's 'tough love' fashion makeover series *What Not to Wear* for Saturday prime time. This premiered in March 2003 as an hour-long show with American fashion stylists as the hosts (Stewart, 2003b). In 2003 TLC also picked up the BBC 2 format *The Good, The Bad and the Ugly*, which follows a professional, a failure and a novice in their attempts to apply for a job, and *Would Like to Meet*, a dating show from FremantleMedia, originally broadcast on BBC 2 (Waller, 2003c). Wall to Wall Television co-produced *Frontier House* and *Colonial House* for the PBS affiliate WNET in 2001 and 2002, two series that turned the clock back to allow American families to recreate the lives of early American settlers. These productions followed the successful airing on PBS of Wall to Wall's Channel 4 series *1900 House*, part of the *House* franchise (see Chapter 4).

Factual formats are an area where British independent producers have made inroads because they have retained rights and in some instances can offer the production experience and skills necessary to make a successful show in the first place – as demonstrated by RDF Media and Wall to Wall. However, US success also exposes smaller British companies to a downturn in revenues if a show is cancelled, as the Television Corporation discovered when Viacom-owned TNN decided in 2002 not to recommission it to produce another American series of its *Robot Wars* format (Vaughan-Adams, 2003; Waller, 2003d). American producers have also woken up to the possibilities of factual entertainment, devising their own celebrity-based reality shows such as *At Home with the Osbournes* (MTV) and *The Anna Nicole Show* (E! Entertainment Television), suggesting that they are catching up quickly and ready to compete (Waller, 2003a). British factual productions and formats may have been needed to kick-start new trends in the American non-fiction market, but with the trend towards domestic production, continued success by British companies is likely to require involvement as locally based producers, selling skills, experience and new ideas directly into the American marketplace.

Children's television

For years the Holy Grail in children's television was to gain access to a Saturday morning animation slot on network television – on ABC, NBC or CBS. The networks provided funding often in excess of $300,000 per half hour for two runs in two years. There was no need to secure overseas pre-sales, and a producer could earn millions in local syndication and overseas. However, there were only three players in the marketplace, and there was little interest in non-American programming. Programming for younger children was largely confined to PBS, whose long-running *Sesame Street* format was the only internationally successful pre-school franchise. The market was dominated by volume cel animation aimed at children aged six to twelve, an area in which British producers had no great experience.

Cable dramatically altered the children's television landscape and by the late 1990s cable channels Nickelodeon, Cartoon Network and the Disney Channel were the dominant forces in American children's television. Domination was secured through consolidation and the withdrawal of the networks from commissioning. Disney acquired ABC in 1995 and Fox Family in 2001 and uses these outlets to air its own programming. Viacom, the owner of Nickelodeon, merged with CBS in 1999. Since December 2000 Nickelodeon has supplied a pre-school block, Nick Junior, to the CBS weekend morning schedule. In 2002, Fox leased its Saturday morning block to 4Kids Entertainment, the supplier of the Japanese animation series *Pokémon* (Johnson, 2002). NBC's Saturday morning block is sourced by Discovery Kids. Children's television in the US is now dominated by three players – ABC/Disney (the Disney Channel, Disney Playhouse, ABC Family, Toon Disney), Viacom/CBS (Nickelodeon, Noggin) and AOL Time Warner (the Cartoon Network). These same three players own or part own 60 per cent of the estimated 100 dedicated children's channels worldwide (Jeremy, 2002).

Consolidation made access more difficult for independent producers. Nickelodeon uses its own studios to produce much of its programming. It produced 450 hours in 2001–02 (30 per cent more than 2000–01) and has an exclusive output deal with Klasky-Csupo Studios, the producer of flagship show *Rugrats* (Ibid.). In 2000–01 ABC only commissioned series from Disney-owned enterprises – DIC, Jumbo Pictures and Walt Disney TV Animation (Anon., 2001b). Opportunities for overseas suppliers are largely restricted to volume Japanese animation series (*Pokémon*, *Medabots* and *Digimon*), which have tie-ins with toy companies and offer channels promising avenues for participation in licensed merchandise (Newhouse Calcaterra and Garrity, 2001).

In this difficult market a small number of British exporters, including HIT Entertainment, Ragdoll Productions and BBC Worldwide, exploited what was then an undersupplied niche, although the market has since become saturated (Fry, 2002a). They developed relationships with the most important pre-school outlets, Nick Junior and PBS, to ensure access to platforms, which could be used to create a market for ancillary rights, the real goldmine for children's programming in America. HIT went on to establish a permanent presence in the US through its acquisition of the Dallas-based Lyrick studios in 2001, the owners of the long-running PBS pre-school series *Barney* (see Chapter 4).

The first pre-school breakthrough occurred in the early 1990s when the Britt Allcroft Company sold *Thomas the Tank Engine* to PBS. This was adapted with local presenters and, airing as *Shining Time Station*, opened up licensing opportunities that convinced other British producers that pre-school was an area where they could compete (Fry and Curtis, 2000). BBC Worldwide followed in 1998 with *Noddy in Toyland*, a half-hour format comprising locally produced live action and puppetry wrapped around a ten-minute stop-frame animation produced in the early 1990s (Fry, 1998, p. 14). Ragdoll's *Teletubbies* became a phenomenon on PBS in 1998. Like the others it offered opportunities for local adaptation with live-action inserts, but it also highlighted a gap in the market for programming aimed at babies and toddlers. It was also available in volume, which made it attractive for scheduling on a daily basis. This in turn created visibility and a national platform for licensing. Although *Teletubbies* was commissioned by the BBC, US rights are retained by Ragdoll, and the programme is reported to have grossed $1 billion from licensing in the US over nine months in its first year (Elliott, 1999, p. 8). *Teletubbies* was still airing in 2003, but the initial furore had died down. In 2001, HIT secured a deal with PBS for a weekend showcase for *Angelina Ballerina*, an animated property about a mouse based on the books by American authors Katherine Holabird and Helen Craig.

PBS is an important outlet for pre-school programming, but slots are limited because of long-running flagship series including *Sesame Street* and *Clifford, the Big Red Dog* (Fry, 2002a). Nick Junior, Nickelodeon's pre-school morning block, which emerged in the mid-1990s, provides a valuable but limited alternative for British-produced series *Maisie* (Polygram/Universal) and the HIT properties *Bob the Builder*, *Kipper* and *Rubbadubbers*. Second-tier outlets include Discovery Kids and Noggin (part of Nickelodeon's bouquet), which airs the BBC's pre-school hit *The Tweenies* and Nick Junior staple *Bob the Builder*. The six to twelve demographic, targeted by Nickelodeon with live action and comedies, remains the most important target audience in America, but constitutes a culturally specific area of American life that British and overseas producers have found difficult to crack.

Funding children's television in the US

With audience fragmentation and declining licence fees, the funding of children's programmes has become more challenging. From network sales of $250,000 per half hour in the late 1980s, licence fees had sunk to $50,000–75,000 per half hour by 2000, although costs of $150,000–300,000 per half hour remained (Fry, 2002a; Newhouse Calcaterra, 2001; Westcott, 2000, p. 18). Larger budget deficits make co-productions, overseas pre-sales or the securing of sponsors essential, unless a producer can fund production on its own – as HIT Entertainment did with *Bob the Builder* (see Chapter 4). The business is no longer based on production, but on the expectation of profits from video/DVD, publishing and toys, which may follow on from a broadcast hit. For example, Ragdoll's 2003 sale of its latest ITV pre-school series, *Boohbah*, to PBS is in fact a three-way deal involving toy manufacturer Hasbro and publisher

Scholastic, which hold the North American master toy licence and publishing rights respectively (Waller, 2003e).

Broadcasters are aware of these opportunities and expect to participate in video and licensing revenues (Caminada, 2001; Fry, 2002a; Jeremy, 2001a, p. 16). They justify reduced financial contributions and participation in ancillary revenues on the grounds of their importance as a platform for ancillary rights exploitation. Giving a broadcaster off-air rights gives them an incentive to keep a show on air, and this was underlined in comments by Brown Johnson, Executive Vice President at Nick Junior:

> Those licence fees [for pre-school programming] have probably gone down to closer to zero to $25,000 per half hour. I mean it's really almost nothing, but if you have your show on a network like Nick Junior, then we'll play it every day, we'll promote it. What we provide is basically millions of dollars' worth of on-air promotion and support because it goes on our dotcom, it goes in our magazine. (Johnson, 2001)

At PBS, the level of financial contribution is believed to be significantly lower than cable, with some producers apparently giving shows away in order to gain access to regular national screenings that can help build an ancillary rights business (Fry, 2002a; Jeremy, 2001a). In return, PBS expects a share of ancillary revenues. In 2001, for example, 17 per cent ($55 million) of PBS funding (excluding programme underwriting by sponsors) came from educational product sales with a further 19 per cent ($62 million) derived from royalties, licence fees and investment income (PBS, 2001).

The adaptation and appeal of British programming

Only a small number of British pre-school properties have been sold into the US market, primarily to PBS (*Teletubbies, Angelina Ballerina*), Nick Junior (*Bob the Builder, Maisie, Rubbadubbers*) and Noggin (*The Tweenies*). Most shows are adapted to appeal to an American audience and these are not recognisably British shows to the audience or their parents. At Nickelodeon and Nick Junior shows are heavily pre-tested with children to gauge the level of children's recall, whether the stories make sense and to what extent they have identified with the characters (Johnson, 2001; Walker, 2002). In the case of PBS, shows must demonstrate educational content. Most shows are re-voiced. At Nick Junior, this is seen as a necessary part of enhancing a property's audience and commercial appeal. Speaking about *Bob the Builder*, Brown Johnson, Executive Vice President of Nick Junior, commented, 'I think it would have been a television success, but to make it a TV hit and a real retail hit, I think having American voices made a big difference' (2001). With saturation in the marketplace, pre-awareness of a property from publishing can be an important factor for buyers (*Maisie* and *Angelina Ballerina*), but some shows (*Bob the Builder* and *Teletubbies*) have no publishing connections.

Stop-frame model animation had been relatively rare in the American market, but *Bob the Builder* was attractive to Nick Junior 'because he speaks himself and the vehicles all speak, it made a difference' (Ibid.). Nick Junior has since acquired HIT's follow-up stop-frame series, *Rubbadubbers*. Executives were keen to emphasise that stories and characters were key rather than any potential revenues from licensing, which strong characterisation might suggest (Ibid.). Access for British pre-school programmes on Nick Junior was also helped by the channel's willingness to take programming in smaller packages and in shorter lengths, rather than the traditional commercial half hour. Nick Junior schedules thirteen-part ten-minute series in a 'chequer board schedule' where two series (e.g. *Maisie* and *Kipper*) are shown on alternate days. The lack of volume was not seen as an insurmountable problem, and the financial risk for British producers of investing in more episodes was acknowledged:

> I would understand from a UK production point of view not wanting to invest that much money in twenty-six half hours, that's a lot of television. That's millions of dollars' worth of production and so I understand wanting to be more circumspect about why they make fewer. (Ibid.)

The success of a small number of pre-school properties in the American market does not extend to live-action series targeted at older children, with one notable exception: *S Club 7 in Miami*, a co-production between pop impressario Simon Fuller's 19TV and BBC Worldwide. Focusing on the adventures of a British pop group in America, it appealed to an older 'tween' audience (ten to twelve years), but was recognisably different from what was on offer elsewhere. According to Joel Andryc, Executive Vice President of Kids' Programming and Development at Fox Family, it was a good example of programming that served the needs of two markets:

> *S Club 7* is a fine example of how someone was able to put together a concept. They hit upon the music, which is very popular and I think very much translates and transcends the boundaries overseas. ... They were able to foresee a couple of years ago the whole thing about pop groups and capitalise on that. Also the way they cast the group – very aspirational with good-looking kids who are slightly older than our intended audience. Kids always want to watch up and a little older. ...
> Also the concept of coming up with something creative that is believable so it doesn't feel like a hundred per cent British import. That they've taken the group of

stars, the British kids and planted them in the US and there's a reason why they're here, that they want to make it big in the US. They want to hit Hollywood. So it serves both of our needs – that it doesn't feel like it's a straight acquisition, because it's shot in the US, but it fits your needs because you have the core group of stars from the UK. (Andryc, 2001)

Entertainment formats

It's funny when Millionaire came out, everyone ... in America thought it was an American show. No one knew that it had originated in Britain. (Schiff, 2001)

The reality of it is that the format business has exploded because it takes into consideration the cultural differences. ... These are all contestants that I recognise as being part of my culture. This host is somebody who I recognise from yonks of watching television. That's what we like in television. We don't want a real foreign flavour to our television. ... Americans don't want to hear a foreign voice anymore than anybody else does. I don't think we're unique in that at all. I think it's true across the board. (Ibid.)

While off-the-shelf sales to the US have become increasingly difficult, there is one area that generated enormous amounts of publicity from 1999. These were sales of British quiz-show formats (*Who Wants to Be a Millionaire?*, *The Weakest Link*), European reality-game-show hybrids (*Big Brother*, *Survivor*) and reality-based talent-show formats (*Popstars*, *Pop Idol*) to American networks. As Hans Schiff, UK Vice President at the William Morris Agency in London indicates, American audiences had no inkling of the British origins of many of the new shows. These were American programmes produced for American audiences and that constituted the core of their success.

The breakthrough occurred in 1999 with the sale of Celador's *Who Wants to Be a Millionaire?* to ABC, followed by the success of reality format *Survivor* (Castaway) on CBS in 2000. The finale of the first *Survivor* series in September 2000, produced by the American Mark Burnett Productions, attracted 72 million viewers. With a 28.6 rating and a 45 per cent share of the eighteen to forty-nine demographic, it became the second most watched show of the year in America after the Super Bowl, securing $600,000 per thirty-second advertising slot (Hazleton, 2000c; Sofley, 2000b).

No British company had much of a format business in America before *Who Wants to Be a Millionaire?*, with the exception of Hat Trick's comedy improvisation format *Whose Line is it Anyway?*, which first aired on ABC in 1998. More than anything else, the success of *Who Wants to Be a Millionaire?* and *Survivor* opened doors to the networks and prime time, doors that had previously been firmly shut. However, it is worth noting that staying on air is as hard as ever, and only a small number of British properties have survived beyond the first series, including:

Whose Line is it Anyway? (Hat Trick) – First aired on ABC in 1998

Who Wants to Be a Millionaire? (Celador) – First aired on ABC in 1999

Survivor (Castaway) – First aired on CBS in 2000

The Weakest Link (BBC Worldwide) – First aired on NBC in 2001

Dog Eat Dog (BBC Worldwide) – First aired on NBC in 2001

Popstars (Target/Screentime) – First aired on WB in 2000

Pop Idol/American Idol (19TV/FremantleMedia) – First aired on Fox in 2002

Yet the potential rewards from a hit are very high. Granada's deal in 2002 with ABC for the reality format *I'm a Celebrity . . . Get Me Out of Here!* was reputed to be worth $15 million over a number of years (Waller, 2002d). BBC Worldwide's contract with NBC for *The Weakest Link* is also reputed to have been worth $15 million if it ran for six years (Wells, 2001). *Pop Idol* was reported to have netted $1 billion in revenue from the United States, with half of this generated from third party deals including artist management, music licensing and sponsorship from Coca Cola, Ford and AT&T (Hodgson, 2003).

However, before 1999 game shows were not seen as prime-time network material, and throughout the 1980s and 1990s they were displaced in daytime syndication by talk shows and court shows (Moran, 1998, p. 48; Schiff, 2001). In the meantime, European players like the Dutch-based Endemol (*Big Brother, Stars in Their Eyes, All You Need is Love*) and FremantleMedia (*Wheel of Fortune, Family Feud*) filled the gap in entertainment format provision in Europe, where they continued to be popular. Yet in the US itself, light entertainment became 'almost extinct' in network prime time from the 1970s onwards because prime-time schedules were built around drama series and situation comedies. When *Who Wants to Be a Millionaire?* arrived there was a realisation that development in this area had been neglected (Schiff, 2001;Van den bussche, 2001). According to Charlie Parsons, co-owner of Castaway Productions and creator of *Survivor*, 'American TV was failing until European formats came to the rescue because corporate laziness had set in and creative people were no longer given their head' (cited in Clarke, 2001). The success of imported formats not only opened the networks' eyes to the possibility of game shows in prime time, but also to the possibility of 'reality' formats that were less about CCTV footage of *Cops* (Fox) or *America's Most Wanted* (Fox), and more about 'ordinary' people interacting under camera surveillance (Dovey, 2001; Fraser, 2002a).

Formats were attractive because they were proven in other territories. They offered savings on development and were initially about one-third to half as expensive to make as a one-hour scripted drama, although the American versions of *The Weakest Link* and *Who Wants to Be a Millionaire?* were reported to have cost about $500,000 per episode (Boddy, 2001; Bruneau, 2001, p. 26; Fry, 2002b). However, success can be undermined by overexposure. *Who Wants to Be a Millionaire?* was phenomenally successful for ABC, but scheduled up to four times a week without using the show as a launch pad for new programming led to a decline in ratings in 2002 and the gradual withdrawal of the show from prime time (Hazleton, 2002c, p. 28). In 2002, NBC decided to 'rest' the BBC format *The Weakest Link* because audiences had fallen from a high of 17.5 million to 7 million (Waller, 2002e). Although these shows no longer feature as heavily in network prime time, new versions have been created for the daytime syndication market, allowing their creators to continue to benefit from exposure in the US marketplace (Smith, 2001).

Selling entertainment formats

Selling entertainment and reality formats to the networks is a different proposition to the sale of completed programmes to cable and PBS because 'It's never about selling the tape, but using the tape to sell the idea' (Schiff, 2001). There are only a small number of people with power in network television and access is nigh on impossible unless you have an agent. The role of American agencies like Endeavor, CAA or the William Morris Agency is crucial in bringing together producers, broadcasters and talent to ensure access to the right people. According to David Lyle at FremantleMedia 'agents can be like doormen, but the tips are bigger' (Lyle, 2001).

The William Morris Agency (WMA), with offices in London, has been important in securing US network access for British scripted and unscripted formats, and was involved in placing *Who Wants to Be a Millionaire?*, *The Weakest Link* and many others. From the broadcaster's point of view an agent is part of the screening process. According to Hans Schiff, in WMA's London office,

> Both from the perspective of knowing what people want and who to go and see as well as knocking on the door and saying, 'Heh I'm a producer you've never heard of. I've got something great. Will you take a meeting with me?' Well by and large the buyers in the US won't because they really as a matter of policy protect themselves against specious lawsuits by saying, 'I'll listen to it if you've got an agent'. (2001)

From the producer or distributors's point of view, an agent's role is not only to help secure the best financial deal but also to secure a degree of creative control for the format owner. According to Schiff:

They should be looking to make a deal where they protect their intellectual property from being damaged, so that they have some creative impact, some creative control, over what the end product looks like. These are now global assets, so it's important that you try to maintain quality control over that as well. (Ibid.)

When *Who Wants to Be a Millionaire?* launched in Britain in September 1998, Michael Davies, Head of Specials at ABC, approached the William Morris Agency in London rather than the producer direct (Smith, 2001). A meeting took place at the end of 1998 and Celador produced a pilot in Britain with American contestants and an American host, Regis Philbin. After approval by Disney, Paul Smith, Celador's Managing Director, went to America in August 1999 with the production bible to supervise the first shows in the initial thirteen-episode run. Launched in the summer of 1999 and produced by ABC's in-house production division, the show became ABC's highest-rating summer series and a further eighteen episodes were ordered. The success of *Who Wants to Be a Millionaire?* opened the door to the networks for others, including Granada (*Boot Camp* to Fox in 2001, *Hotel Hell/Hotel Getaway* to Fox in 2001, *I'm a Celebrity . . . Get Me Out of Here!* to ABC in 2002), BBC Worldwide (*The Weakest Link* and *Dog Eat Dog* to NBC), FremantleMedia, Target, Action Time (*King of the Castle* to CBS in 2002) and the Television Corporation (*Paradise Hotel* to Fox in 2003; *Forever Eden* to Fox in 2004).

After agents, the second key relationship for British producers hoping to break into the network format market has been with established American entertainment producers such as Stone Stanley, LMNO, the Gurin Company, Evolution and Termite Arts which have experience of pitching to and producing for the networks. For example, Granada's *Boot Camp* was produced by LMNO Productions, with Granada benefiting from licensing the format to the producer and from an executive production fee (Waller, 2003a). Similarly the BBC's *The Weakest Link* was sold as a package to NBC, ensuring a more profitable outcome, but the show was produced in the US by the Gurin Company. Received wisdom was that US networks were unwilling to buy an idea without a US producer attached, because they liked to work with production companies that they know will deliver, and who understand the US mass audience with its broad demographic mix (Clarke, 2001; Gurin, 2002; Stephens, 2001).

However, by 2003 Granada had made a strategic decision to move away from licensing its formats to American producers to selling its own production skills and experience. For example, the American version of *I'm a Celebrity . . . Get Me Out of Here!* for ABC was shot in the Australian jungle by Granada's Australian production outpost (Waller, 2003a). This was possible because the format was in high demand, allowing the company to leverage its position to secure a lucrative production deal (Ibid.). The company has since secured orders for further entertainment productions to be undertaken by its LA outpost, Granada Entertainment USA, now merged with Carlton America to form Granada America. These include the six-part reality series *American Princess* for NBC, docusoap *Airline* for A&E, and a pilot of the entertainment format *Saturday Night Take-away* for Fox (Ibid.). Producing entertainment formats for the networks mirrors what had already become a feature of the cable market. Since 2001, RDF Media has made several series of scrap metal challenge *Junkyard Wars* for TLC, an American version of its Channel Four hit *Scrapheap Challenge*. Similarly Mentorn (part of the Television Corporation) produced several American series of *Robot Wars* for TNN and Nickelodeon before this show was cancelled in 2002. For both companies local production in America has become a significant and growing source of revenues (see Chapter 4; also Hughes, 2003).

BBC America

Most export activity in America is focused on programme and format sales. However, the circulation of British programming can also take place through involvement in broadcasting itself. Owned by BBC Worldwide, BBC America was established in 1998 with $100 million of marketing and distribution support from Worldwide's joint-venture partner, Discovery Communications (Hazleton, 2002b; Lee, 2002). Before BBC America, there had never been a foreign-owned English-language channel in the US. Available in 34.5 million American homes by 2003 it constitutes an alternative approach to programming exports.

For BBC Worldwide, BBC America represents an additional strategy to the traditional activities of selling and co-producing programmes, and it is a strategy that the BBC was best suited to pursue because of its library, brand and partnership with DCI. It represents an insurance against selling fewer programmes in future in a consolidating US television landscape. According to Chief Executive Paul Lee, it adds value to the BBC in four ways (Lee, 2002). First, BBC America purchases programmes from BBC Worldwide at market rates with returns benefiting the licence-fee payer. Second, as a commercial channel funded by cable subscriptions and advertising revenues, BBC America promises to return profits to the BBC. Third, BBC America is making a small but growing contribution to BBC productions as a co-production partner. For example, it invested alongside the American channel Comedy Central in the third series of the sitcom *Absolutely Fabulous*. Finally, the channel is a commercial asset.

With classic dramas, older sitcoms and event factual programming sold to cable outlets and PBS, BBC America has focused instead on showing British programming that would not normally get an airing on US networks. In

July/August 2003, the peak-time schedule included lifestyle makeover pro-gramming (*Changing Rooms*, *Ground Force*), factual entertainment (*Faking It*), sitcoms (*Coupling*, *Absolutely Fabulous*), contemporary drama (*Jonathan Creek*, *Red Cap*) and a nightly screening of Channel Four's celebrity talk show *So Gra-ham Norton*. However, as much as providing an alternative sales outlet for British shows, BBC America is also about getting noticed and providing a spring-board for sales of British formats. For example, *Coupling* was re-versioned for NBC, airing in September 2003, albeit to mixed reviews by US critics before it was dropped (Jury, 2003, p. 3). TLC has acquired the formats to *Changing Rooms* and *Faking It*. In September 2003, NBC was negotiating for an Ameri-can pilot of the BBC 2 spoof docusoap *The Office* with US producers Reveille and Universal Network Television (now part of NBC).

The focus on entertainment reflects a different perception of the BBC among the US public than other places in the world, where the BBC is primarily known for its news and the World Service. According to Paul Lee, knowledge of the BBC in the US is confined mainly to older, more highly educated urban-based viewers who watch PBS' *Masterpiece Theatre* or *Mystery!*. For the vast majority of Americans the BBC means very little. As well as providing a showcase for original programming, BBC America was being used to raise the profile of the BBC brand with a younger, urban, upscale audience who were felt to want 'edgier' television than that provided by US channels (Lee, 2002). Lee classi-fied the channel as 'HBO for Basic Cable' with its emphasis on contemporary British drama (*This Life*), 'outrageous' comedies (*The League of Gentlemen*), entertainment (*So Graham Norton*) and lifestyle programming (*Changing Rooms*). Yet for this strategy to succeed the barriers had to be lowered to entice American viewers in. This necessitated the use of celebrities known to Ameri-can audiences to introduce shows (Whoopi Goldberg, Rupert Everett, Chloë Sevigny) and the adoption of a stripped schedule, familiar to American audi-ences. But according to Lee 'being British' was not enough to attract viewers. There had to be a broader appeal, that drew on both familiarity and difference and spoke to a younger, more highly educated target audience:

> Other networks take an eight foot hurdle, English voice and English cadences and turn it into a three foot hurdle with American voices, bite size chunks and easy to watch, but it's basically the same content. We work with being a four or five foot hurdle. In other words there's actually some pleasure in having a hurdle. That's why people are starting to love this network. ... And we can't make it a two foot hurdle because by definition we're full of shows that have English accents. We have done a lot to say this feels like an OK network for you to watch. There are shows that you know and have a relationship with, even if a lot of them are British. (Lee, 2002)

Review

While America is significant as Britain's largest export market, Britain has only a limited presence on American television screens, and is unlikely ever to have a significant presence because British companies are too small to compete with large US-based concerns, which have significant production capability and access to their own channels. There is undoubtedly a special relationship between Britain and America based on the historical commonalities of language and culture, and the anglophile sympathies of some in the American broadcasting community. This gives British players advantages over non-English-speaking exporters.[6] However, this relationship, particularly in respect of co-production funding for ambitious drama, is arguably more important for British producers seeking financial support for distinctively British programmes.

For the vast majority of Americans, British television is marginal, and factual co-productions and the British formats adapted for mainstream US television are not recognised as anything other than American shows. American broadcasters are resistant to foreign-sourced programming like no other nation. With the exception of entertainment formats on the networks, since the late 1960s British programmes have circulated on the periphery, first on PBS and since the 1980s on more narrowly focused cable outlets. British producers have tended to succeed in less commercially attractive niche areas where US dominance is less prevalent, areas such as natural history, wildlife and pre-school television, which are less culturally specific.

To counter the resistance to British-produced programmes, other strategies have been pursued with mixed success. They include producing drama for the US market through US-based subsidiaries (Granada Entertainment USA, Carlton America) and the establishment in 1998 by the BBC of its own dedicated channel for the US market, BBC America. The recent success of formats, which are often hybrids of forms originally developed in the US, and the difficulty of selling 'off-the-shelf' programming, reinforces the notion that to appeal to the US market there is a trade-off involving the suppression of the look and feel of programming that expresses national origins (Sinclair, 1996, p. 45). The US market is interested in Britain as an originator of ideas, innovation and talent,[7] which can stimulate domestic origination, but interest in British content is limited. British drama tends to appeal to a narrower PBS-type audience, characterised by education, wealth and increasingly age, unless it can transcend cultural barriers with a more universal/American appeal based on cast and story. Factual programming is limited to universally appealing events, with maturity among some players, leading away from one-off co-productions towards locally produced formats. British success in children's programming remains firmly entrenched in an oversupplied pre-school market, which is heavily reliant on ancillary revenues from licensed product and video.

This is not to suggest that the American market is unimportant. America, more than any other market, represents the key to international success both in terms of revenues and as a shop window for sales to other markets. This has become apparent with the global success of entertainment formats that have penetrated the mainstream American networks, and with the increased efforts by a small number of independent producers, who are making their mark as producers in the American marketplace. This reinforces the view that sustained economic success in the American mass market ultimately depends on masking the British origins of productions, and on the ability to produce or co-produce drama, entertainment and factual programming locally for American outlets, rather than the sale of programmes produced in Britain for British audiences.

Notes

1. AOL Time Warner Inc. announced the change of its name to Time Warner Inc. in October 2003.
2. General Electric signed an agreement with the French-owned Vivendi Universal in October 2003 to merge NBC and Vivendi Universal Entertainment. The new company is called NBC Universal, and includes the NBC Television Network, Universal Pictures and the Cable networks USA Network, Sci-Fi Channel, CNBC, Bravo and Trio.
3. All three were scripted by Andrew Davies.
4. In 2001, it was estimated that A&E was involved in thirty hours of original US drama (excluding TV movies) (Fine, 2002).
5. In November 2003, it was announced that Granada Entertainment USA and Carlton America would merge to create Granada America, following the merger of parent companies Granada and Carlton. Granada America combines US revenues of £70 million and will spend £4 million a year on the development of reality shows and TV movies for the US market.
6. In the American market a common language does give Britain an advantage over nearly all other exporters with the exception of Canada, which has the added bonus of speaking North American English, a great advantage when selling to US commercial broadcasters.
7. For example, there are increasing numbers of British actors in mainstream television programming, just as there are in film – Jane Leeves in *Frasier*, Mark Addy in CBS' *Still Standing*, John Hannah in ABC's *MDs*, Helen Baxendale in NBC's *Friends*. The NBC transmission of *The Weakest Link* retained the fearsome Anne Robinson, the British presenter, and the US version of *Pop Idol*, *American Idol* on Fox in 2002 retained Simon Cowell, one of the British judges, known for his harsh views.

6

You Can't Sell Everything ... European Particularities

After North America, Western Europe as a region constitutes the largest market for British programming. But unlike America, Western Europe is made up of many different, national markets, serving distinctive linguistic and cultural communities, making the sales process more arduous and fragmented than in the larger and more financially rewarding American market. In 2003, British exports to Europe reached $280 million, 30 per cent of the total (BTDA, 2004). Estimates of Britain's share of imported programmes by volume in the major territories of Germany (3 per cent), France (8 per cent), Italy (1 per cent) and Spain (3 per cent) in 1996–7, place it substantially behind the 66–87 per cent share taken by American imports (DCMS, 1999a, p. 17). This dominance of American imports is reflected in the European Union's (EU) audiovisual trade deficit with North America, which totalled $8.2 billion in 2000, with American television exports to the EU reaching $4.38 billion (EAO, 2002).

In spite of the EU's attempt to create a single market for broadcasting with its *Television Without Frontiers Directive* in 1989 (EC, 1997), European television has remained a largely territory-based affair, because of language differences and the historical origins of radio and later television as national concerns. Of the 1,500 channels circulating in Western Europe in 2002, just fifty nationally based channels accounted for a 75 per cent audience share (Reding, 2002, p. 5). Pan-European television stations that launched in the 1980s proved largely unsuccessful in competition with nationally targeted channels (Collins, 1989; Tracey, 1988, p. 16). American-owned thematic channels (Cartoon Network, CNN, MTV, National Geographic, Discovery, Nickelodeon, Fox Kids, VH1), faced with audience shares that rarely exceeded 1 per cent, have been localised to overcome cultural differences, and compete more efficiently with local rivals (Chalaby, 2002).

Yet at the structural level of ownership European television is increasingly transnational with media conglomerates (the RTL Group, Vivendi Universal, News Corporation) operating channels and participating in media ventures in different countries. The relaxation of ownership rules across Europe promises to extend this trend (Iosifidis, 2005). Nevertheless, it is local markets and the provision of local programming, even if it is based on formats, that remains central to organisations like the RTL Group, which operates television channels in Luxembourg, Belgium, France, Germany, the Netherlands and Britain (Five), for European television is still strongly embedded in local tradition and cultural practices. This underpins substantial variations in television between territories, not only with regard to audience preferences, but also in the way that television schedules are constructed to fit established national routines about where and how particular types of programming are placed and promoted.

Amid this market complexity, this chapter concentrates on the circulation of British programming in the most important Western European territories of Germany (sales of $68 million in 2003), France ($50 million), Spain ($32 million) and Italy ($25 million) (BTDA, 2004). It also considers the smaller territories of Sweden and the Netherlands, which are keen buyers of British programmes, with Britain estimated to account for 12 and 9 per cent respectively of imported programmes in 1996–7 (DCMS, 1999a, p. 17). Based on interviews with buyers between January and July 2002, this chapter positions the circulation of British programming within the context of the variations that exist both between different national markets, and within these markets as well. Within each system, the most notable differences are those that exist between public service and commercial channels. At another level there are also differences between mainstream terrestrial channels and the niche outlets that inhabit the cable and satellite market.

Market overview

Within its short history, television in Western Europe has undergone a radical transformation. One of the chief elements of that transformation has been the shift from a predominantly public service to a commercial model. Where public service monopolies largely prevailed at the beginning of the 1980s, most countries now operate a dual system of commercial and public television. This opening up of television markets resulted in increased opportunities for selling programmes to new commercial channels.

Well into the 1980s public service broadcasters were the chief purchasers of British programming by dint of monopoly in their respective markets. In Germany the main free-to-air public broadcasting outlet is ARD, a federation of ten regionally based stations, whose origins and ethos owe much to the public service station, NWDR, established by British occupying forces in northern Germany in the aftermath of the Second World War.[1] ARD provides a nationally networked television service, *Erstes Deutsches Fernsehen*. ZDF (Zweites

Deutsches Fernsehen), a centrally organised broadcaster, is responsible for a second public television network. The ARD stations, either individually or in collaboration, also provide eight regionally based channels, available throughout Germany on cable and satellite. In France the key public service free-to-air networks are the more mainstream France 2 and France 3 and the information-oriented France 5. Public service television in Italy is represented by RAI, which operates three terrestrial television channels, Rai Uno, Rai Due and, since 1979, the more culturally focused Rai Tre. TVE in Spain is responsible for two national channels, the more mainstream La Primera and the more information-based La 2. There is also a network of independent regional broadcasters, which acquire programming jointly through an organisation called Forta. Public service television in the Netherlands is a complicated affair, with three channels operating under the umbrella of NOS. N2 targets a younger age group with entertainment and sport. N1 is a more mainstream channel for older audiences and N3 has a reputation for culturally progressive and more socially oriented programming. Eight broadcasting organisations with varying degrees of political, religious and social group affiliation provide the majority of programming. These are AVRO, BNN, EO, KRO, NCRV, TROS, Vara and VPRO. Two non-affiliated broadcasters, NPS and Teleac/NOT, cater for multicultural and educational programming respectively on N3. Public service television in Sweden is represented by SVT, which operates two terrestrial television channels, SVT1 and the less mainstream SVT2.

The most lucrative outlets for programme sales are the mainstream commercial free-to-air channels. In Germany the main commercial outlets are controlled by two competing organisations. The Bertelsmann-owned RTL Group controls RTL (100 per cent), RTL2 (35.9 per cent), Vox (99.7 per cent) and the children's channel Super RTL (50 per cent). Its rival, the Kirch Group, which declared insolvency in April 2002, controlled the entertainment channels SAT.1, ProSieben and Kabel 1,[2] as well as the troubled digital pay television platform Premiere World. In France the main free-to-air commercial outlets are TF1, M6 and the pay channel Canal Plus. In Italy the RAI channels compete with the channels of Prime Minister Silvio Berlusconi's company Mediaset – Canale 5, Italia 1 and Rete 4. In Spain free-to-air commercial television is dominated by Telecinco and Antena 3. In the Netherlands the chief rivals to the NOS channels are those of the RTL-owned Holland Media Group (HMG), comprising the general entertainment channel RTL4, the male-oriented RTL5 and the youth-oriented Yorin. The other commercial grouping is SBS Broadcasting, which operates SBS 6, Net 5 and V8. In Sweden commercial television is provided by the free-to-air terrestrial service TV4, and the satellite channels TV3 and Kanal 5 (part of SBS).

The mainstream free-to-air channels, both public and commercial, dominate up to 80 per cent of viewing in most of these countries. Most emphasise local programming, particularly at peak time (Rouse, 2001). What is left is a third tier of smaller channels, both generalist and niche, which on account of low programme budgets are much more highly dependent on imports, but pay less for programming. Some are niche services operated by public service broadcasters. They include KiKa, the children's channel operated by ARD and ZDF, and RaiSat, a separate division of RAI, which provides subscription channels available on digital satellite. There are many more commercial generalist and niche channels, which are largely dependent on cable and satellite distribution. For example, in France the second tier of private channels includes RTL 9 (35 per cent owned by RTL) and those channels that form part of the rival digital pay television platforms Canalsatellite and TPS (Télévision Par Satellite).

Selling fiction

Drama is the most heavily traded and valuable genre, but volume sales of British drama[3] to mainstream channels are very low. In the larger territories of Germany, France, Italy and Spain, buyers from the key terrestrial outlets could only list a limited number of British fiction acquisitions. This short list is dominated by detective series/serials acquired from BBC Worldwide and Granada (see Table 6.1).

Low levels of British drama on European screens are certainly partially attributable to the wrong type of content, programme length and format (see Chapter 3). But closer inspection reveals a range of additional factors that affect acquisitions, reflecting the characteristics of individual territories and a decline in acquisitions on the mainstream networks.

Buyers frequently claimed that British drama fails to meet the requirements for a minimum of thirteen episodes on commercial networks in Italy, France, Spain and Germany. This disadvantage is compounded by longstanding relationships with the major American suppliers, who have driven in long-running series and TV movies on the back of highly desired feature films. However, buyers in Italy and Spain, where output deals for American product were strong in the past, pointed to reduced levels of acquisitions from American suppliers. This was attributed variously to increases in domestic production, a downturn in advertising revenues between 2000 and 2002, surplus stock, and the declining ability of the American studios to include the most attractive feature films in their packages, resulting in more 'cherry-picking' (Grignaffini and Stewart, 2002; Pugnetti, 2002; Ramos, 2002; also EAO, 2001a).

As markets have matured, mainstream channels have sought to raise their profile and ratings with domestically produced drama or entertainment formats in

Table 6.1: Drama purchases by free-to-air television in Germany, France, Italy, Spain 2001–02

Country	Programme
Germany	
ZDF (public)	*The Inspector Lynley Mysteries* (BBC/WGBH)
ProSieben (commercial)	*Coupling* (BBC), *S Club 7* (BBC/19 Entertainment)
RTL (commercial)	*Dangerfield* (BBC), *Silent Witness* (BBC), *The Lost World* (BBC)
France	
FR3 (public)	*Midsomer Murders* (Chrysalis), *Dalziel and Pascoe* (BBC), *Hetty Wainthropp Investigates* (BBC), *Poirot* (Granada/LWT), *Wycliffe* (Granada/HTV), *A Touch of Frost* (Granada/Yorkshire TV), *The Adventures of Sherlock Holmes* (Granada)
TF1 (commercial)	*Silent Witness* (BBC), *Dangerfield* (BBC), *The Lost World* (BBC)
Italy	
RAI (public)	*The Lost World* (BBC)
Mediaset (commercial)	*Poirot* (Granada)
Spain	
RTVE (public)	*The Lost World* (BBC), *The Whistle-Blower* (BBC), *Take a Girl Like You* (BBC)
Telecinco (commercial)	*Invasion Earth* (Granada/Itel), *The Scarlet Pimpernel* (BBC/London Films/A&E)

Source: Interviews with buyers.

peak time. Research by the Eurofiction project in the five largest West European countries shows steady increases in the volume of national first-run fiction broadcast between 1996 and 2000 from 4,127 hours to 5,564 hours (EAO, 2001b, p. 161; EAO, 2001c). These increases have not been sufficient to fill the expansion in transmission hours across Europe, but the trend has worked against all imports including US series, which although still plentiful increasingly occupy a more marginalised position in the schedules (see De Bens and de Smaele, 2001; Rouse, 2001). With the exception of the very best feature films in peak time, US series are now often restricted to daytime or late-night slots on the main free-to-air channels in Germany, Spain, France and Italy. Most buyers testified to this development, and the desire to raise levels of domestic production in peak time is also evident in smaller territories like the Netherlands and Sweden.

For example, in 2002 in Germany, Degeto, the central purchasing arm of ARD, was no longer purchasing any imported drama with the exception of feature films, and was investing in domestic productions for prime-time access (Kunz, 2002; Herfurth, 2002). For British exporters this means that drama sales are mainly confined to limited purchases by the regionally based ARD channels. These purchases included two or three thrillers a year (*Whistle-Blower* and *Ice House* from the BBC; *Prime Suspect* and *Othello* from Granada) by each of the ARD affiliates WDR, BR, SWR and HR (Kunz, 2002). Purchases of any imported drama by ZDF are equally rare. In 2001, ZDF only acquired one drama from Britain – *The Inspector Lynley Mysteries*, a co-produced BBC detective series with US public broadcaster WGBH (Lehmann, 2002). Awareness of the Elizabeth George books in Germany was a factor in securing the sale.

Output deals may be on the wane, but the US continues to dominate fiction acquisitions. A buyer at French commercial broadcaster TF1 estimated that the US accounted for at least 95 per cent of TV movies and 70 per cent of series acquisitions (Leveaux, 2002). At Italian public broadcaster RAI it was estimated that the US accounted for at least 95 per cent of all fiction acquisitions excluding co-productions (Pugnetti, 2002). On the Mediaset commercial channels in Italy, British films accounted for less than 4 per cent of all transmissions, followed by television movies (0.5–1.5 per cent) and series (under 0.5 per cent) (Grignaffini and Stewart, 2002). At TVE in Spain the US was estimated to account for 90 per cent of acquisitions, with 10 per cent coming from Latin America (Ramos, 2002). For commercial outlets in particular, American programming is used to fill airtime cheaply and conveniently during the day or late at night without the time and trouble of concluding numerous contracts for individual TV movies and short series from Britain.

British drama is not noticeable for its presence on European screens, but other European suppliers show a similarly scarce presence. In their two-week survey of six European countries in 1997, De Bens and de Smaele estimated that 8.5 per cent of series/serial transmissions were of European origin (including 2 per cent from Britain), down from 14 per cent in 1988 (2001, p. 65). The US accounted for a 64 per cent share and domestic productions for a further 20 per cent (Ibid.). In a sample week in 1998, Buonanno established levels of European fiction ranging from zero per cent in Britain, to 1 per cent in Spain, 8 per cent in Italy, 9 per cent in Germany and 18 per cent in France (2000, p. 22).

German commercial suppliers have been successful with action and police series (*Kommissar Rex*/Kirch, *HeliCops*/Kirch, *Alarm für Cobra 11*/RTL), chiefly in France and Italy, but less so in Spain, where Latin American *telenovelas* feature more strongly. For example, in 2002 TVE 1 in Spain was scheduling long-running *telenovelas* in the afternoon from 4 to 7pm to appeal to its older female audience (Ramos, 2002). In France more fiction is acquired from Germany than Britain. However, the daytime slots available for German series on

France 2, for example, are also indicative of the need to meet strictly enforced European quotas. Moreover, the enduring popularity of older long-running German police series like *Derrick* (ZDF) and *Ein Fall für zwei* (ZDF) in the French secondary satellite and cable market is attributable to the availability of dubbed versions from earlier terrestrial transmissions (Biancolli, 2002). British distributors did not sell enough volume to the mainstream networks to feed through to the secondary market in the next cycle.

According to one buyer at Mediaset in Italy (responsible for commercial channels Canale 5, Italia 1 and Rete 4), the success of German fiction from commercial suppliers like the Kirch Group could be traced back to basic action adventure plots and stereotypical characters. This was the sort of programming that was no longer made by the major American producers, but was ideally suited to the less demanding daytime schedules of Italian television (Grignaffini and Stewart, 2002). British drama, by contrast, was considered too 'sophisticated' and 'difficult' for this audience (Ibid.).

It is clear that some markets are more resistant to British fiction than others. This would seem to corroborate Straubhaar's views on 'cultural proximity', the idea that audiences will 'tend to prefer programming which is closest or most proximate to their own culture' and will seek substitutes in terms of content, humour, costume and narrative conventions if domestic alternatives are not available (cited in Sinclair, Jacka and Cunningham, 1996, p. 14).

For example, subtitled British programmes work well on public service channels in smaller anglophile and geographically close markets in the Netherlands and Sweden, which are unable to produce large amounts of domestic fiction because of limited budgets and a limited pool of domestic talent.[4] At Dutch public broadcaster NOS buyers spoke about the Netherlands' close cultural affinity with Britain and 'English living styles' (Mulder, 2002), which made it easier for the Dutch to accept British programmes, because they were 'most close … to the Dutch spirit' (Peijnenburg, 2002; also Huisman, 2002). Buyers believed that this acceptance of British programming by Dutch audiences was reinforced by high levels of proficiency in English and the widespread availability of British channels on Dutch cable systems, available in over 90 per cent of homes. Similar sentiments were expressed by buyers at Swedish public channel SVT: 'With British drama, it's a cultural heritage in a way, … that our own television tradition as a whole is much closer to the British and especially the BBC' (Kjellberg, 2002). However, while Dutch and Swedish public television acquire significant amounts of British drama, there are limited sales to commercial channels in these territories, precisely because they seek to distinguish themselves from their public service counterparts with more 'mass appeal' domestic programming and American imports (Easter, 2002).

A greater 'cultural discount' applies to both public service and commercial channels in the major markets of Germany, France, Spain and Italy, where there are not only issues about language (almost all programmes are dubbed), but also about style, the slowness of pace, and content. Buyers in these territories claimed that their audiences were more 'used to' a particular American look, which was 'lighter' and more appealing with casts that audiences recognised and found attractive (Anan, 2002; Leveaux, 2002; Misert, 2002; Ramos, 2002; Grignaffini and Stewart, 2002).

At German commercial channel ProSieben, British drama was felt to have 'that British look which is in most cases not the look our audience is used to', and this was reinforced by unfamiliar casting and 'heavy-going' plots (Anan, 2002). Granada's contemporary relationship series *Cold Feet* was considered a 'fantastic' programme, but insufficiently strong in terms of casting for prime time and too 'sophisticated' for ProSieben's younger daytime audience. A buyer at public service broadcaster France 3 pointed to a lack of cultural proximity and a preference for domestic fiction:

> French people and the French market don't really go well with the English spirit. English social issues are very different from French social issues so we just find that it was better for us to produce our own shows, focusing on our own social issues. The appeal is always bigger when French are producing French dramas. (Dauvin, 2002)

This restricted this buyer's interest to thrillers and detective series, which highlighted French expectations of 'British tradition', or 'mute' comedies like *Mr Bean* (Ibid.).

If current sales of British drama were to be ranked according to their importance in the schedules, the following tentative categorisation is possible.

Event programmes

These are programmes scheduled at peak time as special events. In terms of their broad appeal, high budgets and 'star' casts they are projects that transcend differences of international taste, and are just as appealing to commercial channels as public service channels. The BBC's 2001 production of *The Lost World* (2 x 75 mins or 1 x 140 mins), based on Sir Arthur Conan Doyle's 1912 dinosaur fantasy, provides a good example. With an international cast including Bob Hoskins and Peter Falk, this co-production with the American cable channel A&E was pre-sold to mainstream commercial and public broadcasters across Europe – including RAI (Italy), TVE (Spain), RTL (Germany), TF1 (France), SVT (Sweden) and NCRV/NOS (Netherlands). Such programmes are inevitably attractive as promotional vehicles, but the magnitude of investment, both creatively and financially, makes them a rare undertaking, necessitating co-production finance and pre-sales.

Thrillers/detective series

These programmes often form the mainstay of peak-time drama schedules on BBC 1 and ITV. Focusing mostly on Britain with British casts, they have less appeal than event programming.

In the first instance there are volume sales of up to 100 hours a year to public broadcasters in the smaller territories like KRO (part of NOS) in the Netherlands and SVT in Sweden for peak-time transmission. For example, KRO, transmitting on NOS channel N1, has developed a *Detectives* strand at peak time, 9pm on Wednesdays, based largely on British imports (*Morse*, Carlton; *Dalziel and Pascoe*, BBC; *A Touch of Frost*, Granada; *Silent Witness*, BBC; *The Inspector Lynley Mysteries*, BBC; *NCS Manhunt*, BBC). This initiative helped to overcome the problem of short series lengths, improved promotion possibilities, and gave viewers a recognisable 'appointment to view' (Huisman, 2002).

In the second instance there are negligible sales to mainstream commercial channels in the major territories, where British drama has little significant cultural impact. Granada's *Poirot* was tested on Mediaset's least popular network, Rete 4, before a commitment to buy ten more for £1 million (Granada, 2002b, p. 7; Grignaffini and Stewart, 2002). A transmission in September 2001 at 9.40pm garnered an 8.11 per cent rating (Grignaffini and Stewart, 2002). Familiarity with the Agatha Christie books in Italy was a factor in securing the sale, ensuring that it was 'recognisable' to the audience. More importantly still, 'it didn't look particularly English because a lot of it is shot around Europe' (Ibid.). Following the screening of thirteen episodes in 2002, Mediaset acquired a further eighteen episodes in 2003 for a midweek prime-time slot, together with eight episodes of the period adventure series, *Hornblower* for a prime-time Sunday night slot (Granada International, 2003).

French public broadcaster France 3 has acquired a small number of series with self-contained episodes and a recurring hero, including *Midsomer Murders* and *Dalziel and Pascoe*, for a two-hour European drama slot on Sundays at 9pm. Some of these are repeated as filler in hour-long morning slots during the week. At commercial rival, TF1, rare British purchases were exiled to late-night slots after midnight (*Silent Witness*) or the mid-morning schedule (*Dangerfield*) (Leveaux, 2002). At France 2, Carlton's *Morse* was screened in a two-hour mid-afternoon slot in 2002, usually reserved for German staples, *Ein Fall für zwei* and *Derrick*.

Transmissions of British drama are also marginal on RTL in Germany. *Silent*

Witness was transmitted in a 10.15pm ninety-minute midweek slot in 2000, because its cast and tone were felt to be insufficiently familiar to a German audience. *Dangerfield* aired over thirteen weeks in January 2002 at 11.15pm. In Germany and France imported detective series are not seen as a priority as this is programming produced domestically. Indeed German series like *Siska* (ZDF), *Derrick* (ZDF), *Der Alte* (ZDF) and *Ein Fall für zwei* (ZDF) compete with British product for a limited number of slots for imports in France and also in Italy.

Contemporary drama

Contemporary British drama ranks even less highly, and again is most frequently located in the schedules of Dutch and Swedish public broadcasters. Granada's relationship series *Cold Feet* proved a surprise hit on the least popular Dutch public service channel, N3, where it was originally scheduled in a midnight slot on Sundays. From September 2002 it was set to occupy a prime-time midweek slot (van der Heide, 2002). For the buyer the attraction was that it 'is rather ... classless, it's middle class, but not typically British' (Ibid.). SVT in Sweden acquires contemporary British drama, primarily from the BBC, for peak-time slots. Purchases have included *Clocking Off*, *The Lakes*, *Rescue Me*, *Monarch of the Glen* and *Babyfather* from the BBC, and *Bob and Rose* from Carlton. *Monarch of the Glen*, set in the picturesque Highlands, was thought to appeal to an older audience with its portrayal of 'that kind of Scotland that doesn't exist any more' (Kjellberg, 2002). Yet some purchases also reflected a desire to engage more fully with younger audiences – for example, gay drama *Queer as Folk* from Channel Four, and *This Life* from the BBC.

There is also a market for British drama on Swedish commercial channel TV4, which has an output deal with Granada. TV4 has taken long-running series (*Heartbeat*, *London's Burning*), contemporary drama (*Cold Feet*) and the soap *Emmerdale*, but unlike drama acquisitions at SVT, these programmes are not usually aired at peak time (Redpath, 2002). *Cold Feet*, for example, aired in a noon slot on Saturdays in April 2002. In the Netherlands, contemporary drama has to be exceptionally different to secure a sale to a commercial network. Dutch group HMG was attracted to Channel Four's *Queer as Folk*, because it was

> a soap, brilliantly written, with compelling stories about a subject that's very rarely shown. I don't know whether anyone else has ever made a television programme about gay men in that way as a piece of entertainment. ... It generated vast amounts of publicity, so you knew that even if it didn't rate hugely well, you'd get a lot of publicity from it. ... The schedule works perfectly well without it, but actually it just gives you a slightly better gloss. (Easter, 2002)

However, in spite of an acknowledgment of some cultural affinity (see earlier), even Dutch public broadcasters find some programming too class-based and typically British 'in its language, in its behaviour, in the setting' (Peijnenburg, 2002; also van der Heide, 2002) for what they perceive as their 'more mellowed' society (Huisman, 2002). At SVT a sale of Granada's comedy series for the BBC *The Royle Family* foundered on the perception that this working-class family was being portrayed as 'ignorant' and that Swedish audiences would reject such 'prejudiced' treatment (Kjellberg, 2002). Conversely the rural settings and content of *Ballykissangel* (BBC) were rejected for being 'too sweet' and 'too idealistic', a view at odds with those who believe that British drama is too 'dark' (Ibid.).

Minority/specialist appeal

In terms of volume, but not value, British fiction will do well on those channels where buyers are looking for alternatives to mainstream television and are less concerned about high ratings.

Although regularly co-produced with American funding from WGBH or A&E, period drama, which trades on British heritage, hardly sells at all to mainstream channels in the larger European territories because of its cultural specificity and failure to generate audiences. According to the buyer for the Italian commercial networks of Mediaset, there was no 'time to play around with the audience. I have to give them what they want to watch' (Grignaffini and Stewart, 2002). Sweden proves an exception, with SVT1 airing *Our Mutual Friend* (BBC), *Oliver Twist* (Carlton) and *The Forsyte Saga* (Granada) in a peaktime Saturday slot as an alternative to broader-based entertainment on the other networks (Kjellberg, 2002).

Regular screenings of sitcoms are also confined predominantly to public service channels in the smaller territories of Sweden and the Netherlands. These programmes are viewed as too culturally specific to appeal to mainstream audiences in the larger territories, and sales have also foundered on insufficient episodes for longer runs. In a rare acquisition, German commercial channel ProSieben acquired the BBC sitcom *Coupling* in 2002, but had to wait several seasons for its minimum requirement of twenty-two episodes (Anan, 2002). ProSieben has also acquired a small number of British comedy sketch shows (*Smack the Pony*, *Trigger Happy TV*) that rely on visual gags. These were used in a weekly late-night slot to reinforce a popular daily block of domestic comedy. According to the buyer, British comedy appealed because it was 'much stranger' and the shows demonstrated 'a typical British humour', but their inclusion also has economic benefits, helping to cross-subsidise more costly domestic productions, which have underpinned ProSieben's profile as a channel for younger audiences (Benthues, 2002).

In the Netherlands the attraction of providing an alternative to mainstream channels is true of VPRO, a 'progressive' broadcaster with a penchant for 'edgy' content, and NPS, a culture and arts specialist, which both broadcast on the minority NOS channel, N3. NPS acquired contemporary dramas *This Life* and *Attachments* from the BBC, and series that met its multicultural remit, such as the spoof chat show, *The Kumars at No. 42* and the sketch show *Goodness Gracious Me* (Peijnenburg, 2002). A Dutch version of *The Kumars at No. 42* aired on N3 in 2003. Among VPRO's purchases of thirty to forty hours a year there have been sketch shows (*Smack the Pony, French and Saunders*), sitcoms (*Absolutely Fabulous, The Royle Family*), 'serious' short-run drama (*Nature Boy, Armadillo* from the BBC; and the *Beckett* plays from Channel Four) and adult animation (*Stressed Eric*, Granada). A similar range of titles are purchased by French satellite channel Canal Jimmy, part of Canal Plus' Multithématiques satellite package. Canal Jimmy buys more British fiction than the rest of French television combined, and sees itself as a distinct alternative to the mainstream terrestrial channels for those 'who never watch TV' (Blicq, 2002).[5] Most British purchases are, unusually for French circumstances, broadcast with subtitles. However, potential audiences are low because the channel was available in less than 6 million homes on satellite and cable in 2002 (TBI, 2002, p. 40).

Similarly, with low audiences as part of the Sky Italia digital satellite platform (formerly Telepiù) and restricted budgets ($1,500 an hour), the RaiSat bouquet in Italy has been able to experiment with shows that would not normally get an airing on Italian terrestrial television, including sitcoms (*Absolutely Fabulous*), contemporary drama (*This Life, Attachments, Queer as Folk*) and period drama (*Aristocrats, Great Expectations, David Copperfield*) (Macciocca, 2002). For financial reasons and, unusually for Italian circumstances, some of these are transmitted with subtitles. The satellite sector's propensity to buy in more programming is driven largely by financial necessity, but the differences between mainstream television in the larger territories and niche providers was neatly summed up by RaiSat's buyer:

> in terms of programming I think their [British programmes] diversity is also their strength. ... But I can see there's a problem with language for the rest of the channels. And there are things that are very difficult to translate in Italy. But it's very much based on the culture of the two respective countries, so it would be like bastardising the things that they do, if they tried to change them and divert them in order to be more palatable abroad. So it's the usual European cultural barriers. For me as a pay TV operator, I'm interested in diversity and making proposals that would not be available otherwise in the country. So I'm quite happy to see something that is extremely distinguished and British ... but now if you're talking

about moving TV drama series on terrestrial channels, that's a completely different story, ... the visual language is different, the way people are dressed is different. It's not like the Americans, that we're used to it so much, that we don't even pay attention. But with the British it's colder, more essential. ... It's sometimes a very dry series. It's difficult to get adapted to that. (Macciocca, 2002)

Co-productions with European partners

Drama co-production is important with US partners, but British fiction co-productions with European partners are almost negligible. American and British co-producers insist on shooting in English, rather than 'Babylonese' which allows actors to speak in their native language, with dubbed versions being broadcast in different European territories (Arata, 2002). American and British producers are also hostile to lip-synching where actors whose first language is not English speak in English, and are then dubbed into English. As a result, actors had to be found who could speak English fluently. This limits casting choices, and presents difficulties because each partner in the co-production needs to ensure that a production has 'stars' that appeal to its domestic audience (Arata, 2002; Tettenborn, 2002). There was also a broad feeling among European players that British and American producers tend to want to take control of the development process, providing little of interest to European partners who need to satisfy their own domestic markets.

An exception was provided by Granada, which embarked on its first European drama co-production, *Dr Zhivago*,[6] with E-vision (a joint venture between the German Kirch Group and the Italian commercial broadcaster Mediaset) and US public broadcaster WGBH in 2001. Shot in English in the Czech Republic,[7] it had an Italian director (Giacomo Campiotti), an international cast (Sam Neill, Hans Matheson, Keira Knightley), Russian literary provenance and a British writer, Andrew Davies. This compares with Granada's other period literary project from this time, *The Forsyte Saga*, also scripted by Andrew Davies, but with a British cast and British setting, which engendered no interest from European co-producers.

Dr Zhivago was born out of the desire to widen sources of funding from the small pool of American co-producers usually favoured by British broadcasters (Torrance, 2001). However, such large-scale literary-based projects, which take a long time to set up, are rare and dependent on finding mutually acceptable solutions in terms of international casting, settings and subject matter, which can be sold both domestically and in the international marketplace. With the exception of co-productions between same-language territories, co-produced European drama has to exhibit very great cross-cultural appeal and tends therefore to concentrate on a narrow range of material, based on biblical epics, historical figures (*Napoleon*, GMT Productions/Transfilm/Spice Factory; *Julius Caesar*, DeAngelis/Victory Media) or classic literary works (*Count of Monte Cristo*, *Les Misérables*, E-vision) (Arata, 2002). There is little call for contemporary drama. This is large-scale peak-time event programming limited to a small number of productions. In the case of E-vision, there are usually only two projects a year, which are transmitted on Mediaset's premier channel, Canale 5 (Arata, 2002). For organisations like Mediaset, co-productions are a promotional opportunity to show 'that you can gather a big cast on a project that's yours' (Ibid.). However, the drive to secure consistently large audiences, the difficulty of scheduling events, and the problem of finding the right projects with international appeal made such co-productions an increasingly difficult proposition (Arata, 2002; Tettenborn, 2002).

Fiction formats

> Taking the UK prison drama *Bad Girls* to Spain and remaking it as a local show isn't as simple as slapping *Las Chicas Malas* on the opening titles and dropping a couple of cicadas onto the soundtrack. (Marlow, 2003c)

One solution for overcoming the barriers of cultural difference is to adapt scripted formats in local markets. Within Europe this has proved effective for long-form serial drama in markets that initially had little experience of writing for this type of production (Tracey and Redal, 1995, p. 353). In the early 1990s, Australian producers Grundy (now part of FremantleMedia) entered co-venture arrangements to adapt the format of the Australian soap *The Restless Years* as *Goede Tijden, Slechte Tijden* for RTL4 in the Netherlands, and *Gute Zeiten, Schlechte Zeiten* for RTL in Germany – two serials that were still airing in 2003. More so than entertainment formats, scripted formats allow for greater national variations 'to the point where the adaptation and the original have very little in common', allowing each serial to speak to its national audience (Moran, 1998, p. 140).

There has long been a small market for scripted British formats in the Netherlands, but long-running joint ventures in local drama production on the scale of Grundy or a focused strategy of marketing scripted formats, as has happened in America, are not evident in Western Europe. In 1992–3 the BBC soap opera *EastEnders*, set in a working-class part of London with Cockney characters, was adapted by Dutch producer IDTV as *Het Oude Noorden* for the Dutch public broadcaster Vara. Set in a working-class district of Rotterdam with Dutch characters, it was abandoned after disappointing ratings (Ibid., p. 38). IDTV also produced a Dutch version of the British sitcom *Till Death Us Do Part* (BBC), and took an option on *Steptoe and Son* (BBC) (Ibid.) Dutch producer Endemol has a history of licensing sitcom formats from Britain, including *Man about the House* and *Tom, Dick and Harriet* from Pearson and *The Two of Us* from Granada (van Diepen, 2002). It also licensed from Pearson the format for the ITV police serial *The Bill*, which became *Die Wache* in Germany for RTL. For small territories like the Netherlands fiction formats help overcome the problem of a small pool of writers at home and the expense of developing plot lines from scratch. In some cases the format has continued long after a show has ceased airing in Britain (van Diepen, 2002). In 2003, Mediaset in Italy started developing a local version of Granada's *Cold Feet*. In July 2002, Zeppelin, the Spanish production outpost of Endemol, took an option on *Bad Girls*, originally produced by Shed Productions for ITV, and distributed by Target Entertainment (Marlow, 2003c). But Zeppelin still had to persuade Spanish broadcasters that the drama would work for their audiences, underlining the difficulty of selling scripted concepts in non-English-speaking markets in competition with local ideas.

Selling factual programming

In terms of volume, sales of factual programming far outstrip sales of fiction. But with the exception of prime-time events, factual programming is less valuable in the marketplace. For example, in Italy the prices for factual programming sold to RAI or the Mediaset channels range between $15,000 and $35,000 an hour, compared to prices of $40,000–65,000 for drama series and $25,000–250,000 for television movies (TBI, 2002, p. 482). Sales to satellite channels can be as low $1,500 an hour.

Demand for factual programming is also affected by its low share of transmission time. A survey of thirty-six mainstream generalist channels in six Western European countries in 1997 found that information programming occupied an 11.8 per cent schedule share compared to a 37.4 per cent share for fiction and 17.5 per cent for entertainment (De Bens and de Smaele, 2001, p. 55). But demand for factual programming has been fuelled by an increase in factual channels in the cable and satellite market – including European versions of US channels Discovery, National Geographic and the History Channel, but extending to domestic specialists in France (France 5, Planète, Absat, Histoire, Odyssée), Italy (Planete, RaiSat) and Spain (Odisea, Documania). These outlets pay less than terrestrial television, but do buy large packages because they lack the financial resources to fill their schedules with original productions.

Most factual sales are straight acquisitions, but pre-sales in the larger territories are important for large-scale productions. Co-funding with editorial input is quite rare with European partners, because the British tend to work with

American co-producers, who deliver a greater financial contribution. For European buyers with an editorial function, this was frustrating because they wanted to exercise a degree of influence that ensured relevance for their own audiences. Pre-buying programming without the possibility of editorial influence constituted a greater risk, and where competition was limited buyers preferred to wait and buy material that they could view at their leisure (Lehmann, 2002; Marel, 2002; Pinna, 2002).

All factual buyers testified to the strong position of British suppliers, particularly the BBC. Many named Britain as their largest source of acquired factual programming, ranging from about a third at Rai Tre and SVT, to 90 per cent at Spanish pay channel Canal Plus España (Varela, 2002) and Swedish commercial broadcaster TV4 (Lidén, 2002).

The BBC emerges as the main supplier at the top end of the market for natural history and science, a position reinforced by the demise of the *Survival* wildlife brand in 2001, following the merger of its owner United News and Media with Granada.[8] The BBC's position at the top end of the market rests on the quality of its production resources, its brand and its ability to secure American funding. Its long-term co-production partnership with Discovery in the US has allowed it to invest more in event properties like *The Blue Planet*, *The Human Body* and *Walking with Dinosaurs*. The BBC has recognised that the highest quality films have a market value internationally, which can help to secure larger budgets that contribute to technical innovation and longer shooting times. This adds value to the existing perceived strengths of talent, scriptwriting skills and technical innovation. However, some public service buyers felt that the collaboration with Discovery had led in some cases to a greater emphasis on the 'spectacular' and action sequences at the expense of structure and analytical edge.

Without access to similar sources of co-production finance and home-grown expertise in the form of the BBC's Natural History Unit, other European producers find it difficult to compete. British sources were used to satisfy niche demand for more costly productions. French buyers claimed that their own producers tended to concentrate on social-issue documentaries rather than science, adventure or wildlife, and this meant that they had no choice but to use British programming (Julienne, 2002; Kandel, 2002). Hélène Coldefy, a buyer at France 3, looked to British sources to supply classic 'blue chip', 'pure' wildlife programming without 'human intervention' because there was no tradition of making this type of programme in France (2002).

In Italy a buyer at Rai Uno, which has an output deal with the BBC, drew attention to the BBC's historical investment in wildlife, investment that RAI had eschewed in the 1960s and 1970s (Pinna, 2002; also Maraschi, 2002). Without comparable sources of funding or production resources, RAI had taken 'a strategic choice' to buy in rather than produce. At SVT in Sweden, a buyer pointed to Britain's longstanding documentary tradition which had influenced Swedish documentaries, but also made audiences more accepting of British productions, because 'the British were always ahead of everyone else in telling stories and it's something that we have also imported in Sweden' (Lundberg, 2002). This occurred to the extent that other foreign sources had to 'be told a bit in this English style' (Ibid.), a style defined by another Swedish buyer as a focus on characterisation and personal stories (Lidén, 2002).

Just as European viewers are thought to be used to the look of American drama, buyers, foremost from the public sector, who buy more volume than commercial free-to-air channels, frequently testified to the attraction of British factual programming over American product. This was attributed variously to a perceived superiority in terms of quality, innovation and originality, a 'European edge', storytelling skills, visual style, and an emphasis on the 'human angle' rather than 'the spectacular' (Corsini, 2002; Lidén, 2002; Maraschi, 2002; Marel, 2002; Pinna, 2002; Plym-Forshell, 2002). For one Spanish buyer the disadvantage of the typical American documentary was that these were produced 'as any other programme as a vehicle for advertising', which disrupted 'the flow of the story' (Salas, 2002). A French buyer for pay television channel Canal Plus classified the best British programming as entertainment-led and story-driven,

> It's what I call the English school, it's very good storytelling. It's story-driven. You're hooked by the subjects in the beginning with a strong beginning and a climax in the middle of the film. ... and it works very well on Canal Plus, because people on Canal Plus are paying their subscriptions, because they want to see movies. And they're looking at documentaries in the same way as a movie. So we really need to have the same kind of structure. ... A very good example was the *Africa* story [produced by Tigress Productions]. ... the script was written very carefully. He [the producer Andrew Jackson] had a very clear picture of the story. He could tell me the stories before the first images had been shot, which for me was a ... good way of working. (Cauquelin, 2002)

Unlike most fiction, some factual programming, but not all, is not always easily identified as a product of a particular country, and this makes imports of natural history and science programming particularly attractive, because they can be localised with voiceovers and promoted as original programming. This desire to localise programmes is underlined by an almost universal dislike of onscreen presenters and talking heads in overseas programming by mainstream terrestrial channels. French mainstream channels wanted 'pure wildlife' (Coldefy, 2002) with 'no medium between you and the scene' (Cauquelin, 2002). A perceived trend towards presenter-led wildlife programmes was seen by one French buyer as a means of saving money, because 'filming people talking is cheaper than funding blue chip documentaries' (Ibid.). However, greater levels of proficiency in English and familiarity with subtitles made this less of an issue in Sweden, and broadened the range of programming that was purchased (Lidén, 2002).

As well as adding voiceovers and subtitles for onscreen interviews, programmes are often edited down to fit particular slots, but this process also serves to make programmes more attractive in the domestic market. In Germany, public service broadcasters edit fifty-minute programmes down to fit standard forty-minute slots, and this allows less appealing elements, such as onscreen presenters, to be edited out. At Rai Uno in Italy 'blue chip' science or natural history programming, such as the BBC's *Blue Planet,* are accommodated as one of several items within a two-hour magazine programme, *Superquark*, which includes both acquisitions and domestically produced features. Transmitted over a period of fifteen weeks every summer at 9pm midweek, *Superquark* has become a feature of the Italian broadcast year. Features are presented in a studio by a host, Piero Angela, who has a longstanding reputation and connection with this particular series. The localising process is reinforced with studio discussions and commentary. The two-hour magazine format is peculiar to Italy, and programmes are edited to fit the format both on Rai Uno and Rai Tre, and on Mediaset's two-hour prime-time factual show *La Macchina del Tempo* on Rete 4.

Like fiction, sales of British factual programmes can be ranked and categorised according to their importance in the schedules.

Event programmes

Event programmes are exceptional in terms of their broad appeal and high budgets and are destined for substantial promotion and prime-time transmission. Like event drama, they are projects that are thought to transcend differences of international taste, and are just as appealing to commercial channels as public service channels. The BBC's prehistoric factual entertainment epics *Walking with Dinosaurs* (6 x 30 mins) and *Walking with Beasts* (6 x 30 mins), both products of the co-production agreement with Discovery, fall into this category.

The combination of natural history, computer graphics and entertaining narratives about individual animals had immediate appeal for the factual buyer at German commercial channel ProSieben, who purchased *Walking with Dinosaurs* on the basis of a short clip:

They had shown me this famous two-and-a-half-minute clip, which was an entire little story, ... about Liopleurodon on the beach, which got stranded in a storm. It had all the elements in it. It showed the fantastic animation, it showed the dramatic content and the kind of narration that was planned at that point. ... It actually was produced that way. Often you get some sort of teaser or demo and, well, the end product is quite different. In this case it wasn't ... Tim Haines [the producer] ... he probably realised that it was about time to tell animal stories, and it was basically animal stories, no matter what they looked like, in a bit of a different way. ... (von Hennet, 2002)

Walking with Dinosaurs aired on ProSieben on three consecutive Thursdays at 8.15pm in November 1999, combining two half-hours. *Walking with Beasts* was shown on 24 and 31 January 2002 as two ninety-minute episodes in a peak-time Thursday slot. It secured an audience of 6 million and a 30 per cent share of the target audience of fourteen to forty-nine year olds (von Hennet, 2002; Anan, 2002). With co-production funding from ProSieben and France 3, *Walking with Dinosaurs* was pre-bought by Mediaset (Italy), Canal Plus/Telecinco[9] (Spain), NCRV/NOS (the Netherlands) and SVT[10] (Sweden). As commercial channels, neither ProSieben nor Telecinco had regular documentary slots in 2002, with the exception of 'infotainment' magazines. ProSieben had dropped a regular natural history slot in 1998 (von Hennet, 2002). Telecinco's broadcast of *Walking with Dinosaurs* was the first time the channel had ever aired a factual programme in prime time (Misert, 2002). For both, the shift from the more traditional natural history documentary to the drama of bringing dinosaurs to life as an entertaining spectacle for peak-time audiences was a determining factor in the decision to buy. But like 'event' fiction, the magnitude of investment, both creatively and financially, makes such programmes a rarity dependent on finding internationally appealing subjects and on the pooling of financial resources.

'Blue chip' programmes

'Blue chip' programmes are primarily attractive to public service broadcasters and pay television outlets in France and Spain (Canal Plus, Canal Plus España), who regard the highest quality, high-budget documentaries as a key component in their commitment to information programming. What makes 'blue chip' programmes stand out from less distinguished creations is the scale of the production and the use of sophisticated new filming techniques, including the use of computer graphics (Kaiser, 2002; Plym-Forshell, 2002). Often acquired as pre-sales, natural history tends to dominate – *The Blue Planet*, BBC wildlife specials, *The Life of Mammals* (BBC). The label 'blue chip' also extends to some science programmes (*How to Build a Human, Space,* from the BBC) and programmes dealing with historical or archaeological themes (*Ancient Egyptians*, Wall to Wall). The natural history buyer at SVT, responsible for a weekly prime-time natural history strand on Sundays (*Mitt I Naturen*) on SVT 2, estimated that only thirty programmes a year fell into this category.

However, the label 'blue chip' does not necessarily imply a prime-time slot. In 2002 and 2003, Spanish public broadcaster TVE was airing natural history in a daily one-hour slot on its second channel at 3.45pm. At France 3 in 2002, natural history was confined to a one-hour slot on Sunday mornings (*Échappées sauvages*), with a slot for adventure documentaries at 6pm on Saturdays (*Explore*).

In Germany natural history became a victim of competitive pressures. In the mid-1990s, there was a surge in wildlife transmissions, with commercial channels charging into the market (Marel, 2002; von Hennet, 2002). By the late 1990s, the boom had subsided and most of the commercial channels had withdrawn from the field. However, public service broadcasters also reduced their commitment. There is no longer a prime-time natural history slot on the ARD network, with programming confined in 2002 to an afternoon slot Mondays to Fridays (*Abenteuer Wildniß*), which repeats material from the regional channels. ZDF dropped its weekly prime-time natural history slot at the beginning of 2000 because it was not thought to provide adequate competition against rival drama offerings on ARD and the commercial channels. After a year with no regular slot, a prime-time access slot was reinstated at 6pm on Saturdays in January 2002 (*Wunderbare Welt*), with a further shift in 2003 to a daily afternoon slot during the week. Prime-time transmissions of natural history are now largely restricted to the regionally based channels, operated by ARD affiliates NDR, WDR and BR. WDR, for example, has run a natural history strand, *Abenteuer Erde*, on Tuesdays at 8.15pm since 1995 (Kaiser, 2002).

In France pay television channel Canal Plus invested heavily in classic natural history documentaries from the mid-1980s, when few French channels were interested, and continued to pre-buy the best material in 2002 (including Wall to Wall's *Ancient Egyptians* and *Neanderthal*). However, the repositioning of the channel in 2001 towards its core content of sport and films led to a reduction in the number of natural history slots to one a week on Saturdays at 1.30pm in 2002, shifting to Sundays at 5.10pm in 2003. In Italy blue chip natural history and science programming has continued to find prime-time slots as part of Rai Uno's *Superquark* strand, and the range of topics has been extended to include history (Pinna, 2002).

The difficulty in finding slots for natural history programming is complicated further by buyers no longer wanting straightforward natural history films about animals. SVT in Sweden purchases about forty hours a year, including all the major natural history series from the BBC (*Blue Planet*, *Life of Mammals*, *Wild Africa*, *Indonesia*) (Plym-Forshell, 2002). Over half of its purchases came from Britain. The buyer looked for 'a variation of continents and stories'. But rather than simply an 'enumeration of species' or 'another' film about cheetahs, it was now important to find new angles on animal behaviour and ecologies (Ibid.), a view reiterated by other buyers.

Natural history, science, archaeology, history

More run-of-the-mill wildlife material, and more challenging programmes on science, history and archaeology, are more likely to find their way into the schedules of those public service channels with smaller audiences and a stronger focus on information programming. In France this would apply to public broadcaster France 5, 'a knowledge channel' (Julienne, 2002), which in 2002 only broadcast during the day. At Rai Uno, the highest quality programming is acquired for the *Superquark* strand. A much wider range of programming is acquired by Rai Tre, the most information-focused and more traditionally public service of the RAI channels, with regular magazine slots in peak time or prime time access for natural history, science/the environment and history. Rai Tre had an output deal with Granada in 2002, buying up to twenty-five hours a year of wildlife, adventure, archaeology and history programmes (Corsini, 2002).

Other factual programming and the secondary market

The prospects for lifestyle programming, human interest documentaries and those that focus on the political and social arena are understandably more limited. This is because they tend to emphasise British subject matter, and for cheaper formats broadcasters are more likely to rely on domestic productions. One strategy employed by the BBC has been to package programmes as branded blocks for prime-time transmission, an approach that has worked well on the German commercial channel Vox, which airs BBC Exclusiv in prime time on a weekly basis. At the time of writing (October 2003) there was limited interest in factual formats as opposed to reality and game-show formats, but growing interest in America (see Chapter 5) was beginning to be replicated in Europe. For example, the format for RDF Media's *Wife Swap* was sold in 2003 to M6 in France, TV3 in Denmark and RTL in Germany.

Broadcasters in the smaller territories of the Netherlands and Sweden are prepared to broaden the scope of what they purchase because their own markets are too small to sustain high levels of domestic production. This applies especially to public broadcasters who need to satisfy public service obligations. Dutch culture and arts specialist NPS at NOS acquires a range of documentaries from both the BBC and independent producers for its weekly peak-time documentary strands *Het Uur van de Wolf* and *Dokwerk* on N3. Swedish public broadcaster SVT acquires approximately 50 per cent of its fortnightly global current affairs strand *Dokument Utifrân* (Thursdays 10.10pm) from Britain and approximately 40 per cent is sourced from the BBC (Dahlberg, 2002). *Documentos TV*, a weekly current affairs programme on TVE's second channel in Spain (Wednesdays 11.15pm), acquired 22 per cent of its transmissions from Britain in 2001, including episodes from the BBC strands *Correspondent* and *Panorama* (Erquicia, 2002).

In the smaller territories there are also opportunities with commercial free-to-air broadcasters. Dutch commercial broadcasting group HMG has no regular slots for traditional documentaries. Yet it does make intermittent purchases of personality-led cookery programmes (*Two Fat Ladies*, Optomen; *The Naked Chef*, Optomen; *Nigella Bites*, Channel Four on RTL 4) for daytime transmission, and docusoaps (*Airport*, Chrysalis on Yorin) for peak time (Easter, 2002). Commercial Swedish broadcaster TV4 has sought to distinguish itself from rival SVT's focus on natural history, politics and culture by concentrating on 'human interest' stories for a regular peak-time slot on Wednesdays at 9pm. As a commercial service it was important to TV4 that these programmes had a strong beginning to retain viewer interest and an angle that could be easily promoted. *Designer Vagina*, acquired from Channel Four in 2002, was singled out as one example:

> It was spectacular, it was very edgy ... like something that you've never heard about before ... it feels good that you have a topic that no one else has ever talked about before. It's like you have this 'ah ha' experience, that's interesting, because then often you have a big audience of course. (Lidén, 2002)

Volume sales take place with the growing number of specialist documentary channels on satellite, but prices are low. The decision to buy from British suppliers with large catalogues was a necessity guided by the volume required, what was available in the market and the inability of domestic producers to meet those needs. Planète is part of the Multithèmatiques package on the Canalsatellite digital platform in France. In 2002, Planète was acquiring approximately 1,000 hours a year of factual programming for channels in the package. Half of these were estimated to be British, including 300 hours supplied under an output deal with the BBC (Kandel, 2002). French channel operator ABSAT, which runs factual channels – Histoire, Escales (travel), Animaux, Encyclopèdie (science), Chasse et Peche (hunting) – acquired similarly large packages. At RaiSat in Italy factual programming accounted for about 40–50 per cent of the 300–400 hours of programming acquired for each of the seven thematic satellite channels in the digital package (Macciocca, 2002). The RaiSat channels provide outlets for lower budget docusoaps, lifestyle programming, cookery shows (*Two Fat Ladies*, *The Naked Chef* from Optomen for the cookery channel Gambero Rosso) and material which is too culturally specific for the Italian terrestrial channels (Ibid.). Odisea, part of the Multicanal package on the Spanish digital platform Via Digital, acquires about 500 hours of factual programming a year, with British productions accounting for 35 per cent of its transmission time in 2002 (Salas, 2002).

Selling children's programmes

While factual programming is indicative of British production strength in a niche area, selling children's programming represents a greater challenge. Commercial channels, in particular, are heavily reliant on long-running half-hour animation series from America and increasingly Japan (*Pokémon*, *Digimon*, *Dragon Ball Z*). For example, Italian commercial channel Italia Uno has a tradition of airing Japanese animation as a distinctive alternative to the Disney-sourced fare transmitted by its public service rival, Rai Due. Mediaset, the buying arm for Italia Uno, acquires six or seven twenty-six-episode animated series a year, mostly from Japan (50 per cent) and the US, with Europe accounting for between 20 and 30 per cent of purchases (Mozzetti, 2002).

Since the late 1990s, British suppliers have managed to carve out a niche in the pre-school market, and the larger territories of Germany and France have become important for pre-sales. Born out of the public service view that domestic children's television needs to serve a range of age groups and interests, British pre-school programming has managed to fill gaps in provision in other territories. Modest successes in Europe with programming for younger children have also have been fuelled by successful sales to PBS (*Teletubbies*, *Angelina Ballerina*) and Nickelodeon (*Maisie*, *Bob the Builder*, *Kipper*) in America (see Chapter 5), and the opportunities this has opened up for video and licensed merchandise.

As in America, efforts to cater to an older age group have been less successful – with the exception of the live-action series *S Club 7* – and British export success remains largely focused on programming for younger children. Few broadcasters in Western Europe have any interest in children's fiction, another staple of the schedules of BBC and ITV. This is because schedules are either devoted almost entirely to long-running animation (TF1, France 3, Italia Uno) or this is programming supplied by domestic producers (ZDF, Germany).

Echoing the situation in adult fiction, British children's fiction works best in smaller markets with a public service tradition. Like their British public service counterparts, Dutch and Swedish public broadcasters are committed to a range of children's output rather than simply animation, but are unable to fund suffi-cient amounts of this programming domestically. However, in Sweden there are very specific ideas about what is suitable for a children's audience, reflecting different attitudes to children and the way children interact with adults (Redpath, 2002). According to SVT's buyer, 'Very often I reject British drama because the parents are so terrible. It's like there's no respect between parents and children ... this nagging mum who is so terrible who doesn't appreciate life. She's there all the time in very many British dramas' (Cederborg, 2002).

Although pre-school programming is a British strength, it is not always attrac-tive to commercial channels, because advertisers are not sufficiently interested in this age group. Older children are more attractive to advertisers, because they can express and even act on their consumer preferences. Among commercial outlets in Europe the buyer preference is for half-hour animation, preferably in series of twenty-six episodes rather than the shorter five-minute and ten-minute episodes typical of pre-school programming.

Pre-school properties like *Teletubbies* and *Tweenies* (BBC Worldwide) and *Bob the Builder* (HIT Entertainment) have found greater resonance with public service channels that are required to serve a broader child audience with mixed programming (ZDF, ARD, Rai Tre, TVE, Forta, NOS, SVT) and specialist chan-nels that have developed blocks for younger children (Super RTL and KiKa in Germany; Tiji in France). The commercial priorities of advertising-funded chan-nels means limited pre-school slots on Italia Uno (Mediaset) or TF1 (France) or those public service channels, such as Rai Due or France 3, which are much more directly competitive with commercial counterparts.

A further drawback to the sale of pre-school programming relates to percep-tions about what is suitable for very young children. At Rai Tre buyers believed that Italian parents were uncomfortable letting children under three watch tele-vision (Bollini, Liberi and Di Nitto 2002).[11] At Swedish public broadcaster SVT, the core age group was seven to fourteen. The term 'pre-school' did not mean the same thing because children start school at seven, and again there was a view that very young children should not be watching television (Cederborg, 2002). However, more practical considerations also played a role. The localisation of *Teletubbies* requires the insertion of costly new live-action inserts, and the vol-ume of the series displaced opportunities for other forms of programming which added variety to SVT1's limited slots (6pm–7pm Monday to Friday) (Ibid.).

Key outlets for children's programming

The multi-channel environment and the penetration of localised US-owned channels (Cartoon Network, Nickelodeon, Fox Kids, Disney) has increased seg-mentation of the children's marketplace, but also resulted in downward pressures on licence fees. As in America, television has become a platform for opening up more profitable revenue streams from consumer products, publishing and video. For exporters with a valuable property it is therefore crucial to gain access to channels with the largest audiences and highest market profile.

In Germany, with over 90 per cent of television households connected to cable or satellite (EAO, 2001b), dedicated children's channels Super RTL and KiKa have become the most important outlets. Children's slots on the public channels ZDF and ARD, and the main commercial channels RTL (Disney Club) and SAT.1, are confined to morning blocks at the weekends. RTL2's daily block during the week in 2002 was dominated by Japanese animation (*Pokémon*, *Digimon*, *Dragon Ball Z*). ZDF has purchased British pre-school properties *Angelina Ballerina* (HIT Entertainment), *Fetch the Vet* (Granada/Itel) and *The Forgotten Toys* (Entertainment Rights), but does not acquire volume (Müller, 2002). Launched in 1997 by ARD and ZDF, KiKa airs original programming and archive material from ARD and ZDF[12] as well as long-running British series *Teletubbies* and *Tweenies* for daily transmission. At Super RTL,[13] launched in 1995, pre-school programming airs daily in an early morning block. Launched in 1999, the pre-school block is home to British series *Bob the Builder*, *Rubbadubbers* and *Thomas the Tank Engine* (HIT Entertainment), *Merlin the Magical Puppy* (Entertainment Rights), *Little Monsters* (Sovereign Pictures) and *Dream Street* (Carlton).

In France the children's market is dominated by the morning blocks of the terrestrial channels TF1 and France 3, which between them take a three-quarter share of the audience (Poussier, 2002). France 5 has slots for younger children and Canal Plus has acquired *Teletubbies*, *Andy Pandy* and *Angelmouse* from the BBC for its daily pre-school slot in the mornings. Pre-school programming is difficult to accommodate on TF1 and France 3 because of a shortage of slots, and also because they are obliged by the French regulatory authority, CSA (Conseil Supérieur de l'Audiovisuel), to invest in the production of French animation, which limits what they buy from other sources (Poussier, 2002).[14] At TF1 British purchases included *The Tweenies* and *Little Monsters*. *Little Monsters* met a need for five-minute fillers, and shorter series like *Brambly Hedge* (4 x 26 mins, HIT Entertainment) and *Percy the Parkkeeper* (4 x 26 mins, HIT Entertainment) were screened as specials during the holidays (Ibid.). The buyer at France 3 estimated that between 15 and 20 per cent of its schedule originated from Britain, including *Bob the Builder* (HIT Entertainment), *Rotten Ralph* and *Wallace and Gromit* from the BBC, *Noddy* from Chorion, and *Foxbusters* from ITEL (Dauvin, 2002). Niche services for pre-schoolers include Tiji, a subscription channel for four to seven year-olds, launched in December 2000. Tiji, its older-targeted sister channel Canal J, and Teletoon (available to 1.5 million homes on the TPS digital platform in 2002) are not as attractive to

British exporters. They pay less than their terrestrial counterparts and their low audience reach does not offer a firm basis for licensing campaigns. However, the limited number of pre-school slots on terrestrial television and the need for French channels to fulfil strictly enforced European quotas means that substantial amounts of British pre-school programming have found their way onto Tiji. A survey of Tiji's schedule in the week 18–24 March 2002 shows strong representation by the BBC (*Teletubbies, Dangermouse, Binka, Yoho Ahoy*), HIT Entertainment (*Kipper, Pingu, Oswald, Thomas the Tank Engine*) and Entertainment Rights (*Huxley the Pig, The Forgotten Toys*).

In Italy children's television is dominated by daily blocks on Italia Uno and Rai Due. British exporters have been most successful with *Melevisione*, a two-hour weekday afternoon block for children aged four to seven on Rai Tre, the most 'public service' of the RAI channels. Launched in 1999, *Melevisione* was expressly set up to serve younger children with European programmes (Bollini, Liberi and Di Nitto, 2002). It provides a distinct alternative to the Japanese and American animation targeted at older children in the mornings and afternoons by commercial channel Italia Uno, and Rai Due. British programming was estimated to account for half of all acquisitions and has included *Bob the Builder* and *Brambly Hedge* from HIT Entertainment, *Fetch the Vet* and *Oakie Doke* from Granada, and *Wolves, Witches and Giants* and *Grizzly Tales for Gruesome Kids* from Carlton (Ibid.).

Z@ppelin is a dedicated children's block occupying the daytime hours of Dutch public channel N3. Launched in 2000, it constitutes a more focused public service advertising-free response to Fox Kids in the Dutch marketplace (Willemsen, 2002). It replaced the previous distribution of children's programming over three channels. Serving the full range of children's age groups, it is home to long-running British pre-school series *Teletubbies* and *Tweenies* as well as a range of shorter series and one-offs (*Kipper, Rotten Ralph, Grizzly Tales for Gruesome Kids, Wolves, Witches and Giants*).

In Spain the market is largely dominated by terrestrial television because of the low penetration of satellite and cable. Like Italy the market is focused more on older children, and it is difficult to place pre-school programming. The main buyers of British programmes are public broadcaster TVE (*The Tweenies, S Club 7 in Los Angeles*) with daily blocks during the week on La 2 and weekend blocks on TVE1, and the regional broadcasters who purchase together as Forta (*Teletubbies*). Commercial channel Telecinco (Zon@Disney) had reduced its children's offerings to weekend mornings by 2002, and Antena 3's daily block, *Club Megatrix,* is largely focused on American and Japanese animation. Fox Kids, the most successful children's satellite channel in Spain, had access to 2 million homes on the Via Digital and Canal Satélite platforms in June 2002 (TBI, 2002,

p. 99). It acquired *Teletubbies* and eight series of *Bob the Builder* as a pre-school supplement in the mornings before airing more traditional Fox Kids fare of *Digimon*, *Pokémon* and *Power Rangers* (Ramos and Ortega, 2002).

The appeal of British programming

Animation is expensive (see Chapter 2) and for children's departments, which are strapped for cash, it makes sense to acquire or co-fund rather than produce in-house. In many cases programmes will not be made unless pre-sales have been secured in the largest territories. This involves a high degree of risk by broadcasters, as the Head of Children's Programming at French broadcaster TF1 pointed out:

> We take a huge risk. Usually we decide to buy a series after having read the bible. When it's possible, the synopsis or storylines or scripts, and if we happen to know the producer, it can be a guarantee, but not really. And we can see a trailer of two or three minutes, which is also not a guarantee. (Poussier, 2002)

Sometimes acquisitions are determined by external factors. *Teletubbies* and *Tweenies* were acquired by Dutch educational broadcaster Teleac/NOT to meet its obligation since 1999 to provide a daily block of schools programming on N3 (Willemsen, 2002). Shown between 9.30am and 10.30am both series provided volume at low cost necessary for daily transmissions (Ibid.). They also offered an opportunity to include new live-action sequences, which met Teleac/NOT's educational objectives, and the broadcaster produced over 100 new *Teletubbies* inserts for Dutch children (Ibid.). French commercial broadcaster TF1 acquired *The Tweenies* for a 7am slot on Wednesdays and Sundays to meet a requirement from the French regulatory authority (CSA) that it screen fifty hours a year of children's documentaries or magazine programmes (Poussier, 2002). At Italia Uno the buyer indicated that they might acquire more five- to ten-minute shows from Britain because potential changes in the Italian law meant they would no longer be able to interrupt commercial half hours with advertising (Mozzetti, 2002).

According to the Head of Super RTL in Germany, British success with some pre-school properties stems from a focus on stop-frame model animation (*Bob the Builder*, *Merlin the Magical Puppy*, *Dream Street*). Over time, British suppliers had developed competitive advantages in this area over their rivals. She went on to suggest that this competence had been nurtured by public service tradition and the 'long influence and the long experience of the BBC' (Schosser, 2002). The Head of Children's Programming at French broadcaster TF1 underlined the creative and financial strength of key suppliers like HIT Entertainment, which produced 'very classic, high-quality programmes', such as *Angelina Ballerina* or *Brambly Hedge*, which stood out from their competitors (Poussier, 2002). For German and Dutch public service broadcasters, British programming represented a reliable alternative to what was perceived as the violence inherent in Japanese animation, or low-quality production values from the Far East and Southern Europe (Kuiper, 2002; Müller, 2002). The list of attractions for pre-school programmes included humour, highly developed storytelling skills and the ability to produce programmes that touched children emotionally (Cederborg, 2002; Kuiper, 2002; Poussier, 2002). In this vein, the Head of Children's Television at ZDF commented:

> The quality of scripts, for example, is much better in the UK than somewhere else, and it's on the level of the emotions ... they have to touch you in a way. I think this happens. I think those who either write or those who are the producers, they know a lot about the needs of children and the specific needs in age groups, ... it's a very age adequate programming. (Müller, 2002)

However, the possibility of participating in the merchandising success of a property is also a major attraction. Public service broadcaster France 3 acquired *Bob the Builder* because it was a proven merchandising success in Britain. This led to the purchase of a programme whose audience profile was younger than France 3's target audience, and a France 3 subsidiary was charged with handling the French licensing campaign (Dauvin, 2002). Similarly, for Dutch public broadcaster Teleac/NOT, the acquisition of *Teletubbies* and *Tweenies* was enhanced by a small participation (1–2 per cent) in merchandising income. For commercial broadcaster Super RTL in Germany, the promise of ancillary revenues was also persuasive in its decision to commit to a pre-school block in 1999. Super RTL acts as the German licensing agent for properties like *Bob the Builder* and therefore benefits from its success. In 2001, *Bob the Builder* was the second largest children's property in Germany after *Pokémon,* with licensing revenues estimated at 30–40 million euros (Schosser, 2002). Super RTL therefore has an incentive to keep the show on air in an attractive slot. However, while Germany followed by France offer the strongest opportunities for licensed merchandise, opportunities in Spain and Italy are more limited because there are fewer openings for pre-school programmes and less sophistication in exploiting properties (Bollini, Liberi and Di Nitto, 2002; Mozzetti, 2002).

Selling entertainment formats

In the more competitive and fragmented broadcasting environment that emerged in Europe in the 1990s, the use of entertainment formats has a clear commercial logic. Faced with an expansion of transmission time and the loss to pay television of key sporting events, entertainment formats provide a more cost-effective way of filling schedules with local productions than locally orig- inated drama. For channels trying to stand out in a crowded marketplace, locally produced formats have greater appeal to audiences than cheaper imports. Tried and tested in other markets, risk is reduced, there are savings on development costs, and seriality provides opportunities to build audiences. According to Moran there are also political benefits, because a format adaptation is invariably classed as a domestic production rather than an import (1998, pp. 22–3).

Buyers look for 'an original idea, with elements that could be slightly devel- oped into different cultures' (van Diepen, 2002). For game shows, buyers want something that is both familiar in the mechanics and structure of the show and the build up to the final round, but also original in its underlying concept (Bat- tocchio, 2002; García, 2002; Saló, 2002). Reality shows require an original concept 'that people at home can identify with' (García, 2002). However, most formats are not as successful as *Who Wants to Be a Millionaire?*, and the most elaborate reality formats (*Big Brother, I'm A Celebrity . . . Get Me Out of Here!*) are not necessarily cheap to produce, particularly for smaller territories. For every *Millionaire* there are a far greater number of formats that perform less spectacularly.

American game-show formats (*Wheel of Fortune, Family Feud, The Price is Right*) have a long history in Europe. The key difference in the late 1990s was the use of game shows and reality-based factual entertainment in prime time rather than daytime or prime-time access. The catalyst for change came with the prime-time success of Endemol's *Big Brother* reality format in the Netherlands in 1999, Celador's *Who Wants to Be a Millionaire?* in Britain in 1998 and *Sur- vivor* on CBS in the US in 2000. The successful sale of these formats to American networks fuelled demand in other territories, and British format owners, including BBC Worldwide, Celador, Granada, Action Time and Fre- mantleMedia, were encouraged to meet this growing demand.

British exporters had always been in the business of selling formats, but it was secondary to the business of co-productions and straight sales, with the excep- tion of specialist devisors like Action Time, part of Carlton. Formats were licensed to producers in other countries with no involvement in local produc- tion. Endemol Entertainment UK (formerly Bazal) sold lifestyle formats with a game-show element such as *Ready, Steady, Cook,*[15] *Changing Rooms*[16] and *Ground Force* to broadcasters in Northern Europe. But it had less success in Southern Europe, where there is a preference for studio-based entertainment in prime time rather than lifestyle or factual entertainment formats in local set- tings (Van den bussche, 2001). BBC Worldwide sold the *Top of the Pops* music-show format to RTL in Germany, BNN/N2 in the Netherlands, France 2 and Rai Due (this moved to commercial rival Italia Uno in 2003). In the early 1990s, the consumer-affairs series, *That's Life*, became the BBC's most successful format package in Europe, selling to Germany, Norway, Spain, Belgium and the Netherlands, alongside other entertainment formats such as *Noel's House Party* and *Pets Win Prizes* (Jarvis, 2001; Moran, 1998; van Diepen, 2002). Granada's studio-based entertainment format *Surprise, Surprise*, revolving around 'ordinary' people, has proved a success for Rai Uno in Italy as *Carràmba che sorpresa*, securing a 40 per cent share in January 2002, and entering its seventh season in the Netherlands in 2002 (Mutimer, 2002).

Yet it was the success of *Who Wants to Be a Millionaire?* that placed formats on a new footing with a different approach to exploitation. Rather than simply licensing formats to producers or broadcasters, the emphasis has shifted to the sale of complete packages incorporating production expertise and technical know-how, giving format owners greater control over the end-product (Jarvis, 2001; Van den bussche, 2001). For the most successful formats this control is about creating a global brand with longevity in the marketplace. The production expertise of how to make the show becomes more important than 'the idea in its own right' (Van den bussche, 2001).

In Europe Celador's *Who Wants to Be a Millionaire?* was optioned as a complete package (computers, set, music, software graphics, titles, lighting) by the

Table 6.2: Selected British entertainment formats in Europe

	Millionaire Celador	*Popstars* Screentime (Aus); Target (UK); Zeal (UK)	*The Weakest Link* BBC Worldwide	*Survivor* Castaway	*Greed* Fremantle Media
Germany	RTL	RTL2	RTL	RTL2	ZDF
France	TF1	M6	TF1	TF1	M6
Italy	Canale 5	Italia Uno	Italia Uno	Italia Uno	Rai Due
Spain	Telecinco	Telecinco	TVE1	Telecinco	TVE1
Sweden	TV4	Kanal 5	–	SVT2	SVT2
Netherlands	SBS6	–	RTL4	Net 5	–

Source: *Television Business International*, April/May 2002, p. 16.

Dutch production company Endemol, whose local production outposts went on
to produce the programme in close consultation with Celador across Europe
(see Table 6.2). Endemol acquires third party formats as well as marketing over
400 formats from its own catalogue, including *Big Brother*, *The Soundmix Show*
and *All You Need is Love*. FremantleMedia operates on a similar basis as a local
producer of its formats (*The Price is Right*, *Family Feud*, *Greed*, *Pop Idol*) in key
markets.

BBC Worldwide sold *The Weakest Link* format as a package as well. However,
rather than licensing to an intermediary producer like Endemol, BBC Worldwide has sought to negotiate directly with broadcasters as a co-producer,
contracting local producers (Jarvis, 2001). This allows it to benefit from greater
creative control and financially from a share of the production fee and any production profit as well as a format fee (Ibid.). On hit shows, format owners can
insist on minimum runs and specify how a show is made. For example, ZDF
agreed to make forty episodes of the BBC format *Dog Eat Dog* for $220,000 an
hour (Fry, 2002b).

However, the desire to control the exploitation of a format across different
territories as a distinctive brand stands in tension with the desire by local broadcasters to air programming with local appeal. A highly structured quiz-show
format such as *Who Wants to Be a Millionaire?* or *The Weakest Link* looks almost
identical to the British original with the exception of the local host, local contestants and variations in the questions to reflect local knowledge. By contrast,
reality-based game shows (*Big Brother*) and factual formats (*Faking It*, *Wife
Swap*) require scope for adaptation and are less easy to pin down in terms of
specific elements. Their success in local markets is linked as much to how a concept is interpreted in tune with local preferences as much as the concept itself.
According to David Frank, Managing Director at factual entertainment
specialist RDF:

> The programmes we make rely to a large extent on the production skill of the
> people making them. ... With *Millionaire*, or other studio-based formats, you give
> a kit of parts to Lithuania TV and you end up with something that's still
> recognisable on screen. It's mechanical. With something like *Wife Swap* the real
> skill lies in the production of that show: the casting, the filming and the editing.
> (Cited in Rouse, 2003)

The ability to translate a format in different territories is reflected in the mixed
success of some shows. For example, *The Weakest Link* (*Der Schwächste Fliegt*)
failed to ignite excitement on RTL in Germany and, after initially airing in a daytime slot, it had moved to a weekly 11.15pm slot by January 2002. Its average

share of less than 10 per cent in 2001 was below the average channel share of 15 per cent (Anon., 2002b, p. 17).

The difficulty of adapting formats to local markets is also evident in Italy and Spain, which have never been strong markets for either British programmes or formats.

Format adaptation in Italy and Spain

In Italy, RTI, the production division of Mediaset, was acquiring about one format a year for Canale 5 and Italia Uno in 2002. The number of formats had increased on Italia Uno as a replacement for American drama (Battocchio, 2002). At Telecinco in Spain buyers were looking to buy one format a year – thirteen episodes for a prime-time series like *Who Wants to Be a Millionaire?* at 9.30pm, or up to 200 episodes a year for a prime-time access show at 8pm (Saló, 2002). Spanish producer BocaBoca Producciones options British formats (*The Waiting Game* from Hat Trick, *Find a Fortune* from Granada), which it pitches to the Spanish networks. Of the ten formats it options a year, only one or two are taken up (García, 2002).

Southern Europe illustrates the limits to adaptation and the differences within Europe. According to Fremantle's Head of Entertainment Development and Acquisition, David Lyle:

> Germany, Scandinavia, Holland and England tend to go in one direction, France, Spain and Italy in the other. ... Big entertainment variety shows with troupes of dancing girls still exist in Italy and to some extent Spain. But it's been a while since British viewers saw Bruce Forsythe draping his arm over a couple of bimbettes. ...
> (Cited in Plunkett, 2002)

According to Fabrizio Battocchio, Head of the Format Department at RTI, Italians prefer 'emotional shows' like the 'reality' game-show format *Big Brother* (Canale 5) or entertainment formats like *Surprise, Surprise* (Rai Uno) or Endemol's *All You Need is Love* (Canale 5), preferably with a variety element (Battocchio, 2002). Similarly, Spanish viewers were thought to prefer shows that demonstrate drama and tap into emotions (Saló, 2002), or in the case of reality formats like *Big Brother* expose 'secrets' (García, 2002).

Both Italy and Spain have a tradition of peak-time studio-based entertainment shows, and formats seem ideally suited for these territories. However, weekly prime-time shows need to fill slots of up to two hours and even daily shows in prime-time access last an hour. This is at odds with the half-hour and hour formats favoured in Britain and the US, and formats have to be adapted to fit the slots. But there are also cultural differences at work.

Both *Survivor* on Italia Uno and Telecinco and *The Weakest Link* on TVE in Spain were felt by buyers not to have quite met expectations (Mutimer, 2002). With [shows like] *Survivor*, the elimination format set on a desert island, the absence of a studio setting was seen as a weakness in the Italian market. According to Fabrizio Battocchio at RTI, 'You need to have an emotional centre ... a place where you can see where it's easy to stay' (Battocchio, 2002). According to Battocchio, the most successful shows in Italy have a strong live studio component, which contributes to 'an open-hearted very brilliant kind of show ... far from some Nordic, dark[ness]' (Battocchio, 2002). Entertainment shows had to be segmented and easy for viewers to enter at any stage (Ibid.). Similarly, in Spain, buyers felt that entertainment programmes had to be supported by a studio (García, 2002).

By contrast, *Who Wants to Be a Millionaire?*, with its elaborately specified set, software, lights, graphics and music, did not need much local adaptation at all and was a huge hit in both territories. Launched in May 2000 as *Chi vuol essere milionario?* on Canale 5, it fitted the Italian tradition for studio-based entertainment and signalled 'a big return of the quiz in prime time, with big big prizes. It was an event on its terms, because everybody talked about the show' (Battocchio, 2002). It was both familiar and different and this heightened its appeal. But it was local too with local contestants and a local host (Gerry Scotti) with whom viewers could identify, because he was already known as the presenter of another successful quiz format, *Passaparola* (Ibid.). In Spain the success of *Who Wants to Be a Millionaire?* on Telecinco was attributed to its capacity for drama and emotion with the host as 'your friend', offering the prospect of winning a million (Saló, 2002). The drama was heightened by the tactics employed by contestants to further their progress, including the opportunity to phone a friend for advice, use a lifeline or poll the audience (Ibid.). According to Susana García at Spanish production company BocaBoca Producciones, this potential for drama was evident in the tape used to market the show,

> *Millionaire* for example, the programme that they were using to sell the show ... the girl playing was calling her father to phone a friend. She wasn't crying, but you could see tears in her eyes, and it was a game show, but there was a drama there, a feeling. ... (García, 2002)

Transmitted daily in Italy in prime-time access (6.40pm–8pm) and weekly in prime time at 8.45pm in a two-and-a-half-hour slot, it was the first major format purchase by RTI from Britain, and opened doors for other suppliers (Battocchio, 2002). In 2003, Granada International secured a format sale of

Saturday Night Takeaway for a prime-time slot in the autumn schedule on Italia Uno. At Telecinco in Spain *Who Wants to Be a Millionaire?* began in April 1999. Initially it aired at 9.30pm on Saturdays in a two-hour slot. Extended interviews with the contestants were used to lengthen the show to meet Spanish slot requirements (Saló, 2002). Success in prime time led to a daily prime-time access slot during the week at 7.45pm. However, overexposure dented its appeal. It was no longer airing in June 2002, and its unique success was proving difficult to replicate (García, 2002).

The trend towards 'nasty shows', such as *Fear Factor* (Endemol/NBC), *Temptation Island* (Fox) and *The Chair* (Touchdown/ABC), has rather less appeal in the Italian and Spanish markets. According to Susana García at BocaBoca Producciones, Spanish viewers did not want to see contestants suffer (2002). The idea of a hostile host, and 'walk of shame' for those eliminated by fellow contestants during the course of the British format *The Weakest Link*, was regarded by buyers as somewhat alien to Italian and Spanish television culture. Susana García put the problem down to cultural differences and the limited opportunities for adapting the format to suit local circumstances:

> The thing is everything is the same, the set ... the host treats the contestants the same way as Anne Robinson. That is different in England because of the sense of humour. She's more ironic, and here we don't have the same sense of humour. So people are getting it less, not in a very nice way. (García, 2002)

By contrast, Action Time's parlour game format *The Alphabet Show* represents an example of local adaptation that reflects the preferences of different television cultures, even of those that are thought to be similar – as is the case with Spain and Italy. Based loosely on the original format, the Italian *Passaparola* is screened daily during the week on Canale 5 in prime-time access between 6.40pm and 8pm. The original British format was of little interest to the buyer, but the French version on TFI was updated and this proved attractive to RTI, which licensed it, and expanded the show to last an hour and a half from the original half hour (Battocchio, 2002). Commercial Spanish broadcaster Antena 3 also purchased the format. Here it has aired daily as *Pasapalabra* on weekdays in Spain's later prime-time access slot (8pm–9pm) since July 2000. The Spanish version, using different rounds with contestants answering questions around the alphabet, is based on the Italian version, and bears little resemblance to the British original (García, 2002). For Antena 3 the attraction rested on the build up of tension over several rounds as contestants accumulate time, which they use for the final round (Ibid.). Even so, the Spanish version is different again from the Italian version with less emphasis on the more typically Italian show elements and more emphasis on the game itself (García, 2002; Saló, 2000). In other words the process of adapting a format is complex. The sale of the format is simply the start of that process, and success depends on how that format is adapted for a particular national territory.

Review

While Britain benefits from some degree of cultural affinity with America, which gives it an edge over other suppliers, this cultural proximity is much less evident in Western Europe. Similarities in ethos between British public service broadcasters and their European counterparts mean that public service broadcasters remain important buyers of public service-imbued drama, documentary and children's programming. But mainstream commercial television, with its emphasis on longer-running fiction series and feature films, which are not a strong feature of British catalogues, constitutes a more difficult market for British exporters. Confined largely to the margins of mainstream schedules in the major territories or the secondary cable and satellite market, British programmes are not widely promoted in the media, and there are few opportunities to capture the imagination of the public. Programmes produced in Britain therefore have no great cultural impact.

The 'underperformance' of British television drama, the most recognisably British genre, is a consequence of the popularity of domestic production and the historical strength of US imports, rather than any failure to produce the 'right' type of programmes. Moreover, any large-scale attempt to emulate US suppliers in terms of number of episodes and programme content is no guarantee of success. Several buyers pointed out that Britain was at its worst when it tried to emulate American drama – where it could not compete in terms of budgets and casting. With the exception of public broadcasters in the smaller, anglophile markets of Sweden and the Netherlands, drama sales are limited because drama's distinctive 'Britishness' is hard to disguise. Co-production offers only a limited solution, because there are few drama projects that have cross-cultural appeal.

Britain does best in those areas where the US is less strong and where it can carve out a distinctive niche. Programming for younger children is one such area. Factual programming represents another area. The sort of high-profile factual programmes that work best for British exporters in West European markets are those whose British origins can be disguised and add kudos to a channel profile – natural history, wildlife and science. However, there is little sense of further collaboration beyond pre-sales, and slots for factual programming are limited predominantly to public service outlets and niche channels in the secondary market. Commercial mainstream outlets will buy programmes that meet their commercial priorities, as large-scale event programmes like *Walking with Dinosaurs* have demonstrated, but these are limited to a small number of programmes.

As in America, the key to success seems to lie in suppressing the look and feel of programming that expresses national origins. This is seen most clearly in the phenomenal success of some formats (*Who Wants to Be a Millionaire?*, *The Weakest Link*), but is also evident in factual events (*Walking with Dinosaurs*), event drama (*The Lost World*) and animation (*Bob the Builder*), which are not recognised as British and can be adapted by dubbing and re-voicing to hide any further remnants of otherness. The recent success of entertainment formats in prime-time slots underlines the growing importance of tailoring programming to fit local situations. But there are tensions relating to the extent to which formats can be adapted to meet local requirements and the desire of format owners to maintain control over the exploitation of their brands on a global scale. As we saw in Italy and Spain, there are also cultural hurdles relating to the ideas and motivations underlying some formats, which do not always translate into other cultures.

Notes

1. The US and French occupying forces also adopted public service broadcasting in their zones, in contravention of their domestic experience of commercial and state-owned broadcasting respectively. In the Soviet zone, which became the German Democratic Republic, broadcasting became part of the state-owned apparatus. Since unification in 1989, broadcasting in the former GDR has been integrated into the dual system of private and publicly owned broadcasting.

2. ProSiebenSat.1 Media was acquired from KirchMedia by the American Saban Capital Group in August 2003.

3. Drama as defined here includes fiction made specifically for television, including series, serials, situation comedies and television movies, but not feature films.

4. At SVT in Sweden, for example, Britain accounted for 20 per cent of the 27 per cent of airtime devoted to overseas transmissions, behind the US with 32 per cent (SVT, 2001, p. 10).

5. Canal Jimmy's acquisitions include the sitcoms *Absolutely Fabulous* (BBC), *Hippies* (BBC), *Chambers* (BBC), *Babes in the Wood* (Carlton), *Small Potatoes* (Target), *Father Ted* (Channel Four); comedy entertainment *Da Ali G Show* (Channel Four); drama *The Young Person's Guide to Becoming a Rock Star* (Channel Four), *Bob and Rose* (Carlton), *This Life* (BBC); and lifestyle programming *Two Fat Ladies* (Optomen).

6. Broadcast on ITV in 2003.

7. Although co-productions with European partners are rare, this has not prevented historical drama being filmed in cheaper Eastern European locations. The BBC's

four-part dramatic portrayal of Charles II, *Charles II: The Power and the Passion* (2003 with A&E), was filmed in the Czech Republic, and Carlton's co-production with WGBH, *Boudicca*, was filmed in Romania (Burrell, 2003).

8. *Survival* was re-branded as *Granada Wild*, and production was moved from Norwich to Bristol in 2001.

9. Simultaneous pre-sales are possible in Spain, and pay channel Canal Plus España acquired a pay television window before transmission on the free-to-air channel Telecinco.

10. The sequel *Walking with Beasts* was pre-sold to commercial rival TV4.

11. *Teletubbies* was initially acquired by Rai Tre, but by 2002 had moved to Rai Due.

12. ZDF supplies KiKa with approximately 200 hours of new programming and 1,250 hours of archive material a year (Müller, 2002). ZDF acquires between ten and twenty animation and live-action series a year of thirteen to twenty-six episodes (Lehmann, 2002).

13. SuperRTL is 50 per cent owned by Disney, and 25 per cent of the daytime schedule is delivered by Disney. Fifty per cent of its programming is acquired, 35 per cent is co-produced and 15 per cent produced in-house (Schosser, 2002).

14. In 2002, TF1 was required to invest up to FF55 million a year in six to eight French animated series (Poussier, 2002).

15. The rights to *Ready, Steady, Cook* were shared between BBC Worldwide and Endemol Entertainment UK, and the format has sold to Vox in Germany, TV4 in Sweden, SBS6 in the Netherlands and Antena 3 in Spain for daytime transmission.

16. *Changing Rooms* sold to to RTL4 in the Netherlands, SVT in Sweden and ARD in Germany (Van den bussche, 2001).

7

Old Friends and New Markets – Australia, New Zealand and East Asia

The Asia Pacific region demonstrates at a stroke the significance of cultural proximity, driven by language, historical and cultural links. In spite of their geographical distance from Britain, the former British settler societies of Australia and New Zealand remain significant export destinations for British programmes, underpinned by the persistence of cultural and linguistic ties. In 2003, Australia and New Zealand combined accounted for $76 million of Britain's television exports, over 8 per cent of the total, in second place after America, and more than the $68 million generated in Germany, a much more populous country and Britain's largest European market (BTDA, 2003).

Sales to Asia totalled $62 million in 2003, but are fragmented across many more economically disparate territories including the more heavily populated markets of Japan, China and India. Between 1988 and 1993 the number of television households in the region grew by 70 per cent, and fuelled by an economic boom there were exponential increases in both domestic and transnational commercial television services (Cunningham and Jacka, 1996, p. 28; Hong and Hsu, 1999; Waterman and Rogers, 1994).

Television was already well developed in the economic powerhouse of Japan and the free-market enclave of Hong Kong. But economic growth and the emergence of a wealthy middle class in other territories whetted the appetite of Western companies to tap into a burgeoning market of 3 billion people – including a market of almost 1.3 billion in China (Hong and Hsu, 1999, p. 226; Iwabuchi, 2000, p. 143; Scott, 2001, p. 34). However, with domestic producers supplying over 75 per cent of programming (Waterman and Rogers, 1994) and following an economic crisis in 1997, Asia has failed to live up to earlier optimistic forecasts. According to Chadha and Kavoori, sales growth in Asia has been stagnant, accounting for only 10–15 per cent of global sales revenues (2000, p. 427).

Cultural and political barriers, combined with a preference for local programming, give local and regional producers an edge, making Asia an intensely difficult market to crack, in contrast to Australia and New Zealand, which are more consistent outlets for British product. This chapter provides an overview of the presence of British television programmes in Australia and New Zealand and Britain's most important markets in East Asia, including Japan, South Korea, China and Hong Kong. It considers the changing characteristics of television in these territories and the implications of change for the continuing presence of British programmes.

Television in Australia and New Zealand

Like Britain, Australia and New Zealand both operate a dual system of public and commercial television, with public broadcasters the ABC (Australian Broadcasting Corporation) and TVNZ (Television New Zealand) both modelled in the image of the BBC. Although bound to each other by geographical proximity, economic ties and shared historical links with Britain, Australia and New Zealand are, according to Lealand, 'fundamentally unalike in the way each perceives itself and its relation to its immediate external environments' (Lealand, 1996, p. 215). In terms of television exchanges New Zealand also exhibits some degree of tension with its larger neighbour, whose programmes have a significant presence in New Zealand television schedules (Ibid.).

The ABC, established in 1932, has operated one television channel since 1956 and competes with the 'Americanised' schedules of the commercial networks Seven, Nine and Ten in a highly competitive marketplace. Subject to commercial competition in television from the start, ABC usually comes fourth behind its commercial rivals in the ratings, securing a share of 15.5 per cent between January and June 2002 (TBI, 2002, p. 199). Funded by direct government grant, it has also proved vulnerable to inadequate funding and government pressure (Barker, 1997, p. 35; George, 2001a, p. 14). The Special Broadcasting Service (SBS), a publicly owned multicultural channel, funded by advertising, was established in 1980. Attracting 2 per cent of the audience, SBS is 'deliberately minoritarian', reflecting the gradual shift in Australia from its historical Anglo-Celtic roots towards a more multicultural society, fuelled by recent waves of immigration from Asia and Europe (Jacka and Johnson, 1998, p. 218). Foxtel is the dominant pay television platform, available in 790,000 cable and satellite homes in 2002, ahead of rivals Austar and Optus (George, 2002a, p. 36). The ABC launched ABC Kids and the youth network Fly, Australia's only digital channels, in 2001, but lack of financial support from the government led to their closure in the summer of 2003. A British channel presence is evident with UKTV, a joint venture channel, owned by BBC Worldwide, Foxtel and FremantleMedia, available in 1.2 million homes in 2003.

In the early years of Australian television (1956–65) imports from America and Britain dominated, accounting for over 50 per cent of transmissions (Barker, 1997, p. 35; Jacka and Johnson, 1998, p. 212). Serving a small population (19 million), the ability to support local production was limited, and there has always been heavy reliance on imports. According to Barker there is a 'sense in which Australian television has been subject to internationalizing influences since its inception' first because of imports and second because the ABC and the commercial television networks were modelled respectively on British public service and American commercial institutions (1997, p. 36). Indeed the first ABC television operatives and announcers were sent to the BBC for training, and from the start the ABC had an exclusive agreement for first refusal on BBC programmes (Jacka and Johnson, 1998, p. 209).

Commercial expansion in a second phase (1965–75) led to an increase in local production on both public and commercial networks to fill expanded schedules and attract audiences which had become 'fed up with the increase in American imports' (Barker, 1997, pp. 35–6). This has continued and between 1992 and 1998 levels of imports declined from 48 per cent to 41 per cent as all channels have sought to promote domestic productions in prime time (Easter, 2003; Rouse, 2001, p. 38). Local content rules stipulate that 50 per cent of transmissions on commercial free-to-air television between 6am and midnight must be Australian, with minimum levels of first-run Australian drama, documentaries and children's programmes. The drama quota is determined by a points system weighted towards high-budget programmes (George, 2001b, p. 44). In 2001–02, over 60 per cent of the ABC's transmissions between 6am and midnight were locally produced (ABC, 2002, p. 51). Between 1968 and 1994, British programmes accounted for 22 per cent of ABC content, surpassing American suppliers with a 15 per cent share (O'Regan, 2000, p. 308).

According to Moran there are still strong links between Australia and the 'mother country' (1998, p. 50). Initially the relationship with Australia was predominantly one-way, based on British exports and some British involvement in co-productions, particularly with the ABC and Channel Seven (Ibid., p. 51). Until 1974 Australian regulation even allowed British programmes to count as Australian content (Ibid.). This influence extended to the imitation of ideas or 'informal borrowing' (O'Regan, 2000, p. 313). From 1956 ABC emulated, but did not pay for the right to develop, its own programming based on the BBC formats for current affairs programmes *Panorama* (*4 Corners* in Australia) and the science format *Tomorrow's World* (Moran, 1998, p. 27; Jacka and Johnson, 1998, p. 212).

In the 1980s, the relationship changed when Australia emerged as a more significant exporter of programmes and formats in its own right, particularly to Britain (Cunningham and Jacka, 1996, pp. 124–6). With the success of long-running serials such as *Neighbours* (Grundy) on BBC 1 and *Home and Away* (Channel Seven) on ITV in the mid-1980s, Australian exporters met demand for daily serials in British schedules increasingly targeted at a younger demographic in prime-time access. But even here there was a congruence of interests. According to Moran, popular daily soap operas did not emerge as a viable programming form on Australian commercial television until 1972 (1998, p. 51). Their development was influenced by British television writers working in Australia and by Australian-born producer and writer Reg Watson, who had devised the British daily serial *Crossroads* for ATV in 1964, working subsequently for Grundy (Ibid.). Watson originated *Neighbours*, which became a hit on BBC 1 in 1986.

Since the peak of Australian exports to Britain in the mid-1980s, programme exchanges between the two countries have reverted back to more familiar patterns, with British programmes featuring prominently in the schedules of the ABC, but very much less so on the commercial networks. This relationship has attracted criticism. According to O'Regan, some Australian critics have argued that the ABC is too 'slavish in its adoption of British models, its preparedness to employ English migrants at the expense of those of a non-English-speaking background, and its implicit devaluation of local life experiences not drawn from a particular middle-class and Anglophile cultural experience' (2000, p. 316).

Unlike the ABC, TVNZ, with two channels, has always dominated television in New Zealand. TV One caters for an older audience, with high levels of British drama. In 2002, 56 per cent of TV One content screened in prime time was locally originated (TVNZ, 2002). TV2, established in 1975, caters for a younger audience, with significant amounts of American and Australian fiction. Established in 1936, TVNZ held a television monopoly until 1988, but has maintained dominance of the ratings with a 60 per cent share between January and August 2002 in spite of the introduction of commercial rival TV3 in 1989, and later Prime Television (TBI, 2002, p. 246).

Always funded predominantly by advertising, TVNZ underwent a transformation in 1989 when it was restructured as a 'state-owned enterprise operating on commercial profit-making principles', thus removing the public service objectives at its core and requiring it to deliver a dividend to the government (Lealand, 1996, p. 216).[1] Economic rationalisation changed New Zealand from being a resolutely public service ecology to an aggressively market-led television environment dominated by ratings without, according to some commentators, a concurrent rise in diversity, choice, domestic production or even competition (Bell, 1995; Herman and McChesney, 1997, p. 181).

Lealand suggests that the transformation of New Zealand into a 'deregulatory laboratory' economy in the 1980s also contributed to a break in its traditional trading relationship with Britain. In terms of television, there is now a greater emphasis on cultural exchange with Australia, the largest source of television imports in New Zealand after America (Lealand, 1996, p. 215). Reflecting this change, the proportion of British imports on New Zealand television declined from 17.1 per cent in December 1989 to 12.5 per cent in December 1993, while Australian imports rose from 5.1 per cent to 12.9 per cent (Ibid., p. 218).

British programmes in Australia and New Zealand

Imports by Australia and New Zealand are dominated by purchases from America, followed by Britain, and in the case of New Zealand from Australia, with little purchased from other sources. In spite of the comparatively small revenues to be earned from such small markets, Australia and New Zealand are attractive to British exporters because they acquire a broad range of content (Alvarado and Stewart, 1985, p. 18).

The vast majority of sales take place with public service broadcasters the ABC and TVNZ. Both have long-running first-look output deals with the BBC and Channel Four across all genres, and the relationship reflects a shared public service ethos and aesthetic preferences. However, this institutional proximity with the BBC needs to be placed in the context of the ABC's more marginal position in Australian society and TVNZ's more commercial outlook, funded as it is by advertising.

All the Australian commercial networks have output deals with the American majors. But Britain is considered sufficiently important as a programming market for the Nine Network and Channel Seven to employ buyers based in London. These not only acquire small amounts of British programmes to supplement larger purchases of American product, but also serve to ascertain trends in a market that is still considered a source of innovative programming and new trends (Easter, 2003).

Drama

Unlike Europe and America, sales to broadcasters in Australia and New Zealand, and particularly to the ABC and TVNZ, are driven by sales of British drama, including contemporary drama. But increases in domestic production, outlined earlier, have made sales of the most valuable peak-time drama more difficult (Easter, 2003; Hansen, 2003; O'Regan, 2000, p. 308; Roberts, 2003). According to Sue Masters, Head of Drama at Ten, and a former head of drama at the ABC, this trend reflected a desire to serve domestic audiences with domestic programming:

We do not make enough drama. We are competing all the time [on domestic channels] with the best from the UK and the US, which produce much greater volumes. But I don't know anyone who is trying to emulate US or UK production. The people I work with want to find our own voice and tell Australian stories well. (Cited in George, 2003a, p.10)

Most British sales are straight acquisitions. Pre-sales are rare, except for return-ing series with known casts, such as *Teachers* (Channel Four/ABC) or *Prime Suspect* (Granada/Channel Seven) (Hansen, 2003; Roberts, 2003). *Dr Zhivago*, Granada's international co-production of 2002, was acquired as a pre-sale by the Nine Network in 2002, but this was quite exceptional. Co-productions are infrequent, because of the problems of finding drama that works in more than one market (George, 2002b). They are also rare because of the difficulties in meeting conditions relating to Australian creative control set down by the Aus-tralian Film Finance Corporation (FFC) before a production can be considered as an official co-production, and therefore eligible for FFC funding (George, 2001b, p. 42; George, 2002b, p. 90). Only independent Australian companies can access FFC funding, so foreign-owned companies like Granada and Grundy (part of the RTL Group) are required to find local partners (George, 2001b, p. 43). In 2000, *Do or Die* (Southern Star/Warner Sisters/BSkyB), a backpacker drama, shown on Channel Seven, became the first Australian-initiated official British/Australian co-production for ten years (George, 2001b, p. 44). With a small domestic market, Australian producers have continued to look to Britain as a source of funding for their own productions, with Channel Four, for example, pre-buying the long-running Australian youth series *The Secret Life of Us* (Southern Star/Ten) in 2000 (George, 2001b).

The ABC is the main Australian outlet for British drama, acquiring almost 75 per cent of its 349 hours of first-run fiction from overseas in 2002 (ABC, 2002, p. 145). FremantleMedia's long-running ITV police serial *The Bill*, broad-cast at 8.30pm, functions as a flagship programme on Saturdays and Tuesdays. With little interest from commercial networks, the ABC is also the key outlet for period drama on Sunday evenings (*Daniel Deronda*, BBC; *The Forsyte Saga*, Granada), contemporary drama (*Linda Green*, BBC; *Teachers*, Channel Four; *Cutting It*, BBC), and sitcoms during the day (*Birds of a Feather*, FremantleMedia; *As Time Goes By*, BBC). Demand is highest for mainstream or family drama, with less call for anything that is 'too edgy' or 'too dark' (Roberts, 2003). The most prestigious dramas appear to outperform the ABC's average share. In 2002 peak-time transmissions of *Shackleton* (Channel Four), *Murder Rooms: Tales of the Real Sherlock Holmes* (a BBC/WGBH co-production distributed by High Point Film and Television) and *The Lost World* (BBC) achieved 21.4 per cent, 22.3 per cent and 21.2 per cent audience shares respectively (ABC, 2002, p. 54). SBS buys little British drama because of the ABC's output deals with the BBC and Channel Four, but does take material that is too risqué for the mainstream channels, including Channel Four's gay drama *Queer as Folk*, shown in peak time.

The Australian commercial networks are more aligned with American suppliers and have few available slots. Emulating American stripped scheduling, and targeting younger audiences with American imports (soaps, talk shows) during the day and domestic productions at peak time, they acquire very little (Easter, 2003; Hansen, 2003; George, 2003b). With BBC and Channel Four product taken by the ABC, they have traditionally acquired programming, primarily murder mysteries and detective series, from the ITV distributors.

Seven, in which Granada holds a 10 per cent stake, and with whom it has a minimum spend output deal, has always acquired the most. Previous acquisitions have included *Taggart, Inspector Morse, Cracker, A Touch of Frost* and *Prime Suspect*, the latter garnering a 37.2 per cent share when it was first screened in 1995 (O'Regan, 2000, p. 307). But interest and purchases have declined because these programmes are perceived by buyers as slow and tend to attract older audiences. According to Tim Worner, Head of Production and Programming at Seven, 'Often this type of programming is too dark, gritty and intimidating for a broad audience and we need it to have accessible characters' (cited in George, 2003b, p. 9). The shift away from murder mystery and detective franchises is reflected in a desire for younger-rating contemporary drama. Ten, which 'resolutely' caters for sixteen to thirty-nine year-olds, acquired the racy and glamorous ITV peak-time series *Footballers' Wives* (produced by Shed Productions and distributed by Target) in 2002 because it 'was very Ten in its style' (David Mott, Head of Programming, Ten, cited in George, 2003b, p. 9). Likewise, Seven's purchase of Granada's relationship drama *Cold Feet*, which was airing in 2003 in a 9.30pm slot on Tuesdays, met its requirements for 'commercial' contemporary fiction with broad appeal.

According to Australian buyers for the commercial networks, ITV has been supplying less of the *Prime Suspect*-like franchises that used to work in Australia. British drama that cast British soap stars, such as Ross Kemp in *Ultimate Force* (distributed by Chrysalis), has less resonance in the Australian marketplace because British soaps (*EastEnders, Coronation Street*) do not air on Australian free-to-air television, and the casts were therefore unknown. The most attractive dramas contained known stars such as Billy Connolly or James Nesbitt, whose role in *Cold Feet* motivated Seven to acquire the BBC police drama *Murphy's Law* (1 x 90 mins) from Target in 2001.

Much higher volumes of British drama are sold to TVNZ's TV One, including long-running soaps, programmes that fail to sell in volume elsewhere. In 2003 *EastEnders* (12.25–1pm), *Crossroads* (1–1.30pm) and *Emmerdale* (3.40–4.10pm) were all stripped in daytime five days a week. *Coronation Street*, one of TV One's most highly rated shows, airs weekly on Mondays, Tuesdays and Fridays at 7.30pm. High levels of acquisitions are driven by economic necessity in such a small market of 3.8 million people. The attraction of British fiction on the first channel also extends to peak-time transmissions of contemporary drama (*Cold Feet, Monarch of the Glen*, BBC; *Bad Girls, Footballers' Wives*, Shed Productions; *The Vice*, Carlton) and the showcasing of imports in the sponsored Sunday night strand, *Lexus Sunday Night Theatre*.

While TV One demonstrates a strong British drama presence, this does not extend to TV2, with its younger audience profile. This is the home of domestically produced soap *Shortland Street* (Grundy, 7pm, Mondays to Fridays), daytime transmissions of Australian imports (*Home and Away, Neighbours*), American imports (*The Young and the Restless, Days of Our Lives*) and reality formats in peak time (*Big Brother, Fear Factor*), which attract younger viewers. Commercial channels TV3 and Prime (which airs *The Bill* twice a week in peak time) focus on American imports because most of the main British suppliers have output deals with TVNZ, the dominant player in the marketplace.

Factual programming

Factual sales exceed sales of drama in terms of volume. Channel Four, for example, sells approximately 100–130 hours a year to Australia, of which two-thirds is factual material (Roberts, 2003). Institutional and cultural proximity means that the ABC and TVNZ take a much broader range of British material than the commercial channels, with a predominance of purchases from public service counterparts the BBC and Channel Four. Commercial channels in Australia and New Zealand do not have regular slots for documentaries, reflecting their traditional focus on entertainment and the public perception that more serious public service-imbued educational and information programming belongs on the ABC, SBS and TVNZ (see Bonner, 2003, p. 138).

The ABC tends to concentrate on event series (*Walking with Dinosaurs, The Human Face*), and documentaries on history, science and religion (Roberts, 2003). A history strand was introduced on Sunday evenings in 2001 with *The Six Wives of Henry VIII* (Channel Four), hosted by British historian David Starkey, achieving a higher than average share of 22.8 per cent. *Elizabeth I* (Channel Four), a four-part series, gained an average share of 21.5 per cent in the same slot (ABC, 2002, p. 54). With a less pronounced public service remit and a dependency on advertising as its main source of income, TVNZ takes a more commercially oriented approach to factual programming and is 'not very

likely to take a high science series or arts documentary' even on its main channel, TV One (Roberts, 2003). The best of foreign programming, for example
Sars: Killer Bug (Channel Four), which aired in May 2003, are showcased in *Reel
Life* a weekly prime-time strand on Wednesdays, but science programmes such
as the BBC series *Space* are far more likely to be aired during the day.

Intermittent acquisitions by the commercial channels tend to focus on factual
entertainment for prime-time access or after prime time in tightly stripped
schedules where slots are at a premium. The Nine Network acquires ten to
twenty hours a year from Britain, including observational programming (*Airport,
Chrysalis*) and more risqué programmes such as *Beautilicious* or *Vain Men*
(Channel Four) for late-night viewing (Easter, 2003; Roberts, 2003). Seven
acquired Granada's celebrity special *Living with Michael Jackson* in 2002, but
the remainder of its infrequent purchases have been focused predominantly on
factual entertainment – such as the *From Hell* series (*Builders from Hell, Divorces
from Hell* etc.) sold by Granada International. Personality-led cookery programmes are popular with commercial channels. In 2003, Ten was airing both
the reality-based *Jamie's Kitchen* (FremantleMedia) and cookery show *The
Naked Chef* (Optomen), no doubt anticipating that the youth of the presenter,
Jamie Oliver, would appeal to its core audience.

Formats

While sales of factual programming are limited, sales of entertainment and factual formats have grown to meet the demand for local origination of 'ordinary'
television involving 'ordinary' people (Bonner, 2003). Alongside internationally
franchised peak-time hits such as *Who Wants to Be a Millionaire?* (Nine in
Australia; Prime in New Zealand), *Boot Camp* (Nine), *Survivor* (Nine), *The
Weakest Link* (Channel Seven) and *Pop Idol* (Channel Ten in Australia; TV2 in
New Zealand), Australia in particular, has proved a fruitful outlet for factual
entertainment and lifestyle formats.

The enduring popularity of Australian house and garden shows such as *Burke's
Backyard* on the Nine Network, which has aired on Friday nights since 1987,
and *Better Homes and Gardens* on Channel Seven, meant that the market was
strongly receptive to house and garden makeover formats from Britain. Gardening makeover show *Ground Force* (Endemol Entertainment UK) proved so
popular on Channel Seven that it inspired a controversial Nine Network imitation in 2000, *Backyard Blitz* (Bonner, 2003, p. 180). *Changing Rooms* (Endemol
Entertainment UK), a format where couples are challenged to decorate rooms
in each other's houses under the guidance of designers, became a hit for the
Nine Network because it depicted recognisable local types and locations, and
referenced recognisable national characteristics and myths (Ibid., p. 183). The

interest in factual entertainment formats has now been extended to other
lifestyle programmes involving 'ordinary people'. *Life Laundry*, a Talkback/Fre-
mantleMedia format, which follows members of the public as they declutter
their homes and lives under the guidance of lifestyle professionals, was acquired
by Channel Seven in 2003 for reversioning as *Your Life on the Lawn*. *Britain's
Worst Driver*, a game-show–factual hybrid, originally produced by the TV Corporation for Five, was sold as a format to Seven in 2002. Both the original
versions and format rights of RDF Media's *Faking It* and *Wife Swap* were purchased by the Nine Network in 2003. The airing of the original British versions
functioned as a test run for possible local adaptations (Easter, 2003), suggesting that audiences need to be primed for their reactions before any commitment
to a more costly local adaptation (see also Bonner, 2003, p. 178).

The growing importance of format sales is reflected in limited involvement by
British companies in local production. In 2003, Granada Australia's adaptation
of Talkback's *The Kumars at No. 42* was screened in peak time as *Greeks on the
Roof* on Channel Seven, following the airing of the original on the ABC
(Hansen, 2003). Launched in 2001, Granada Australia is responsible for selling
formats into the Australian market alongside its production activities, which
have included producing episodes of the British productions *Cold Feet* and *I'm
a Celebrity . . . Get Me out of Here!* in Australia. The Chrysalis TV Group (now
All3Media) has a majority 60 per cent stake in New Zealand's South Pacific Pictures, the producers of *Shortland Street* for TV2, and the New Zealand version
of *Pop Idol*.

Children's programmes

Sales of British children's programmes in Australia are mainly confined to the
ABC, which has regular morning and afternoon slots for pre-school programming that meet a public service remit. Imports feature heavily, accounting for
almost 74 per cent of the 1,645 hours devoted to children's programmes in
2001–02 (ABC, 2002, p. 145). *Bob the Builder, Maisie, Thomas the Tank Engine,
Angelina Ballerina, Basil Brush* and *The Fimbles* feature strongly alongside Australian programmes (*Bananas in Pyjamas, Round the Twist*) and American imports
(*Sesame Street, The Charlie Brown Specials, The Bear in the Big Blue House*).
British sales to commercial channels are rare because of a lack of slots restricted to weekend mornings, a preponderance of domestic production to meet
domestic quotas, and output deals with American suppliers such as Seven's deal
with Disney (Easter, 2003). The lack of interest by advertisers in the pre-school
market is also a barrier for sales to the commercial channels.

However, in New Zealand commercial channel TV3 has carved out a pre-
school niche, with British imports accounting for over half of all transmissions

for children. It has become home to *Teletubbies, Thomas the Tank Engine, Brum, Bob the Builder* and *Angelina Ballerina* in a daily Monday to Friday slot between 6.30am and 9.30am. Sales to TVNZ's second channel, TV2, are less frequent (*Percy the Parkkeeper*, HIT; *Ace Lightning*, BBC), and a weekday morning block for pre-schoolers shows a preponderance of American imports (*Blues Clues, Clifford, the Big Red Dog*).

In both territories merchandising and licensing opportunities drive revenues much more than programme sales, which function as a platform for activities in ancillary markets. The ABC usually picks up the licensing, video and DVD rights to the shows it acquires. In its first year in 1999 *Teletubbies* generated sales of 1 million books for BBC Worldwide in both territories (BBC Worldwide, 1999). During the same period, *Teletubbies* reached number one in the Australian video charts and BBC Worldwide launched the *Teletubbies* magazine, the first local version of a BBC magazine in the region (Ibid.).

Television in East Asia

In contrast to Australia and New Zealand, the television systems of East Asia demonstrate enormous diversity in terms of language, culture and wealth. Changes to the television environment in the 1990s were much more dramatic than in either Europe or North America in the 1980s. Before liberalisation, most Asian countries were resistant to imports because of linguistic, political and cultural barriers, and there were only limited regional exchanges of programming (Waterman and Rogers, 1994, p. 107).[2]

Many markets in the region (notably China, Malaysia and Singapore) were dominated by one or two state-owned networks, and there was no strong tradition of media independence (Banerjee, 2002, pp. 524–5; Man Chan, 1997, pp. 96–7). Japan and Hong Kong were already operating as open and commercialised television systems. Both, alongside South Korea, have been politically influenced by Western/Anglo-American powers in the decisive post-war period, but remained largely resistant to the allure of Western imports (Kwak, 1999, p. 256).

The catalyst for change came with the introduction of cross-border satellite channels, foremost Star TV in 1991, which undermined the ability of national systems to resist external cultural influences. Even in more mature markets such as Japan, the launch of Star TV demonstrated that the Japanese media industry was no longer a self-contained domestic market (Iwabuchi, 2000, p. 144). The appearance of transnational channels not only destabilised monopolistic television systems in many territories, but also posed challenges to the more authoritarian regimes in the region. Governments in countries with a less pronounced tradition of media autonomy, such as Malaysia, Singapore and China, voiced concern about their cultural autonomy in the face of a Western media onslaught, viewing Western media and cultural products as a threat to Asian values and traditions (Chadha and Kavoori, 2000, p. 417).

Economic liberalisation and the commercialisation of broadcast media led to a massive increase in channels across the region, a swift growth in advertising, and a significant albeit short-term increase in imported programmes (Richards and French, 2000, p. 16). National responses to this situation varied. They involved a mixture of encouraging local programming and commercial television, and depending on the degree of market and political openness, on a variety of measures aimed at limiting Western influence (Sinclair, Jacka and Cunningham, 1996, p. 3; Chadha and Kavoori, 2000; Hong and Hsu, 1999, pp. 233–5).

However, the strategy of encouraging local production reaped dividends because of a marked preference for local and regionally produced programming in local languages, which forced transnational operators like Star TV to localise their programme schedules (Chadha and Kavoori, 2000, pp. 424–5). Star TV was available in an estimated 300 million homes in fifty-three countries in 2001 (Frater, 2001, p. 36). News Corporation acquired a majority stake in 1993, and the strategy of the multi-channel operation changed. To counter strong local competition, sub-regional language channels were developed with more locally sourced programming that appealed to national variations in language and culture (Thomas, 2000, p. 97). For example, the Phoenix Chinese Channel, a 'blend of traditional Chinese culture with the westernised ethos of Hong Kong' (Thussu, 2000, p. 213), was launched in 1996 as a joint venture between Star TV and the Chinese Phoenix Satellite Television Company. Broadcasting in Mandarin, the principal language of China, Phoenix represents a prime example of the realisation that to succeed in the Chinese-speaking market, Western corporations need to provide local programming in local languages and work with local partners (Thussu, 2000, p. 212; Lee, 2000, p. 190).

Chadha and Kavoori have argued that imports and transnational corporations have in fact not had a pervasive presence or influence in the region. This is because of a complex interplay of national gatekeeping policies (bans on satellite dishes, censorship, equity restrictions on foreign investment, quotas), a strong preference for local content, as well as the countervailing forces of local competition (2000, p. 428; also Banerjee, 2002, p. 533; Hong and Hsu, 1999, p. 233).

Rather than being swamped by Western cultural products, there has been a shift in priorities in many territories 'from the exclusive needs of the nation, however vaguely expressed to commercialism and infotainment' (Richards and French, 2000, p. 25). This has been driven by changes in the financial structure of television and a swift growth in advertising, rather than transformation of ownership (Hong and Hsu, 1999, p. 230). According to some commentators, these changes have resulted in a decline in public broadcasting and a lack of genuine diversity, as many Asian countries have appropriated and integrated the American model of commercial and competitive media without political reform (Banerjee, 2002, p. 533; Chadha and Kavoori, 2000, p. 429). Equally, however, commercialisation has weakened the ability of some governments, notably China, Singapore and Malaysia, to maintain ideological positions in the face of market pressures arising from the commercialisation of television (Hong and Hsu, 1999, p. 227; Karthigesu, 1994).

Television systems in Japan, Hong Kong, South Korea and China

The wealthy, mature and open Japanese market is dominated by public service broadcaster NHK and five private sector terrestrial networks – NTV (Nippon Television), Fuji TV, Tokyo Broadcasting System (TBS), TV Asahi and TV Tokyo 12. In spite of a lack of restrictions on imports, the Japanese terrestrial television market is highly resistant to foreign programming, which accounts for less than 5 per cent of total transmissions (Iwabuchi, 2000, p. 144; Man Chan 2000, p. 254). NHK, with a 7.5 per cent terrestrial share in 2001 (TBI, 2002, p. 231), operates two national terrestrial channels, two broadcast satellite channels (BS1 and BS2) and, since 1991, a Hi-Vision service. The communications satellite market launched in 1989, and after a period of consolidation, is now led by the SkyPerfecTV platform of over 300 services, available in an estimated 10 per cent of television households in 2002 (Nakamura, 1999, p. 310; Rea, 2000, p. 8; TBI, 2002, p. 232). The launch of advertising-supported digital satellite services by the free-to-air commercial broadcasters in late 2000 fragmented the market still further, but these have failed to ignite consumer interest and television is still dominated by the mainstream networks (Hansen, 2003; Weatherford, 2003). Animal Planet Japan, a joint venture channel between BBC Worldwide, Discovery Communications and the Japanese Jupiter Programming Company, was available in 1.7 million satellite homes in 2003 (BBC Worldwide, 2003a).

TVB (Television Broadcasters Ltd), a commercial free-to-air broadcaster with an 80 per cent audience share, is the key player in Hong Kong, followed by commercial rival ATV (Asia Television) (Scott, 2001, p. 35). Established in 1967, it produces up to 85 per cent of its own transmissions (Thomas, 2000, p. 95). Until 1997 Hong Kong was a British colony, when it became a Special Administrative Region of China. The colonial past has left a legacy of English-language services. However, Pearl, operated by TVB, and World, run by ATV, play a marginal role because of audience preferences for Cantonese programmes on the mainstream channels Jade (TVB) and ATV Home (Lee, 1991, p. 60; Kwak, 1999, pp. 263–4). I-Cable (formerly Wharf Cable) was launched in 1993 and provides multi-channel television with a mixture of local, international and transnational services.

As a small market of 5.8 million people, Hong Kong is not a significant export destination. Its importance rests much more on its role as a regional media production centre and launch pad for accessing other territories in the region, particularly China (Kenny, 2001; Man Chan, 2000, p. 254; Thomas, 2000). Star TV launched from Hong Kong in 1991, but has since been joined by a range of Hong Kong-initiated services, broadcast in Mandarin, which provide transnational competition to Star TV in Greater China and to the Chinese-speaking communities of South-East Asia. TVB, owner of the world's largest library of Chinese-language programmes, launched TVBS, a Mandarin-language satellite service in 1993. Other sources of Hong Kong-based Mandarin language competition include Time Warner's joint venture Chinese Entertainment Television (CETV), launched in 1994 with a formula of 'no sex, no violence and no news' (Kenny, 2001, p. 282), and CTN (Chinese Television Network), a Mandarin equivalent of CNN. The existence of these channels has not dented the share of local channels, but reinforced Hong Kong's position as a media hub exporting culturally proximate content to others in the region (Hong and Hsu, 1999, p. 234; Man Chan, 2000, p. 258; Thomas, 2000, p. 106).

Terrestrial television remains the overwhelming choice for viewers in South Korea, a market of 14.5 million television homes. The government-funded public corporation KBS (Korea Broadcasting System) operates two channels, which combined had a 43 per cent share in 2000 (TBI, 2002, p. 257). The commercial free-to-air service MBC (Munwha Broadcasting Corporation), with a 28 per cent audience share in 2000, is 70 per cent owned by a public foundation, but funded by advertising. Government-controlled EBS (Educational Broadcasting System) was established in 1990 as an educational service. Commercial free-to-air service SBS (Seoul Broadcasting System) was launched in 1991 as an entertainment channel, and transformed South Korean broadcasting into a mixed system (Lee, 2002, p. 285). Domestic productions dominate transmissions on the terrestrial networks and there is a ceiling of 15 per cent on imports, which are usually scheduled outside the prime-time period of 7pm to 10pm (Lee and Joe, 2000, pp. 138–9). Foreign influence is further limited because ownership of most businesses, including the television industry, is restricted to local concerns or joint ventures (Driscoll, 2003; Thomas, 1999, pp. 251–2). Cable television was established in 1995, but has had difficulties in securing subscribers (Lee, 2002, p. 285). In 2002, multi-channel cable television was available in 25 per cent of households (TBI, 2002, p. 257). SkyLife, a digital satellite platform, with over seventy channels, launched in March 2002 with a year-end target of 400,000 subscribers (Ibid.).

China operates a three-tier structure of television, headed by state broad-caster CCTV (China Central Television). Beneath CCTV there are government-owned provincial networks, with Beijing TV and Shanghai TV reaching in excess of 200 million and 130 million people respectively (Anon., 1999). Hundreds of county- and city-based cable channels cater to more local areas (Anon., 1999; Scott, 2001, p. 34). A poll undertaken in 2001 in sixty-two cities shows that provincial free-to-air networks are most popular, with a 34 per cent share, followed by CCTV (32 per cent), cable channels (14 per cent) and city-based channels (13 per cent) (TBI, 2002, p. 213). Cable penetration was estimated to stand at 28 per cent in 2001 (Carter, 2003a, p. 29).

CCTV operates eleven channels. CCTV1, available in 310 million television households, is the most popular with a 20 per cent share (Carter, 2003a, p. 29). CCTV2 offers educational, social and business programming. CCTV3, 5, and 6 are encrypted pay television channels focusing respectively on music/opera, sport and films. CCTV4 targets Chinese audiences overseas and CCTV9 is an English-language channel. CCTV10 and 11 provide cultural and educational content. CCTV8 focuses on drama and entertainment with a daily prime-time programming block supplied by Encore Media, part of the American Liberty Media corporation.

The decentralisation, marketisation and corporatisation of Chinese television in the mid-1990s led to an explosion of television stations at provincial and local level. This had the effect of undermining central control by the government and the Chinese Communist Party (CCP) in favour of commercially driven decisions and content, particularly at the lower levels (Bin, 1998, p. 249; Hong, 2000, p. 300; Keane, 2001; Pan and Man Chan, 2000, p. 257; Thomas, 1999, pp. 248–9). A shift away from ideological content towards entertainment pro-gramming was further reinforced by the withdrawal of government subsidies in the 1990s, rendering stations more dependent on commercial revenues, and forcing them to cater more effectively to popular tastes (Hong, 2000, p. 292; Pan and Man Chan, 2000, p. 240; Wei, 2000, p. 332).

However, there are still tensions between state control and the dynamics of the market in a system that is still comprised of government-owned media. According to Lull, the commercialisation of Chinese television has resulted in a contradiction and ideological conflict 'between the blatant materialism and indi-vidualism' of content driven by advertising and material goals and other content that 'advocates traditional socialist values' (Lull, 1997, pp. 264–5). This conflict is evident in the failure of Chinese media to function as genuinely independent social institutions and in continued tight party control over news content (Bin, 1999; Hong, 2000, p. 302).

For those entering the Chinese market this has presented difficulties because in spite of the marketisation of television the Chinese Communist Party still regards the media as a political tool and ideological state apparatus (Hong, 2000, p. 302). News Corporation notoriously dropped the 'politically unsuitable' BBC World satellite channel from the Star TV package in 1994 in an attempt to assuage Chinese political sensitivities.[3] According to Louis Boswell, China and Hong Kong manager for BBC Worldwide, 'TV in China is meant to be a healthy medium. They don't want "spiritual pollution" ' (cited in Carter, 2003a, p. 30). To achieve output that is 'wholesome and spiritually uplifting', foreign acquisitions are therefore highly selective, and all imports must be submitted for approval by the authorities before transmission (Carter, 2003a, p. 30; Driscoll, 2003).

The Chinese approach involves policies that are both open and resistant to Western influences. The imposition of 15 per cent quotas on imports exists alongside strategies designed to promote domestic production and exports (Chadha and Kavoori, 2000, p. 419; Hong, 2000, pp. 297–9). The market has been partially opened to foreign players, including Star TV and Time Warner's CETV, whose channels have long been available illegally on cable systems and in border areas, but are now officially sanctioned in hotels, selected cable networks and some designated areas (Carter, 2003a, p. 29; Doward, 2003; Thomas, 1999, p. 249). Nevertheless, China has a long way to go before it can be described as actively encouraging foreign investors and foreign programming. Although its political and ideological functions have been reduced in favour of economic and entertainment objectives, television remains a state-owned political tool. There are substantial trading opportunities, but significant barriers remain, as testified by the attempts of British exporters to break into the world's most populous television marketplace.

British programmes in Japan, South Korea, Hong Kong and China

> I hear your comments about Japan and China being very difficult, but they're no more difficult than a Chinese or Japanese company going into London or New York to do the same things. It's mutual. . . . In Los Angeles there's a guy who goes to London about three or four times a year. He'll come to Japan once every three or four years. And I said, 'Why don't you come to Japan more often?' And he said, 'But Jim it's so far.' I said, 'It's further to London than it is from LA to Japan.' But he said 'No, that's not what I meant. It's so far away, thinking wise. It's just difficult.' (Weatherford, 2003)

At the end of the day, making programmes is a business. When you work out your budget you work out who you're going to sell to. Most programme producers aren't going to worry about whether it's suitable for Asia or not, because it's not that big a financial slice of the cake. They're going to say, 'Will it sell to Australia, will it sell to France, Germany, Spain and Italy or the US?' That's where the budget is going to be covered. Even if I sold it to eight countries in Asia I still would barely be able to meet the fee that you would get from Australia in a single blow. (British Sales Executive, 2003)

The preceding comments highlight the degree of apprehension among exporters about the Asian market, based on perceptions of cultural difference and its capacity for generating revenues. According to one US executive, based in Japan, success demands perseverance:

You just stick with it and have to show you're committed to the market and not just there for the sale. It's all about developing relationships, sitting down and talking to the people for hours on end. ... You have to know as much about the market as they do in order for them to feel comfortable with you. (Weatherford, 2003)

But sales trips by British exporters to Asia appear to be infrequent, except by the larger players, because the volume of sales and the returns do not justify the expense. Face-to-face contact is frequently limited to meetings at the sales conventions, MIP-TV or MIPCOM. This has drawbacks in developing relationships and understanding how the territories function. BBC Worldwide, the leading distributor in the region, has offices in Hong Kong and Japan. But other British distributors, including larger operations like Granada International, Chrysalis (now All3Media) and Channel Four International, make extensive use of local agents.

Agents are not used in all territories, and direct access to broadcasters in South Korea and Hong Kong is quite straightforward. But sales executives regard local agents as key to accessing the complicated Chinese market. Agents here are not only necessary to secure access to the right executives, but are also essential for negotiating a path around China's complicated censorship rules (Carter, 2003a, p. 29; Driscoll, 2003). These require the approval of individual episodes, and British programmes that deal 'with sex, drugs or criminals getting away with it' have often fallen foul of the rules (Driscoll, 2003; Grant, 2003). According to Stephen Driscoll, Senior Sales Executive at Carlton International, the relationships that a Chinese agent has with the broadcasters are crucial:

That agent does a lot of things I can't do. He puts all the scripts into Chinese. He fills out all the paperwork. He goes through all the censorship process and does all that paperwork. By him doing it he saves the TV station from having to go through the hassle of doing it. So he saves them a workload, and it's all done professionally. It's a system that operates very differently than we do in other countries, but it works for them, and it would be very rude to walk in and say 'you know you don't want to do it like this. You've got to buy off me direct.' And they'll say 'no thank you, don't come back.' (Driscoll, 2003)

Most exporters try to sell on a territory-by-territory basis to the terrestrial networks rather than to transnational operators such as Star TV, HBO Asia and Hallmark, because the rewards are higher, but sales are limited. With the exception of Japan, licence fees are not high. A common practice in the region is for broadcasters to buy programmes with commercial airtime instead of cash (Carter, 2003a, p. 30). Nor is this a market for co-productions or pre-sales, except for a limited number of high-profile 'prestige' documentary programmes with the major Japanese broadcasters, and even these are not necessarily shown in prime time (Rea, 2000, p. 7; Iwabuchi, 2000, p. 155). Smaller or less mature territories like China lack the financial resources to become involved in co-productions, notwithstanding the difficulties in all territories of locating projects with cross-cultural appeal (Driscoll, 2003; Roberts, 2003). In some countries, particularly China, copyright protection is not effective, making it difficult to develop reality and game-show formats (Fraser, 2002b).

Drama
Sales of British drama are negligible because of a preference for domestic and American productions, compounded by a lack of cultural proximity. According to one sales executive, buyers found some British drama distinctly unattractive, 'It's a different sensibility. There are laws on censorship. We don't do glossy programmes very well. We try to make them too hard hitting and realistic and people look at them and say, "They're all ugly and why on earth would we want that. We want good-looking people"' (Driscoll, 2003).

The only Western programmes to play a major role are Hollywood films, giving American suppliers an edge because feature film sales can be tied into other product, including long-running series (Rea, 2000, p. 7). The heaviest demand is for action movies that resemble the most popular programmes in the region (Cunningham and Jacka, 1996, p. 198), produced in volume in Hong Kong, Taiwan and increasingly South Korea (Chadha and Kavoori, 2000, p. 426). For instance, Carlton International built a strong video and DVD business in Asia, particularly in Japan, based on the popularity of its library of American action-adventure movies (Driscoll, 2003).

NHK's purchases of British drama are intermittent, comprising mainly detective series and mysteries. In the mid-1990s, Granada sold crime thrillers

Cracker and *Prime Suspect*, with *Prime Suspect III* achieving a 4.6 per cent share in 1995 (O'Regan, 2000, p. 307). More recent purchases have included *Poirot* (Granada), *Midsomer Murders* (Chrysalis), *Inspector Morse* (Carlton) and the historical epic about the Arctic explorer *Shackleton* (Channel Four/A&E in association with ABC). However, these are more likely to air on NHK's satellite channels than the free-to-air services.

In China the hurdles of censorship are compounded by a lack of interest in series as opposed to television movies. Yet Carlton's rural medical series *Peak Practice,* and *Inspector Morse* (4 x 120 mins), were acquired in 2002 by Encore International, part of the American Liberty Media corporation. Encore manages slots for foreign programming on its daily *Jiayi* prime-time block at 9.45pm on CCTV8, which is available in 80 million homes (Carter, 2003a, p. 30; Driscoll, 2003; Waller, 2002f). In 2002, *Peak Practice* became *Jiayi*'s highest-rating drama series (Waller, 2002f). In Hong Kong TVB and ATV buy the best American dramas for their low-rating English-language channels, but not much from Britain. In Korea infrequent sales, usually of television movies, take place with cable stations (Dramanet, Q Channel, OCN – Orion Cinema Network) rather than the terrestrial networks, whose schedules are dominated by local productions (Driscoll, 2003; Hansen, 2003; Waterman and Rogers, 1994). Sales of period drama are limited to educational broadcasters in the region, including EBS in South Korea.

Factual programming

The volume of factual programme sales is low because of a lack of slots in markets where 'the bulk of the available programming tends to be purely entertainment oriented, with comparatively little content devoted to educational, cultural or non-commercial children's programming' (Chadha and Kavoori, 2000, p. 429; also Driscoll, 2003). In addition to commercial considerations, sales to some territories in the region (China, Malaysia, Singapore) are also limited by what is deemed politically acceptable (Ibid.; Cunningham and Jacka, 1996, p. 204). Straight sales of uncontentious programmes about wildlife and science, which do not focus on Britain, work best in all markets, with little demand for anything else. For example, CCTV has taken event and natural history programming from BBC Worldwide, including *Walking with Dinosaurs*, *The Human Body* and *Ultimate Killers* (C. Johnson, 2001). Reality-based footage shows on crime, or shows about luxury lifestyles, work well on some cable and transnational satellite channels (Driscoll, 2003).

Of all the markets in the region, Japan offers the greatest potential rewards. NHK's science division has been a buyer and co-producer of science and natural history programmes for many years, but limited slots on the terrestrial

networks were cut at the beginning of 2003, reducing access to its satellite outlets, which pay less, and have lower audiences (Roberts, 2003). TV Asahi, the
most news and information-oriented of the Japanese commercial networks,
functions as a co-producer on a small number of 'event' programmes, including Wall to Wall's *Ancient Egyptians* and *Walking with Dinosaurs*. Japanese
commercial network NTV acquired Granada's celebrity special *Living with
Michael Jackson* in 2002.

Formats

The most high-profile entertainment formats have launched in the largest
markets. TBS airs *Who Wants to Be a Millionaire?*, the first Western game show
ever sold to Japan, and the format has also been sold to China and Hong Kong.
A Mandarin version of *The Weakest Link* was launched in China in February
2002, a deal having been struck with the advertising company Mindworks, to
produce the show with Beijing-based Nanjing TV for syndication to regional
stations (Carter, 2003a, p. 29). The format was sold to Fuji Television in Japan
in 2002.

However, the entry of Western entertainment formats has not been universally welcomed, reflecting the widely held view among political figures and
government agencies that foreign media constitute a threat to Asian culture and
values (see Chadha and Kavoori, 2000, p. 417). Robert Chua, the co-founder
of China Entertainment Television (CETV), has attacked formats like *The Weakest Link* and *Fear Factor* as 'degratainment television'. This was because they
'attack people's dignity and encourage the audience to enjoy others' pain and
discomfort' and made 'a spectacle of negative emotions including aggression,
rudeness and a desire to humiliate' (Waller, 2002g).

The cross-cultural limitations of adapting *The Weakest Link* are partially born
out by the experience of TVB's Cantonese-language channel Jade in Hong
Kong. TVB was one of the first in the region to take *The Weakest Link*, stripping
it five nights a week in the autumn of 2001 at 8.30pm against *Who Wants to Be
a Millionaire?*, which debuted on rival ATV in May 2001 (Anon., 2001c). But
The Weakest Link only lasted one season. According to Stephen Chan, Assistant
General Manager of TVB, *The Weakest Link* 'was a typical case of cultural differences. ... The show started off with poor ratings and we faced a lot of
criticism for the confrontational host. Although the BBC has very strict rules
about the show, we adapted it and ratings went up' (cited in Waller, 2003f). But
the failure of formats like *Who Wants to Be a Millionaire?* and *The Weakest Link*
to survive beyond their first season was also attributed to the audience's tendency to become quickly bored with stripped shows (Ibid.). Other cultural
barriers include a reluctance to lose face by appearing on such programmes, and

the lack of emotion expressed by Hong Kong participants even when winning 'big money' prizes (Ibid.). Having experimented with straight quizzes, TVB decided to revert back to in-house formats based around local celebrities, which are more popular with viewers.

British participation in the local production of formats is rare because of a lack of cultural and institutional proximity, reinforced by reliance on agents rather than direct relationships with broadcasters and producers. In China involvement in local production is only possible by securing a local partner, which allows foreign players to bypass tighter censorship and scheduling restrictions on foreign imports (Carter, 2003a, p. 30). To gain experience of the Chinese market, Granada entered a three-year joint venture in 1999 with Beijing-based Yahuan Audio and Video Production Company (YAVPC) to provide production expertise and finance on *Joy Luck Street*, a soap based loosely on *Coronation Street*. Launched in August 2000, the show aired three times a week on eighty local cable networks on a barter basis. The adaptation presented some challenges, not least the need to appeal to both urban and rural audiences (Ibid.). Initially script teams in Britain sent material to Beijing to be worked on by Chinese scriptwriters until the show became established, but careful consideration needed to be given to ideological sensibilities. According to Gary Knight, Executive Director of Commercial Ventures at Granada Enterprises:

> Lots of affairs in a plotline is fine, as is people doing wrong – so long as they are eventually punished. ... But we always have to be careful how figures of authority are dealt with – they can be criticised but again, only if they are shown to have done wrong. (Cited in Carter, 2003a, p. 30)

Children's programming

Selling children's programmes to the Far East is difficult because Japan and increasingly South Korea are prominent exporters of animation within the region (Iwabuchi, 2000; Cooper-Chen, 1999; Jeremy, 2001b).[4] Japan, in particular, has made its cultural presence felt globally as well through the export of long-running action-adventure animation series (*Pokémon, Dragon Ball Z, Digimon*) and computer games, supported by sophisticated licensing campaigns (Jeremy, 2001b).

As in other regions of the world, the British presence is confined primarily to the export of programmes for younger children. But even here there are limitations based on different perceptions of what is deemed to be 'cute' or appealing in comparison with local and regional productions, which are often action-based and targeted at older audiences. According to one sales executive:

If you go in as a British distributor and try to sell to these people, they're going to say, 'Why on earth do we want this? It's not cute to look at. It's not full of action.' And basically kids like cute or violent. And some of the British stuff is just a bit too quirky for that. (Driscoll, 2003; also Weatherford, 2003)

Yet children's programming does represent a good example of the different strategies required to access Asian markets. As in other territories, terrestrial television, rather than the satellite sector, is the Holy Grail for pre-school programming because it constitutes a platform for ancillary rights exploitation. Indeed, some properties already have an established presence in the lucrative Japanese market, based on earlier broadcast airings. The 1960s supermarionation series *Thunderbirds*, sold by Carlton International, was re-launched in 2002 on NHK 2 and cable and is a major property for the Japanese licensing agent Tohokushinsha in the DVD market (Driscoll, 2003). The enduring success of *Pingu* and *Thomas the Tank Engine* in the Japanese consumer products market was one of the motivating factors behind the purchase of these properties by HIT Entertainment in 2001 and 2002 respectively (HIT Entertainment, 2001; HIT Entertainment, 2002). In 2002, *Thomas the Tank Engine* was re-launched on Fuji TV, and HIT Entertainment renewed a master licence over five years for *Pingu* with Sony Creative (HIT Entertainment, 2002, p. 14).

However, the success of some properties needs to be viewed against the domination of local and regional productions. In Japan domestic animation is estimated to account for almost all animation transmissions (Jeremy, 2001b, p. 5). NHK's long-running daily pre-school block *Together with Mother*, and Fuji TV's weekly *Ponkikki* slot for younger children on Saturday mornings, provide few sales opportunities because most content is sourced locally (Weatherford, 2003). The best opportunities lie with the smallest commercial network, TV Tokyo 12, which acquired an estimated 15 per cent of its animation from overseas in 1999 (Jeremy, 2001b). British acquisitions have included *Bob the Builder* and for a short while *Teletubbies*, which has also sold to broadcasters in South Korea and Hong Kong (BBC Worldwide, 1999).

The key to securing a terrestrial slot in Japan and building an ancillary rights business is to find sponsors, 'which is very difficult if you're a foreign company unless you have a property that people want to spend big bucks to support' (Weatherford, 2003). This requires local partners, who put together the sponsors that fund the time slot. For *Bob the Builder* HIT concluded an all-rights deal in 2000 with ShoPro (Shogakukan Production) part of Shogakukan Inc., one of the largest Japanese publishing companies. Although the property was unknown in Japan, its success in other markets proved decisive (Jeremy, 2001b, p. 5). ShoPro produce a sponsored half-hour weekly show for TV Tokyo 12,

which airs every Wednesday at 7.30am. *Bob the Builder*, the only imported programme, features as a ten-minute segment. As part of the all-rights deal, ShoPro
organises the television broadcast, the video release, locates partners for merchandising and handles publishing in-house.

China has the potential to be a huge market with an audience of over 300
million children. BBC Worldwide sold *Teletubbies* to CCTV in 2002, the first
BBC pre-school series to be broadcast in China (BBC Worldwide, 2002). However, other players are more wary because licence fees are low, and the market
for licensed products is characterised by piracy, which makes exporters careful
about what they release onto the market (Weatherford, 2003). These concerns
were underlined by one sales executive:

> I'm nervous about selling to China, because I don't think the protection for
> copyright is very effective. And my fear is that you'd not only lose a large part of
> your Chinese business, but once the pirates start manufacturing to satisfy demand,
> they're going to look at the export potential for those illegal products and then you
> start detracting from other developed territories. ... It's fine to sell dramas and
> documentaries [to CCTV], but the revenues generated by video and licensing, if
> you can't protect those revenue streams, there's very little point in going in and
> there are dangers in going, in that those illegal products will find their way to other
> territories.

By contrast, South Korea constitutes a more reliable market with consistent
demand for educational programming, including pre-school material on KBS,
EBS and SBC. In order to protect its own animation industry, South Korea has
sought to limit Japanese animation to one third of transmissions on the free-to-
air channels (Cooper-Chen, 1999, p. 299). This has benefited Western
producers to a degree, and *Bob the Builder*, *Teletubbies* and most recently *The
Fimbles* have all aired on KBS. But like Japan, sales are often dependent on all-
rights deals with local partners who can secure sponsorship to fund broadcast
slots.

For instance, in 2001 HIT Entertainment secured a 130 x half-hour format
deal with KBS for its American-produced property *Barney*, which airs five days
a week in an afternoon slot. KBS produces the show using the original characters, but the scripts have been modified to appeal to a young Korean audience.
However, as is the case with Japan, the deal rested on selling all rights to a
Korean partner – in this case the Korean licensing agency RJ Wood, who locate
sponsors and exploit ancillary rights with local partners for video, publishing and
merchandising – to make the project financially worthwhile. A fee is paid for the
format and guarantees are given against licensing, merchandising and videocas-

sette. Television sales are therefore just the start of more profitable revenue streams from character merchandising.

Review

Television in Australia, New Zealand and East Asia reasserts the importance of cultural specificities. British programmes do have a strong presence on Australian and New Zealand screens because of the commonalities of language, culture and history, which have encouraged British exporters to target both countries as export destinations. In East Asia, by contrast, the British presence is marginal because of limited cultural affinities, reinforced by a preference for local programming and the growing strength of regional producers. The limited financial returns from Asia mean that greater attention is given to more financially rewarding and culturally proximate markets in North America and Western Europe, which play a greater role in the funding of productions.

This is not to say that Asia is unimportant as a market. Japan is an important territory for some children's properties and a limited number of factual co-productions, and China undoubtedly represents a growing market, but it seems unlikely that Britain will ever gain a significant audiovisual presence in the region. This opportunity belongs largely to those transnational players (Star TV/News Corporation, Time Warner, Liberty Media), who have established channels and joint ventures in the region and have a longer-term strategy of penetrating markets with localised media product, targeted at different language markets, foremost China. With the exception of BBC Worldwide's participation with Discovery in Animal Planet Asia and Animal Planet Japan, and the global distribution of news channel BBC World, there are no British players with the financial or programming resources to target the Asian market on the scale of global players like News Corporation or regional players like TVB.

Yet even in Australia and New Zealand, the British presence remains largely confined to public service outlets in the traditionally strong areas of drama, factual programming and programming for younger children. The presence of British drama on the ABC and TVNZ's TV One is much stronger than on any other overseas outlets, based on longstanding relationships with British suppliers. Sales of British programmes to commercial outlets are limited by a lack of congruence between these channels' commercial priorities, which involve the targeting of younger audiences, and the public service origins of many British programmes. British drama skews too old. There are only limited slots for factual programming, and programming for younger children is of little interest to advertisers. In this respect Britain does indeed function as a complementary public service alternative, as a niche purveyor of 'high' culture in the form of documentaries, 'oddball' comedy, detective series and thrillers. Quiz, talent and lifestyle formats represent the key growth area for British sales to commercial broadcasters in Australia and New Zealand, but to derive the full economic benefits from these, British players need to investigate the possibilities of local production more closely.

Notes

1. A small licence fee goes to a separate organisation, New Zealand On Air, for distribution to targeted areas such as public radio, and small levels of production intended to foster New Zealand's culture and identity (Herman and McChesney, 1997, p. 183; Lealand, 1996, p. 216).

2. A survey undertaken in 1989 found that over 91 per cent of programmes in South Korea, over 94 per cent of programmes in Japan and 61 per cent of programmes in Hong Kong were produced domestically, with the vast majority of imports coming from the US (Waterman and Rogers, 1994, pp. 100–1).

3. In 2002, BBC World was granted a licence by the Chinese State Administration for Radio, Film and TV (SARFT) for distribution in hotel rooms and foreign compounds in China (Broadcast, 2001).

4. By 1992 animation constituted 58.3 per cent of Japan's television exports of 19,456 hours, primarily to other Asian, European and North American markets (Cooper-Chen, 1999, p. 295).

Conclusion

This study began with the idea that a mixed system of public and private broadcasting incorporating public service principles for both publicly funded and commercially funded free-to-air television gave British television an advantage in international markets. Britain's broadcasting ecology resulted in the production of a broad range of programming, which satisfied domestic demand as well as providing scope for exploitation of *some* programming in the international marketplace. The export of costume dramas and natural history programming allowed Britain to assume the role of a public service 'quality' British alternative to mass-market fiction and entertainment from America. However, as we have seen, the tendency in television systems the world over, including Britain, has been to prioritise commercial television and locally produced programming, affecting what is produced domestically and the type of television that circulates in global markets.

Britain is a significant exporter of television programmes and formats, and via the BBC there is a small presence in channels aimed at overseas markets. But Britain, positioned neither at the periphery nor at the centre of television trade flows, is not really a global player of magnitude because it lacks the distribution and hardware capability to secure a more permanent presence for its programming in global markets, in contrast to American-based transnational players. Programmes produced in Britain are more likely to feature as 'filler' in foreign schedules. With the exception of some formats (*Who Wants to Be a Millionaire?*) and factual events (*Walking with Dinosaurs*), British programme exports do not exert a cultural impact that captures the imagination of overseas buyers and audiences. Moreover, although the revenues from television programme exports are significant and growing, it is also important to recognise that they represent only a small proportion (£430 million in 2001) of total industry revenues of £7.7 billion in 2001 (ITC, 2002a, app. 1, p. 3).

It is also clear that the most attractive British programmes and formats in international markets are not always those that best reflect the diversity of British society because the need to overcome cultural barriers diminishes the inclusion of social, political and cultural content aimed specifically at British audiences. Much of the 'ordinary' day-to-day television produced for the British domestic market has very little international potential. The domestic context of British production, largely funded by free-to-air broadcasters, has prioritised production for domestic audiences to satisfy advertiser interests and/or meet public service obligations. Popular soaps (*EastEnders*, *Coronation Street*) and entertainment and factual programmes dealing with domestic themes are undoubtedly popular in the domestic marketplace, but are too culturally specific to attract overseas audiences, who have a preference for their own locally produced 'soaps' and entertainment.

However, financial pressures arising from channel proliferation and market fragmentation have made overseas revenues more important, encouraging broadcasters and producers to promote entertainment-based formats, high-profile drama, factual productions and children's programmes that have a wider value internationally. In terms of cultural goals, the danger lies in a shift towards programming that is more attuned to the international marketplace at the expense of distinctive and diverse programming created specifically for British audiences.

Those properties that work best internationally are increasingly those that mask their British origins through local production, production technique and the choice of subject matter in a process comprising the global production of the local and the localisation of the global. Producers either 'draw on the codes and conventions' of the 'globally popular' to increase the appeal of their products in international markets – seen most clearly in universally popular wildlife, natural history and science programming, animation and action-based drama, which can be re-voiced and indigenised. Or they seek to localise their products to appeal to a differentiated global market – seen in the local adaptation of entertainment, fiction and factual formats. It is those programmes and formats that suppress national origins that have the greatest potential overseas and it is in these programmes and formats that the bulk of British trade is increasingly accomplished. But programmes that focus predominantly on Britain – most drama, situation comedies, news, current affairs, documentaries and formats in their original form – have little overseas appeal because of their cultural specificity.

As we have seen, the reception and presence of British programmes overseas is affected by a variety of factors. These include the regulatory environment, levels of domestic production, the context of reception (scheduling, promotion), the culture of distinctive nationally based television ecologies, and the views of those who purchase programmes, who are making decisions based on their understanding of domestic audiences, channel requirements and the prevailing television culture. Trade flows are indeed much more diverse and complicated than the crudity suggested by cultural imperialism.

British detective series, high-budget literary adaptations and landmark factual programming are prized where, for reasons of cost, there are no domestic alternatives. However, the demand for British detective series and costume dramas seems to be diminishing in the face of a preference for local productions and the ageing audiences these British programmes attract, marginalising their presence still further to public service outlets. The demand for factual programming is limited by a lack of slots in overseas schedules, and by a preference for a narrow range of content with low cultural barriers, such as wildlife, natural history and science programming, which are increasingly dependent on securing co-production funding in America. Exports of children's television are characterised by the success of a small number of global pre-school brands (*Teletubbies*, *Bob the Builder*), where broadcast exposure functions as a platform for generating ancillary revenues from video and consumer products.

Analysis of trade flows more than ever underlines the importance of cultural proximity, the significance of domestic production in national markets and the impact of cultural discount, where programmes rooted in one culture will be less appealing in another. In the case of Britain, the English language has proved to be a decisive factor affording preferential access to those territories that form part of the wealthy English-language geolinguistic region – foremost North America, but including Australia and New Zealand. Conversely, a lack of cultural proximity, reinforced by language differences, and combined with a preference for local production, have contributed to the more uneven impact of British programming in other markets, notably in Asia and Western Europe.

But even in its most culturally proximate markets – those sharing commonalities of language, culture and history – the bulk of programming produced in Britain still circulates on the margins on public service outlets and niche channels in the cable and satellite sector. In America, for example, there is strong interest in British ideas, innovation and talent, but not necessarily British content, which is rarely shown outside the confines of PBS or the basic cable channels. Institutional proximity means that public service-imbued drama and factual programming appeals to those channels that share a public service ethos with Britain, but do not have the resources to fund a full range of public service programming themselves. They include PBS in America, public service channels in the smaller anglophile markets of Sweden and the Netherlands, and public service channels in the culturally proximate territories of Australia and New Zealand. However, this is a declining and ageing market, and it is noticeable that programming produced in Britain has failed to make any significant impact on more mainstream commercial channels in Western Europe, America, Australia, New Zealand and the Far East.

The growing significance of domestic programming in Britain's major export markets is reflected in the declining importance of sales of completed programmes and the growth in revenues from the licensing of consumer products, video/DVD, co-production, the sale of formats and local production. Although sales of completed programmes still predominate (40 per cent of sales in 2003), the shift towards other revenues signifies a change in strategies to overcome cultural discount and the low prices available from sales of completed programmes.

For historical and literary-based drama and factual event programming, exporters have sought co-production finance from America and pre-sales in the larger European markets. Co-production funding is beneficial because it allows the pooling of financial resources and improved access to other markets. But it offers only a partial solution to the pressures on domestic funding because co-productions tend to be restricted to a small number of high-cost productions with cross-cultural appeal. There are also drawbacks relating to the downward pressures on domestic licence fees in the expectation of co-production finance. One solution might be to emulate American exporters by producing more American-style drama, which might attract a wider range of co-production partners, but there is no guarantee that these will fare better in the international marketplace, notwithstanding the risk of alienating domestic audiences.

Another strategy involves a focus on global brands, seen most clearly in the children's market and in the marketing of formats, where ancillary revenues from product licensing, exploitation in other media and sponsorship are becoming more important than revenues from sales to broadcasters. But this strategy also carries risks for the domestic market. The decline in licence fees for children's programmes worldwide is largely due to the expectation of export success and the assumption that producers will be able to top up income from foreign and ancillary earnings. This works against those programmes, such as children's drama or information programming, that have little potential to generate ancillary revenues.

To overcome the difficulties of selling programmes made in Britain and meet the industrial imperative for cheaper locally produced programmes, exporters are paying greater attention to the exploitation of fiction, game-show, reality and makeover formats, which allow for local adaptation and customisation. In pursuing this strategy, Britain is no longer predominantly a complementary provider of public service-type programming, which maintains and reproduces Britain's literary and cultural heritage, but a supplier of universally appealing concepts whose British origins are masked, and which are internationally integrated from the start in an interplay of the global and local. Hybridisation occurs to create something new but recognisable in overseas markets. These are programmes that can be indigenised by the receiving culture, and they are markedly different from the identifiably British historical or literary-based drama on which Britain's international success was assumed to rest in the past.

Formats and local production are one way of overcoming the reluctance to buy productions made in Britain, but there are some disadvantages. Local production in overseas territories contributes less to the financial well-being of the British production sector as opposed to the local market where the format has been sold. Moreover, a shift towards domestic productions that can be formatted in overseas markets runs the risk of developing a narrower range of content with international potential at the expense of diverse programming created specifically for British audiences. Nor are formats a complete solution for overcoming cultural discount and the industrial and cultural barriers in national markets. In America, for example, the adaptation of scripted formats for the networks in the 1990s has yet to deliver a sustained hit in an intensely competitive market for network programmes. Moreover, some formats falter in foreign markets, as demonstrated in Southern Europe and Asia, because the underlying concept, rooted in one culture, fails to connect with the style and values to which audiences have become accustomed, regardless of local production.

The narrow demands of the international marketplace do not always fit easily with the more varied demands of the British domestic market, which suggests that there are inherent dangers in prioritising international concerns and a narrow range of exportable programming over domestic concerns in respect of policy. The public service rationale behind free-to-air television was meant to ensure that British audiences see their lives and the pluralistic nature of British society reflected on screen. But this conflicts with what is assumed to work in international markets.

As we saw in Chapter 3, television exports briefly became an object of concern for the Labour government in 1999, in its efforts to promote Britain as a 'brand' in a media and communications economy increasingly characterised by global flows of finance, information and images. However, the idea that television exports might function as a showcase for Britishness and British life is contradicted by the realities of an international marketplace where 'Britishness' is not a major selling point. The debate merely served to highlight the tension between the culturally specific and varied demands of the domestic market, and industrial goals associated with international competitiveness and the production of internationally attractive programmes and concepts, which need to satisfy a broader range of cross-cultural tastes and circumstances.

A more significant impact on export performance is likely to come with the implementation of the 2003 Communications Act and its fundamental reform of the broadcasting sector. The debate surrounding the passage of the legislation served to open up broader issues connected with export performance and the domestic market.

The Labour government's acceptance of the forces of globalisation has led to a shift from a focus on exports and the promotion of domestic broadcasters as global champions towards the relaxation of foreign ownership rules for commercial free-to-air television. This has been done in the expectation that inward investment from America will allow British companies to break out of the confines of the domestic market and perform more effectively internationally as part of larger global concerns. However, Labour's embrace of globalisation and the benefits of inward investment sits uneasily next to the idea of national culture and British television serving British audiences with programming designed specifically for those audiences.

The decision to allow American investors to acquire commercial free-to-air broadcasters (ITV, Five) may lead to a better global performance, with inward investment resulting in a better-funded industry, better programmes and more exports. But there is no evidence that this will happen, and it raises questions about what type of programming is likely to be made for diverse British audiences in future. Even if American imports do not end up dominating the schedules of free-to-air commercial channels, there is a risk that commercial television will be geared even more towards an internationally or US-focused programme mix that serves American commercial interests, leaving less room for programming that is resolutely national or local in its address.

Proposals, arising from amendments to the Communications Act, to change the way that programme rights are allocated between broadcasters and independent producers also promise to have profound implications for the export sector and the role of broadcaster-distributors, in particular. The BBC's commercial arm, BBC Worldwide, is Britain's only significant global player, accounting for over 50 per cent of British television export revenues, and with significant international partnerships and overseas channel interests. Encouraged by successive governments, it has promoted its role as a national champion in global markets. But its dominance in the programme-supply market has affected the capacity of other players to be effective exporters. Changes in the rules, allowing independent producers to retain more secondary rights in the programmes they have created, promise to weaken the international activities of broadcaster-distributors, foremost BBC Worldwide, many of whose international hits have come from the independent sector. However, questions remain as to whether independent producers have the capacity to make a significant impact in international markets. A small number of the larger independent production companies have already demonstrated their willingness to engage on the international stage, but it is significant that their activities are predominantly focused on format sales and local production in the USA, the most culturally proximate, largest and richest of Britain's overseas markets – underlining the importance of the American market above all others.

To conclude, there are limits to the scale of Britain's overseas presence. In spite of globalising trends, this survey of British television in overseas markets demonstrates the continued importance of ethnicity, the strength of local production, the context of reception and the role of gatekeepers who regulate the flow of imports. In this respect the implementation of policies to raise levels of exports can only ever have a limited impact. However, the reform of British television and its orientation away from public service principles towards commercial priorities is already having an impact on the type of programmes and formats produced for the domestic market, with implications for what is exported. This is mirrored by a shift in priorities in Britain's major markets towards the commercial model and infotainment. With the passage of the Communications Act in 2003, British television stands on the threshold of significant changes. The possible integration of British commercial broadcasting and independent production companies as part of larger global/American concerns suggests that global imperatives will have a greater impact on British production in future. However, the impact of inward investment on export performance is likely to be less significant than the impact on Britain's own national television ecology.

Bibliography

ABC (Australian Broadcasting Corporation), *Annual Report 2001–2002*. (Sydney: ABC, 2002). Available in PDF format at <www.abc.net.au/corp/ar/02> (accessed 23 September 2003).

Acheson, K., and Maule, C., *Much Ado About Culture: North American Trade Disputes* (Ann Arbor: University of Michigan Press, 1999).

Aksoy, A., and Robins, K., 'Hollywood for the 21st Century: Global Competition for Critical Mass in Image Markets', *Cambridge Journal of Economics*, vol. 16, 1992, pp. 1–22.

Alvarado, M., 'The "Value" of TV Drama. Why Bother to Produce it?', *Television and New Media*, vol. 1, no. 3, 2000, pp. 307–19.

Alvarado, M., and Stewart, J., *Made for Television: Euston Films Limited* (London: BFI, 1985).

Anan, Nadja (Head of Series and Animation, ProSieben Television), Telephone Interview, 7 February 2002.

Anderson, B., *Imagined Communities* (London: Verso, 1983).

Andryc, Joel (Executive Vice President, Kids' Programming and Development, Fox Family), Interview, Los Angeles, 19 September 2001.

Ang, I., *Watching Dallas* (London: Methuen, 1985).

Ang, I., 'Globalisation and Culture', *Continuum*, vol. 8, no. 2, 1994, pp. 323–5.

Ang, I., *Living Room Wars* (London: Routledge, 1996).

Anon., 'World's Biggest Market Still Tough Nut to Crack, but Regional TV Gains Strength', *Broadcasting & Cable's TV International*, 1 November 1999, p. 5.

Anon., 'More Upheaval for CITV as Granada Rejigs Kids', *Broadcast*, 9 November 2001a, p. 1.

Anon., 'Vertical Integration Hits Animation Market', *Screen Digest*, May 2001b, p. 157.

Anon., ' "Link" vs. "Millionaire" ', *Variety*, 6 August 2001c, p. 55.

Anon., 'Major Local Difficulties. Mipcom was Tough for the US studios', *The Financial Times,* 22 October 2002a, p. 26.

Anon., 'Breaking the Law of Averages', *TBI's Guide to Formats*, April/May, 2002b, p. 17.

Anon., 'Granada America to Absorb Carlton's US Brand', 7 November 2003. Available at <www.c21media.net/news/detail.asp?area=2&article=18112> (accessed December 2003).

Appadurai, A., 'Disjuncture and Difference in the Global Cultural Economy', in M. Featherstone (ed.), *Global Culture* (London: Sage, 1990), pp. 295–311.

Arata, Giovanna (Head of International Productions, Mediatrade, Gruppo Mediaset), Interview, Milan, 12 June 2002.

Baker, M., 'Dyke: a Long-running TV Drama', *Broadcast*, 21 November 1997, pp. 16–17.

Banerjee, I., 'The Locals Strike Back? Media Globalization and Localization in the New Asian Television Landscape', *Gazette*, vol. 64, no. 6, 2002, pp. 517–35.

Barker, C., *Global Television: An Introduction* (Oxford: Blackwell, 1997).

Barker, C., *Television, Globalization and Cultural Identities* (Buckingham: Open University Press, 1999).

Battocchio, Fabrizio (Head of Format Department, Reti Televisive Italiane, Gruppo Mediaset), Interview, Milan, 11 June 2002.

BBC (British Broadcasting Corporation), *Initial Submission to the Government's Communications Review* (London: BBC, 4 July 2000).

BBC, *ITC Review of the Programme Supply Market. Evidence from the BBC* (London: BBC, 18 October, 2002). Available in PDF format at <www.itc.org.uk/uploads/BBC1.pdf> (accessed December 2002).

BBC Worldwide, *Annual Report 1998/1999* (London: BBC Worldwide, 1999). Available at <www.bbcworldwide.com/report99> (accessed December 2003).

BBC Worldwide *Annual Report 1999/2000* (London: BBC Worldwide, 2000). Available at <www.bbcworldwide.com/report2000> (accessed December 2003).

BBC Worldwide, *Annual Review 2000/2001* (London: BBC Worldwide, 2001). Available at <www.bbcworldwide.com/review> (accessed December 2003).

BBC Worldwide, *Annual Review 2001/2002* (London: BBC Worldwide, July 2002a). Available at <www.bbcworldwide.com/aboutus/corpinfo/annualreps/ annualreport2002/default.htm> (accessed December 2003).

BBC Worldwide, *The ITC Review of the Programme Supply Market in British Broadcasting* (London: BBC, October 2002b). Available in PDF format at <www.itc.org.uk/uploads/BBC_Worldwide.pdf> (accessed December 2002).

BBC Worldwide, *Report and Financial Statements for the Year ended 31 March 2002* (London: BBC Worldwide, 2002c).

BBC Worldwide, *Annual Review 2002/2003* (London: BBC Worldwide, 2003a). Available at <www.bbcworldwide.com/aboutus/corpinfo/annualreps/ annualreport2003/default.html> (accessed December 2003).

BBC Worldwide, *Report and Financial Statements for the Year ended 31 March 2003* (London: BBC Worldwide, 2003b).

BBC Worldwide, ' "Walking with . . ." Brand is Monster Hit for BBC Worldwide', BBC Worldwide Press Release, 15 July 2003c. Available at <www.bbc.co.uk/pressoffice/commercial/worldwidestories/pressreleases/2003/07_july/walking_with_brand.shtml> (accessed December 2003).

Bell, A., 'An Endangered Species: Local Programming in the New Zealand Television Market', *Media, Culture and Society*, vol. 17, 1995, pp. 181–200.

Benthues, Jobst (Head of Entertainment, ProSieben Television), Interview, Munich, 18 February 2002.

Biancolli, Nathalie (Fiction Acquisitions, AB Groupe), and Queme, Isabelle (Documentary Acquisitions, AB Groupe), Interview, Paris, 19 March 2002.

Biltereyst, D., and Meers, P., 'The International Telenovela Debate and the Contra-Flow Argument: A Reappraisal', *Media, Culture and Society*, vol. 22, 2000, pp. 393–413.

Bin., Z., 'Greater China', in A. Smith (ed.), *Television. An International History* (Oxford: Oxford University Press, 1998), 2nd edn, pp. 247–53.

Bin, Z., 'Mouthpiece or Money-spinner? The Double Life of Chinese Television in the Late 1990s', *International Journal of Cultural Studies*, vol. 2, no. 3, 1999, pp. 291–305.

Blair, T., *New Britain: My Vision of a Young Country* (London: Fourth Estate, 1996).

Blanchard, S., 'The "Wrong Type" of Television: New Labour, British Broadcasting and the Rise and Fall of an Exports "Problem" ', Paper Presented at AHRB Seminar, Birkbeck College, London, September 2001.

Blicq, Annette (Head of Acquisitions, Canal Jimmy), Interview, Paris, 22 March 2002.

Boddy, W., 'The Quiz Show', in G. Creeber (ed.), *The Television Genre Book* (London: BFI, 2001), pp. 79–81.

Bollini, Mussi (Head of Children's Programmes, Rai Tre), Liberi, Annalisa (Children's Programmes Acquisition, Rai Tre) and Di Nitto, Laura (Children's Programmes, Public Relations and Promotion, Rai Tre), Interview, Rome, 13 June 2002.

Bonner, F., *Ordinary Television* (London: Sage, 2003).

Bourdieu, P., *Distinction: A Social Critique of the Judgement of Taste* (London: Routledge, 1984).

Boyd-Barrett, O., 'Media Imperialism: Towards an International Framework for the Analysis of Media Systems', in J. Curran, M. Gurevitch and J. Woollacott (eds), *Mass Communication and Society* (London: Arnold, 1977), pp. 116–35.

Boyd-Barrett, O., 'International Communication and Globalization: Contradictions and Directions', in A. Mohammadi (ed.), *International Communication and Globalization* (London: Sage, 1997), pp. 11–26.

Boyd-Barrett, O., 'Media Imperialism Reformulated', in D. Thussu (ed.), *Electronic Empires* (London: Arnold, 1998), pp. 157–76.

Branston, G. and Stafford, R., *The Media Student's Book* (London: Routledge, 2003), 3rd edn.

Broadcast, 'BBC Gets China Licence', *Broadcast*, 12 January 2001, p. 6.

Bruneau, M-A., 'Up for the prize', *Television Business International*, January/February 2001, pp. 26–31

Bruneau, M-A., 'The Main Event', *Television Business International*, October/ November 2002, pp. 59–64.

BTDA (British Television Distributors Association), 'Brit TV Still Proving a Hit Overseas', Press Release, 20 September 2000. Available at <www.btda.org> (accessed March 2003).

BTDA, *News from the BTDA*, June, no. 3, 2001. Available in PDF format at <www.btda.org> (accessed December 2003).

BTDA, 'Big Jump in Demand for UK TV Programmes Stateside', Press Release, 12 June 2002. Available in PDF format at <www.btda.org> (accessed March 2003).

BTDA, 'Better Year for Overseas TV Sales in 2002', Press Release, 19 March 2003. Available at <www.btda.org> (accessed December 2003).

BTDA, 'UK TV Exports approach $1 billion for the First Time', Press Release, 13 May 2004. Available at <www.btda.org> (accessed June 2004).

BTDA Board, 'A Funding Lifeline', *News from the BTDA*, 5 March 2002.

Buonanno, M. (ed.), *Imaginary Dreamscapes. Television Fiction in Europe* (Luton: University of Luton Press, 1998).

Buonanno, M. (ed.), *Continuity and Change. Television Fiction in Europe* (Luton: University of Luton Press, 2000).

Burrell, I., 'Foreign Film Makers are Lured to Britain as Industry Enjoys Boom', *The Independent*, 25 November, 2003, p. 10.

C21, Programme Prices Map 2003. Available at <www.c21media.net/resources/ index.asp?area=45> (accessed December 2003).

Caminada, Charles (Chief Operating Officer, HIT Entertainment), Interview, London, 4 June 2001.

Cantor, M., and Cantor, J., 'American Television in the International Marketplace', *Communication Research*, vol. 13, no. 3, 1986, pp. 509–20.

Carlisle, Candace (Chief Operating Officer, BBC Sales Company), Interview, New York, 11 September 2001.

Carlton Communications plc, *Response to the Consultation on Media Ownership Rules* (London: Carlton, January 2002a). Available in PDF format at <www.culture.gov.uk/creative/media_ownership_replies.html> (accessed December 2003).

Carlton Communications plc, *Annual Report and Accounts 2001/2002* (London: Carlton, November 2002b). Available in PDF format at <www.carltonplc.co.uk/carlton/financials/reports> (accessed December 2003).

Carlton International Media Ltd, *Directors' Report and Accounts for the Year ended 30 September 2001* (London: Carlton, 6 September 2002).

Carter, M., 'Breaking Through the Wall', *Broadcast International*, 21 March 2003a, pp. 29–30.

Carter, M., 'The World at his Feet', *Broadcast*, 6 June 2003b, p. 31.

Cassy, J., 'Sexy Again in the City', *The Guardian G2*, 12 May 2003, pp. 4–5.

Cauquelin, Christine (Head of Documentaries, Canal Plus), Interview, Paris, 21 March 2002.

Cederborg, Annika (Acquisitions Executive, Children and Youth, SVT Programme Acquisitions), Interview, Stockholm, 23 April 2002.

Celador International Ltd, *Financial Statements for the Year ended 30 September 2002* (London: Celador, 6 December 2002).

Celador Productions Ltd, *Financial Statements for the Year ended 30 September 2002* (London: Celador, 6 December 2002).

Chadha, K., and Kavoori, A., 'Media Imperialism Revisited: Some Findings from the Asian Case', *Media, Culture and Society*, vol. 22, 2000, pp. 415–32.

Chalaby, J., 'Transnational Television in Europe. The Role of Pan-European Channels', *European Journal of Communication*, vol. 17, no. 2, 2002, pp. 183–203.

Channel Four, *Channel 4's Relationship with the Independent Production Sector. A Creative and Commercial Partnership, Submission to the ITC Review of the Programme Supply Market* (London: Channel Four, 11 October 2002a). Available in PDF format at <www.itc.org.uk/uploads/Channel_4.pdf> (accessed December 2002).

Channel Four, *Submission to the DCMS/DTI Consultation on the Draft Communications Bill* (London: Channel Four, August 2002b). Available at <www.communicationsbill.gov.uk/responses_organisations.html> (accessed December 2003).

Channel Four, *Report and Financial Statements 2001* (London: Channel Four, 2002c).

Channel Four, *Report and Financial Statements 2002* (London: Channel Four, 2003)

Channel Four, *Report and Financial Statements 2003* (London: Channel Four, 2004).

Channel Four International Ltd, *Annual Report for the Year ended 31 December 2002* (submitted 1 April 2003).

Chapman, G., 'Towards a Geography of the Tube: TV Flows in Western Europe', *Intermedia*, vol. 15, no. 1, January 1987, pp. 10–21.

Chris, C., 'All Documentary, All the Time? Discovery Communications Inc and Trends in Cable Television', *Television and New Media*, vol. 3, no. 1, February 2002, pp. 7–28.

Clarke, S., 'Selling to the US: Promised Land', *Television Europe*, 1 May 2001. Available at <tvinsite.com/television-europe/index.asp?id=27593&article ID=CA83297> (accessed 24 May 2001).

Clarke, S., 'Crunch Time for Drama Schemes', *Financial Times*, 14 October 2002.

Coldefy, Hélène (Conseiller de Programmes, France 3), Interview, Paris, 21 March 2002.

Collins, R., 'Wall-to-Wall "Dallas"? The US–UK Trade in Television', *Screen*, 1986, pp. 66–77.

Collins, R., 'The Language of Advantage: Satellite Television in Western Europe', *Media, Culture and Society*, vol. 11, 1989, pp. 351–71.

Collins, R., *Television: Policy and Culture* (London: Unwin Hyman, 1990).

Collins, R., Garnham, N., and Locksley, G., *The Economics of Television* (London: Sage, 1988).

Cooper-Chen, A., 'An Animated Imbalance. Japan's Television Heroines in Asia', *Gazette*, vol. 61, no. 3–4, 1999, pp. 293–310.

Corsini, Piero (Acquisitions, Rai Tre), Interview, Rome, 14 June 2002.

Cunningham, S., and Jacka, E., *Australian Television and International Mediascapes* (Cambridge: Cambridge University Press, 1996).

Cunningham, S., and Jacka. E., 'Neighbourly Relations? Cross-Cultural Reception Analysis and Australian Soaps in Britain', in A. Sreberny-Mohammadi, D. Winseck, J. McKenna and O. Boyd-Barrett (eds), *Media in Global Context* (London: Arnold, 1997), pp. 299–310.

Currie, D., and Siner, M., 'The BBC: Balancing Public and Commercial Purpose', in A. Graham et al., *Public Purposes in Broadcasting* (Luton: University of Luton Press, 1999).

Curtin, M., *Redeeming the Wasteland: Television Documentary and Cold War Politics* (New Brunswick: Rutgers University Press, 1995).

Dahlberg, Olof (Executive Editor – Documentaries, SVT News and Factual Programmes), Interview, Stockholm, 25 April, 2002.

Dahlgren, P., 'Key Trends in European Television', in J. Wieten, G. Murdock and P. Dahlgren (eds), *Television Across Europe* (London: Sage, 2000), pp. 23–34.

Dauvin, Pauline (Programme Advisor for Youth Department and Fictions Acquisitions, France 3), Interview, Paris, 21 March 2002.

David Graham & Associates, *Out of the Box: The Programme Supply Market in the Digital Age – A Report for the Department for Culture, Media and Sport* (Taunton: David Graham & Associates, 2000).

David Graham & Associates, *Response to the Draft Communications Bill* (Taunton: David Graham & Associates, August 2002). Available at <www.communicationsbill.gov.uk/responses_organisations.html> (accessed December 2003).

Davis, Stephen (President and Chief Executive Officer, Carlton America), Interview, Los Angeles, 20 September 2001.

DCMS (Department for Culture, Media and Sport), *Creative Industries Mapping Document* (London: DCMS, 1998).

DCMS, *Building a Global Audience: British Television in Overseas Markets – A Report by David Graham & Associates* (London: DCMS, 1999a).

DCMS, *The Report of the Creative Industries Task Force Inquiry into UK Television Exports* (London: DCMS, 26 November 1999b).

DCMS, *Creative Industries Exports: Our Hidden Potential* (London: DCMS, 1999c).

DCMS, 'Chris Smith Announces Inquiry Team', Press Release 105/99, 8 April 1999d.

DCMS, 'More Than a Tenth of Global TV Exports Shown at Prime Time are British', Press Release 287/99, 24 November 1999e.

DCMS, *The Future Funding of the BBC* (London: DCMS, 1999f).

DCMS, *Action Plan – Response to TV Exports Inquiry* (London: DCMS, 19 July 2000a).

DCMS, *Creative Industries Task Force Television Inquiry Phase II, Terms of Reference* (London: DCMS, 19 July 2000b).

DCMS, *Creative Industries Mapping Document* (London: DCMS, 2001a).

DCMS, 'Creative Industries: "A Multi-Billion Pound Growing Force"', Press Release 68/01, 13 March 2001b.

DCMS, 'Government Sharpens Focus on Creative Exports', Press Release 81/02, 26 April 2002a.

DCMS, 'Tessa Jowell Announces Review of TV Programme Production Sector', Press Release 170/02, 20 August 2002b.

DCMS, 'Tessa Jowell Responds to ITC Programme Supply Review', Press Release 8/03, 15 January 2003.

De Bens, E. and de Smaele, H., 'The Inflow of American Television Fiction on European Broadcasting Channels Revisited', *European Journal of Communication*, vol. 16, no. 1, 2001, pp. 51–76.

de Sola Pool, I., 'The Changing Flow of Television', *Journal of Communication*, vol. 27, 1977, pp. 139–49.

Dilnott-Cooper, Rupert (Director, Carlton International Media), Interview, London, 20 June 2001.

DNH (Department of National Heritage), *The Future of the BBC: Serving the Nation, Competing Worldwide* (London: HMSO, 1994), Cm 2621.

DNH, *Copy of the Royal Charter for the Continuance of the British Broadcasting Corporation*, May 1996, Cm 3248.

Dorfman, A., and Mattelart, A., *How to Read Donald Duck* (New York: International General Editions, 1975).

Dovey, J., 'Reality TV', in G. Creeber (ed.), *The Television Genre Book* (London: BFI, 2001), pp. 134–7.

Doward, J., 'Sun King Rising in the East', *The Observer*, Business, 12 January 2003, p. 16.

Doyle, G., *Understanding Media Economics* (London: Sage, 2002).

Driscoll, Stephen (Senior Sales Executive, Asia, Carlton International Media), Telephone Interview, 28 May 2003.

DTI/DCMS (Department of Trade and Industry/Department for Culture, Media and Sport), *Regulating Communications: Approaching Convergence in the Information Age* (London: DCMS/DTI, 1998), Cm 4022.

DTI/DCMS, *A New Future for Communications* (London: DCMS/DTI, 2000), Cm 5010.

DTI/DCMS, *Consultation on Media Ownership Rules*, (London: DCMS/DTI, November 2001a). Available in PDF Format at <www.culture.gov.uk/global/consultations/2001> (accessed December 2003).

DTI/DCMS *Summary of Responses to the Consultation on Media Ownership Rules* (London: DCMS/DTI, November 2001b). Available in PDF Format at <www.culture.gov.uk/global/consultations/2001> (accessed December 2003).

DTI/DCMS, *The Draft Communications Bill – The Policy* (London: TSO, May 2002a), Cm 5508-III.

DTI/DCMS, *Communications Bill* (London: TSO, November 2002b), Bill-6-I.

Dupaigne, M., and Waterman, D., 'Determinants of US Television Fiction Imports in Western Europe', *Journal of Broadcasting and Electronic Media*, vol. 42, no. 2, 1998, pp. 208–21.

EAO (European Audiovisual Observatory), 'TV Fiction Programming: Prime Time is Domestic, Off Prime Time is American', based on the fifth Eurofiction survey, *Television Fiction in Europe. Report 2001*, 9 October 2001a. Available at <www.obs.coe.int/about/oea/pr/pr_eurofiction_bis.html.en> (accessed December 2003).

EAO, *Statistical Yearbook* (Strasbourg: EAO, 2001b).

EAO, 'European TV Fiction Production in Decline', 9 October 2001c. Available at <www.obs.coe.int/about/oea/pr/pr_eurofiction.html.en> (accessed December 2003).

EAO, 'The Imbalance of Trade in Films and Television Programmes between North America and Europe Continues to Deteriorate', 9 April 2002. Available at <www.obs.coe.int/about/oea/pr/desequilibre.html.en> (accessed December 2003).

Easter, Geraldine (Head of London Office, Holland Media Group), Interview, London, 4 January 2002.

Easter, Geraldine (UK and European Representative, Nine Network, Australia), Telephone Interview, 3 June 2003.

Eaton, Rebecca (Executive Producer, WGBH, *ExxonMobil Masterpiece Theatre* and *Mystery!*), Interview, Boston, 11 September 2002.

EC (European Commission), *Directive 97/36/EC amending the 1989 'Television without Frontiers' Directive*, OJ L 202 (Brussels: European Commission, 30 July 1997).

EC, *Principles and Guidelines for the Community's Audiovisual Policy in the Digital Age*, COM 657 final (Brussels: European Commission, 14 December 1999).

EC, *Fifth Communication from the Commission to the Council and the European Parliament on the Application of Articles 4 and 5 of the Directive 89/552/EEC 'Television Without Frontiers' for the Period 1999–2000*, COM (2002) 612 final (Brussels: European Commission, 8 November 2002).

Egger, Toni (Vice President, Development, Discovery Health Channel), Interview, Bethesda, 16 September 2002.

Elliott, K., 'American Dream', *Broadcast International*, 1 October 1999, p. 8.

Elliott, K., 'The Deal Maker', *Broadcast International*, 19 January 2001, pp. 8–10.

Elliott, K., 'The BBC's Rights and Wrongs', *Broadcast*, 7 March 2003, pp. 20–1.

Erquicia, Pedro (Director of Current Affairs and Investigative Programmes, Televisión Española, TVE), Interview, Madrid, 24 June 2002.

Featherstone, M., 'Global Culture: An Introduction', in M. Featherstone (ed.), *Global Culture* (London: Sage, 1990), pp. 1–14.

Fejes, F., 'Media Imperialism: An Assessment', *Media, Culture and Society*, vol. 3, 1981, pp. 281–9.

Ferguson, M., 'The Mythology about Globalization', *European Journal of Communication*, vol. 7, 1992, pp. 69–93.

Fichandler, Mark (Senior Director, Development and International Co-Production, Courtroom Television Network), Interview, New York, 19 September 2002.

Fine, Delia (Vice President of Film, Drama and Performing Arts Programming, A&E), Telephone Interview, 8 October 2002.

Fiske, J., *Television Culture* (London: Routledge, 1987).

Frank, Matthew (Managing Director, RDF International), Interview, London, 21 November 2001.

Fraser, F., 'US Networks Look to the UK', *C21*, 30 October 2002a. Available at <www.c21media.net/news/detail.asp?area=2&article=4602> (accessed December 2003).

Fraser, F., 'Tackling the China Problem', *C21* 30 October 2002b. Available at <www.c21media.net/news/detail.asp?area=2&article=4600> (accessed December 2003).

Frater, P., 'Asia's Rising Star', *Broadcast International,* 30 March 2001, p. 36.

Freedman, D., 'National Culture or International Trade? The Labour Government's Media Policies', in S. Nagel (ed.), *Handbook of Global International Policy* (New York/Basel: Marcel Dekker, 2000), pp. 311–34.

Frith, S., 'Introduction: Mr Smith Draws a Map', *Critical Quarterly*, vol. 41, no. 1, 1999, pp. 3–8.

Fry, A., 'Youthful Inventions', *Broadcast Supplement*, 3 April 1998, p. 14.

Fry, A., 'Made-for-TV – Television Movies and the US networks', *Broadcast International*, 30 March 2001, pp. 52–3.

Fry, A., 'Preschool TV: Underage Achievers', *C21*, 1 October 2002a. Available at <www.c21media.net/features/detail.asp?area=2&article=4314> (accessed December 2003).

Fry, A., 'How Much is that Format in the Window?', *C21*, 6 March 2002b. Available at <www.c21media.net/features/detail.asp?area=2&article= 2717> (accessed December 2003).

Fry, A, and Curtis, H., 'A Slice of American Pie', *Broadcast International*, 21 January 2000, pp. 5–9.

Fukuyama, F., *The End of History and the Last Man* (London: Hamish Hamilton, 1992).

Fuller, C., 'Difficult to Cure', *Television Business International*, October/November 2002, pp. 44–8.

García, Susana (Observatorio de Mercados, BocaBoca Producciones), Interview, Madrid, 24 June 2002.

Garnham, N., *Capitalism and Communication* (London: Sage, 1990).

George, S., 'Australian ABC of Public Service TV', *Broadcast International*, 5 October 2001a, pp. 14–15.

George, S., 'Making a Drama Out of a Cash Crisis', *Broadcast International*, 30 March 2001b, pp. 42–3.

George, S., 'Can a Fat Cow Drive Digital?', *Broadcast International*, 12 April 2002a, pp. 36–7.

George, S., 'Drama from Down Under', *Television Business International*, October/ November 2002b, pp. 88–90.

George, S., 'Creating the News at Ten', *Broadcast International*, 21 March 2003a, p. 10.

George, S., 'The Leaders of the Australian Pack', *Broadcast International*, 21 March 2003b, pp. 8–9.

Gillespie, M., *Television, Ethnicity and Cultural Change* (London: Routledge, 1995).

Golding, P., and Harris, P. 'Introduction', in P. Golding and P. Harris (eds), *Beyond Cultural Imperialism* (London: Sage, 1997), pp. 1–9.

Graham, A., and Davies, G., *Broadcasting, Society and Policy in the Multimedia Age* (Luton: University of Luton Press, 1997).

Granada, *Annual Report and Accounts 2000* (London: Granada, 2000).

Granada, *ITC Review of the Programme Supply Market. Granada Submission* (London: Granada, October 2002a). Available in PDF format at <www.itc.org.uk/uploads/Granada.pdf> (accessed December 2002).

Granada, *Annual Report and Accounts 2002* (London: Granada, 27 November 2002b).

Granada International, 'Dramatic Italian Deal for Granada International', Press Release, 19 June 2003. Available at <www.int.granadamedia.com/cs/international/news_story.asp?id=61752> (accessed 17 September 2003).

Granada/Carlton, *Second Interim Results, 12 Months ended 30th September 2003*. Available as PDF file at <www.granada.com> (accessed 26 November 2003).

Grant, Peter (Senior Sales and Marketing Executive, Chrysalis Distribution), Telephone Interview, 28 May 2003.

Grignaffini, Giorgio (Head of Programming, Mediaset) and Stewart, Zelda (Acquisitions Executive, Mediatrade, Gruppo Mediaset), Interview, Milan, 12 June 2002.

Guback, T., *The International Film Industry* (Bloomington: Indiana University Press, 1969).

Guback, T., and Varis, T., *Transnational Communication and Cultural Industries* (Unesco: Reports and Papers on Mass Communication, 1982), no. 92.

Gurin, P., 'An American's View of the UK', *Broadcast*, 18 January 2002, p. 17.

Hall, S., 'Encoding/Decoding', in S. Hall et al. (eds), *Culture, Media, Language* (London: Hutchinson, 1980).

Hall, S., 'The Question of Cultural Identity', in S. Hall, D. Held and T. McGrew (eds), *Modernity and its Futures* (Cambridge: Polity Press, 1992).

Hall, S., 'The Centrality of Culture: Notes on the Cultural Revolutions of Our Time', in K. Thompson (ed.), *Media and Cultural Regulation* (London: Sage, 1997), pp. 207–38.

Hall, S., and Jacques, M., 'Les Enfants de Marx and de Coca-Cola', *New Statesman*, 28 November 1997, pp. 34–6.

Hamelink, C., *Cultural Autonomy in Global Communications* (New York: Longman, 1983).

Hannerz, U., *Transnational Connection* (London: Sage, 1997).

Hansen, Glen (Vice President Sales, Australia, New Zealand, Latin America, Granada International), Telephone Interview, 29 and 30 May 2003.

Hat Trick Productions Ltd, 'ITC Review of the Programme Supply Market. Submission from Hat Trick Productions Ltd', October 2002. Available in PDF format at <www.itc.org.uk/uploads/Hat_Trick.pdf> (accessed December 2002).

Hazleton, J., 'Playing Syndication Games', *Broadcast International*, 21 January 2000a, pp. 14–15.

Hazleton, J., 'US Cable's Own', *Television Business International*, December 2000b, pp. 10–12.

Hazleton, J., 'Remade in the USA', *Television Business International*, October 2000c, pp. 51–6.

Hazleton, J., 'Crossing the Pond', *Television Business International*, October 2001, pp. 65–70.

Hazleton, J., 'Bought in the USA', *Television Business International*, April/May 2002a, pp. 40–4.

Hazleton, J., 'A Very Special Relationship', *Broadcast*, 18 January 2002b, pp. 16–17.

Hazleton, J., 'From Millionaire to Weakest Link?', *Broadcast International*, 12 April 2002c, p. 28.

Herfurth, Hans Wolfgang (Head, International Relations/Programme Purchase, WDR), Interview, Cologne, 22 February 2002.

Herman, E., and McChesney, R., *The Global Media: The New Missionaries of Global Capitalism* (London: Cassell, 1997).

Hesmondhalgh, D., *The Cultural Industries* (London: Sage, 2002).

HIT Entertainment plc, *Annual Report and Accounts 1996* (London: HIT, 1996).

HIT Entertainment plc, *Annual Report and Accounts 1997* (London: HIT, 1997).

HIT Entertainment plc, *Annual Report and Accounts 1998* (London: HIT, 1998).

HIT Entertainment plc, *Annual Report and Accounts 1999* (London: HIT, 1999).

HIT Entertainment plc, *Annual Report and Accounts 2001* (London: HIT, 2001).

HIT Entertainment plc, *Annual Report and Accounts 2002* (London: HIT, 2002).

HIT Entertainment plc, *Annual Report and Accounts 2003* (London: HIT, 2003).

Hobson, D., *Crossroads: Drama of a Soap Opera* (London: Methuen, 1982).

Hodgson, J., ' "Pop Idol" Scores a $1bn Hit in US Market', *The Observer*, Business, 7 September 2003, p. 1.

Holmwood, L., 'Funny Business', *Broadcast*, 21 February 2003, p. 13.

Holt, J., 'Vertical Vision: Deregulation, Industrial Economy and Prime-time Design', in M. Jancovich and J. Lyons (eds), *Quality Popular Television* (London: BFI, 2003), pp. 12–31.

Homewood, Alison (Sales Director EMEIA – Europe, Middle East, India, Asia, BBC Worldwide), Interview, London, 15 November 2001.

Hong, J., 'Reconciliation Between Openness and Resistance. Media Globalization and New Policies of China's Television in the 1990s', in G. Wang, J. Servaes and A. Goonasekera (eds), *The New Communications Landscape* (London: Routledge, 2000), pp. 288–306.

Hong, J., and Hsu, Y-C., 'Asian NICs' Broadcast Media in the Era of Globalization. The Trend of Commercialization and its Impact, Implications and Limits', *Gazette*, vol. 61, no. 3–4, 1999, pp. 225–42.

Horsman, M., and Marshall, A., *After the Nation State* (London: HarperCollins, 1994).

Hoskins, C., Finn, A., and McFadyen, S., 'Television and Film in a Freer International Trade Environment: U.S. Dominance and Canadian Responses', in E. McAnany and K. Wilkinson (eds), *Mass Media and Free Trade* (Austin: University of Texas Press, 1996), pp. 63–91.

Hoskins, C., and McFadyen, S., 'The US Competitive Advantage in the Global Television Market: Is it Sustainable in the New Broadcasting Environment?', *Canadian Journal of Communication*, vol. 16, no. 2, 1991, pp. 1–12. Available at <www.wlu.ca/~wwwpress/jrls/cjc/BackIssues/16.2/hoskins.html> (accessed December 2001).

Hoskins, C., McFadyen, S., and Finn, A., *Global Television and Film: An Introduction to the Economics of the Business* (Oxford: Oxford Univerity Press, 1997).

Hoskins, C., McFadyen, S., Finn, A., and Jäckel, A., 'Film and Television Co-production. Evidence from Canadian-European Experience', *European Journal of Communication*, vol. 10, no. 2, 1995, pp. 221–43.

Hoskins, C., and Mirus, R., 'Reasons for the US Dominance of the International Trade in Television Programmes', *Media, Culture and Society*, vol. 10, no. 4, 1988, pp. 499–515.

Hoskins, C., Mirus, R., and Rozeboom, W., 'US Television Programs in the International Market: Unfair Pricing?', *Journal of Communication*, vol. 39, no. 2, 1989, pp. 55–75.

Howton, Judith (Head of Sales, Carlton International Media), Interview, London, 24 October 2001.

Hughes, P., 'Looking to Create a Virtuous Circle', *Broadcast International*, 21 March 2003, p. 20.

Huhn, Manuela (Programme Acquisitions Executive, RTL Television), Interview, Cologne, 21 February 2002.

Huisman, Mignon (Head of Programme Acquisitions and Co-productions, KRO), Interview, Hilversum, 31 January 2002.

Iosifidis, P., 'The Legal and Regulatory Context – National Approaches,' in P. Iosifides, J. Steemers and M. Wheeler (eds), *European Television Industries* (London: BFI, forthcoming 2005).

ITC (Independent Television Commission), *Communication Reform White Paper. ITC Response to Consultations on Proposals for Reform* (London: ITC, June 2000). Available in PDF format at <www.communicationswhitepaper.gov.uk/dti-dcms_comms-reform_submissions2.html> (accessed December 2003).

ITC, *A Review of the UK Programme Supply Market* (London: ITC, 26 November 2002a). Available at <www.itc.org.uk> (accessed December 2002).

ITC, *Consultation on Media Ownership Rules. ITC Response* (London: ITC, 22 January 2002b). Available at <www.culture.gov.uk/creative/media_ownership_replies.html> (accessed December 2003).

Iwabuchi, K., 'To Globalise, Regionalise or Localize Us, That is the Question. Japan's Response to Media Globalization', in G. Wang, J. Servaes and A. Goonasekera (eds), *The New Communications Landscape* (London: Routledge, 2000), pp. 142–59.

Jacka, E., and Johnson, L., 'Australia', in A. Smith (ed.), *Television: An International History* (Oxford: Oxford University Press, 1998), 2nd edn, pp. 208–22.

Jarvik, L., *PBS: Behind the Screen* (Rocklin, CA: Forum, 1997).

Jarvis, Colin (Director of Programming and Operations, International Television, BBC Worldwide), Telephone Interview, 12 December 2001.

Jenkinson, D., 'US Series Don't Cut it in European Primetime', *C21 Media*, 9 October 2002. Available at <www.c21media.net/news/detail.asp?area=2&article=4429> (accessed December 2003).

Jeremy, D., 'Toy Sales are Go!', *Broadcast International*, 19 January 2001a, p. 16.

Jeremy, D., 'Drawing Lessons from Japan', *Broadcast International*, 30 March 2001b, pp. 4–5.

Jeremy, D., 'Clash of the Child Titans', *Broadcast International*, 12 April 2002, pp. 24–8.

Jezequel J-P., and Lange A., *Economy of European TV Fiction*, Executive Summary (Strasbourg: European Audiovisual Observatory, December 2000).

Johnson, Brown (Executive Vice President, Nick Junior, Nickelodeon), Interview, New York, 10 September 2001.

Johnson, C., 'Eastern Promise for BBC', *C21*, 9 October 2001. Available at <www.c21media.net/news/detail.asp?area=2&article=1705> (accessed December 2003).

Johnson, C., '4Kids Triumphs in Fox Block Bidding War', *C21*, 23 January 2002. Available at <www.c21media.net/news/detail.asp?area=2&article=2408> (accessed December 2003).

Joint Committee on the Draft Communications Bill, *Draft Communications Bill*, Volume 1 Report, 25 July 2002, HL Paper 169–I, HC 876–I (London: The Stationery Office, July 2002).

Julienne, Ann (Acquisitions and International Co-productions, France 5), Interview, Paris, 20 March 2002.

Jury, L., 'Made in Britain, Sold to America as the New *Friends*. But Can *Coupling* Survive a Critical Mauling?', *The Independent*, 27 September 2003, p. 3.

Kaiser, Dieter (Editor, Natural History, WDR), Interview, Cologne, 22 February 2002.

Kandel, Francis (Programming Manager, Planète), Interview, Paris, 22 March 2002.

Kapner, S., 'US TV Shows Losing Potency Around World', *New York Times*, 2 January 2003.

Karthigesu, R., 'Broadcasting Deregulation in Developing Asian Nations: An Examination of Nascent Tendencies using Malaysia as a Case Study', *Media, Culture and Society*, vol. 16, 1994, pp. 74–90.

Keane, M., 'Broadcasting Policy, Creative Compliance and the Myth of Civil Society in China', *Media, Culture and Society*, vol. 23, 2001, pp. 783–98.

Keighron, P., 'Independent Spirits', *Broadcast International*, 30 March 2001, p. 38.

Keighron, P., 'Piecing Together the Big Picture', *Broadcast International*, 12 April 2002a, pp. 22–3.

Keighron, P., 'Deal of the Decade', *Broadcast*, 5 April 2002b, p. 15.

Keighron, P., 'Attack of the Clones', *Broadcast International*, 21 March 2003, pp. 13–18.

Kenny, J., 'Hong Kong Television. A Virtual Leader in Asia', *Television and New Media*, vol. 2, no. 3, 2001, pp. 281–94.

Kjellberg, Gudrun (Acquisitions Executive, Fiction, SVT), Interview, Stockholm, 25 April 2002.

Kuiper, Els (Programme Buyer, Youth, VPRO), Interview, Hilversum, 1 February 2002.

Kunz, Hildegard (Acquisitions, Bayerischer Rundfunk), Interview, Munich, 18 February 2002.

Kuzmyk, J., 'Drama: Speaking My Language', *C21*, 23 July 2002. Available at <www.c21media.net/features/detail.asp?area=2&article=3808> (accessed December 2003).

Kwak, K-S., 'The Context of the Regulation of Television Broadcasting in East Asia', *Gazette*, vol. 61, no. 3–4, 1999, pp. 255–73.

Labour Party, *Create the Future: A Strategy for Cultural Policy, Arts and the Creative Economy* (London: The Labour Party, 1997).

Lealand, G., *American Television Programmes on British Screens* (London: Broadcasting Research Unit Working Paper, 1984).

Lealand, G., 'New Zealand', in S. Cunningham and E. Jacka, *Australian Television and International Mediascapes* (Cambridge: Cambridge University Press, 1996), pp. 214–27.

Lee, J-K., 'The Asian Financial Crisis and the Tribulations of the South Korean Media', *Gazette*, vol. 64, no. 2, 2002, pp. 281–97.

Lee, P., 'The Absorption and Indigenization of Foreign Media Cultures. A Study on a Cultural Meeting Point of the East and West: Hong Kong', *Asian Journal of Communication*, vol. 1, no. 2, 1991, pp. 52–72.

Lee, P., 'Television and Global Culture', in G. Wang, J. Servaes and A. Goonasekera (eds), *The New Communications Landscape* (London: Routledge, 2000), pp. 188–98.

Lee, Paul (Chief Operating Officer, BBC America), Interview, Bethesda, 12 September 2002.

Lee, S-C., and Joe, S. K., 'Key Issues in the Korean Television Industry. Programmes and Market Structure', in D. French and M. Richards (eds), *Television in Contemporary Asia* (London: Sage, 2000), pp. 131–49.

Lehmann, Volker (Director Acquisitions, ZDF Enterprises), Interview, Mainz, 20 February 2002.

Leveaux, Sophie (Creative Director Service Acquisitions, TF1), Interview, Paris, 21 March 2002.

Lidén, Maria (Acquisitions Executive, Documentaries, TV4), Interview, Stockholm, 24 April 2002.

Liebes, T., and Katz, E., *The Export of Meaning: Cross Cultural Readings of Dallas* (Oxford: Polity Press, 1993), 2nd edn.

Lull, J., 'China Turned On (Revisited). Television, Reform and Resistance', in A. Sreberny-Mohammadi, D. Winseck, J. McKenna and O. Boyd-Barrett (eds), *Media in Global Context* (London: Arnold, 1997), pp. 259–68.

Lundberg, Jan (Acquisitions Executive, Documentaries, SVT), Interview, Stockholm, 23 April 2002.

Lyle, David, 'LA Confidential', *C21*, 15 March 2001. Available at <www.c21media.net/features/detail.asp?area=2&article=525> (accessed December 2003).

Macciocca, Luca (Acquisitions Executive, RaiSat), Telephone Interview, 10 June 2002.

Machill, M., 'Background to French Language Policy and its Impact on the Media', *European Journal of Communication*, vol. 12, no. 4, 1997, pp. 479–509.

McChesney, R., 'Media Convergence and Globalisation', in D. Thussu (ed.), *Electronic Empires* (London: Arnold, 1998), pp. 27–46.

McLuhan, M., *The Gutenberg Galaxy* (New York: McGraw-Hill, 1962).

McQuail, D., 'Western European Media: The Mixed Model Under Threat', in J. Downing, A. Mohammadi and A. Sreberny-Mohammadi (eds), *Questioning the Media* (London: Sage, 1995), pp. 147–64.

Maday, Charles (Senior Vice President, Historical Programming, the History Channel), Interview, New York, 18 September 2002.

Man Chan, J., 'National Responses and Accessibility to STAR TV in Asia', in A. Sreberny-Mohammadi, D. Winseck, J. McKenna and O. Boyd-Barrett (eds), *Media in Global Context* (London: Arnold, 1997), pp. 94–106.

Man Chan, J., 'No Culture is an Island. An Analysis of Media Protectionism and Media Openness', in G. Wang, J. Servaes and A. Goonasekera (eds), *The New Communications Landscape* (London: Routledge, 2000), pp. 251–64.

Maraschi, Fabiana (Sales Manager, Videoshow), Interview, Rome, 14 June 2002.

Marel, Renata (Manager, Health and Nature Department, ZDF), Interview, Mainz, 20 February 2002.

Marlow, J., 'A Stateside Story', *Broadcast International*, 5 October 2001, p. 8.

Marlow, J., 'Harvesting the Fruits of Teamwork', *Broadcast International*, 4 October 2002, pp. 22–3.

Marlow, J., 'Earning the Rights', *Broadcast*, 6 June 2003a, p. 23.

Marlow, J., 'Show Me the Money', *Broadcast International*, 21 March 2003b, pp. 5–6.

Marlow, J., 'Breaking Away from Cultural Roots', *Broadcast International*, 21 March 2003c, p. 19.

Mattelart, A., Delcourt, X., and Mattelart, M., *International Image Markets* (London: Comedia, 1984).

Methven, Nicola ,'Carlton buys ITC Library for £90m', *Broadcast*, 22 January 1999, p. 14.

Miller, D., 'The Consumption of Soap Opera: *The Young and the Restless* and Mass Consumption in Trinidad', in R. Allen (ed.), *To Be Continued . . . Soap Opera Around the World* (London: Routledge, 1995), pp. 213–33.

Miller, J., *Something Completely Different: British Television and American Culture* (Minneapolis: University of Minnesota Press, 2000).

Mills, P., 'An International Audience?', *Media, Culture and Society*, vol. 7, 1985, pp. 487–501.

Misert, Tamara (Acquisitions Manager, Telecinco), Interview, Madrid, 26 June 2002.

Moran, A., *Copycat TV: Globalisation, Program Formats and Cultural Identity* (Luton: University of Luton Press, 1998).

Morley, K., and Robins, K., 'Spaces of Identity: Communications, Technologies and the Reconfiguration of Europe', *Screen*, vol. 30, no. 4, 1989, pp. 10–34.

Morley, K, and Robins, K., *Spaces of Identity: Global Media, Electronic Landscapes and Cultural Boundaries* (London: Routledge, 1995).

Morris, Mike (Marketing Director, Channel Four International), Interview, London, 4 July 2002.

Mozzetti, Francesco (Acquisitions Manager, Children's Programmes, Mediatrade, Gruppo Mediaset), Interview, Milan, 12 June 2002.

MPAA (Motion Picture Association of America), *2001 US Economic Review*. Available at <www.mpaa.org/useconomicreview/2001Economic/sld032.htm> (accessed 28 January 2003).

Mulder, Frank (Director of Programme Acquisitions and Sales, NOS), Interview, Hilversum, 31 January 2002.

Müller, Suzanne (Head of Children's Programmes, ZDF), Interview, Mainz, 20 February 2002.

Mullin, Rita (Director of Development, Discovery Health), email correspondence, 1 October 2002.

Murdock, G., and Golding, P., 'Digital Possibilities, Market Realities: The Contradictions of Communications Convergence', in L. Panitch and C. Leys (eds), *The Socialist Register* (London: Merlin Press, 2001), pp. 111–30.

Mutimer, T., 'Formats Must Tune into National Psyche', *C21*, 4 February 2002. Available at <www.c21media.net/news/detail.asp?area=2&article=2474> (accessed December 2003).

Nakamura, K., 'Japan's TV Broadcasting in a Digital Environment', *Telecommunications Policy*, vol. 23, no. 3–4, 1999, pp. 307–16.

Newhouse Calcaterra, Jill (Vice President of Marketing, Nelvana Communications Inc.) and Garrity, Colin (Manager of Marketing and Sales, Nelvana Communications Inc.), Interview, Los Angeles, 21 September 2001.

Nordenstreng, K., and Varis, T., *Television Traffic – a One-Way Street* (Unesco, Reports and Papers on Mass Communications, 1974), no. 70.

Oliver, M., 'Scenarios for Convergence and the Internet. Implications for Content and Content Providers', White Paper Special Papers, June 2000. Available at <www.communicationswhitepaper.gov.uk/cwp_Consultation/scenarioscontent.pdf> (accessed December 2003).

ONS (Office of National Statistics), 'UK Film and TV Industry 2001 – Import and Export of Services', 24 October 2002. Available in PDF format at <www.statistics.gov.uk/pdfdir/film1002.pdf> (accessed November 2002).

ONS, 'International Service Transactions of the Film and Television Industries, 2002', 30 October 2003. Avilable in PDF format at <www.statistics.gov.uk/pdfdir/film1003.pdf> (accessed June 2004).

O'Regan, T., 'New and Declining Audiences: Contemporary Transformations in Hollywood's International Market', in E. Jacka (ed.), *Continental Shift* (Sydney: Local Consumption Publications, 1993), pp. 74–97.

O'Regan, T., 'The International Circulation of British Television', in E. Buscombe (ed.), *British Television: A Reader* (Oxford: Clarendon Press, 2000), pp. 303–21.

O'Sullivan, T., Dutton, B., and Rayner, P., *Studying the Media* (London: Arnold, 1998), 2nd edn.

PACT (Producers Alliance for Cinema and Television), *The Courage to Compete. Releasing Britain's Creative Potential* (London: PACT, 1998).

PACT, *Consultation on the Scope of the White Paper on Communications Reform* (London: PACT, June 2000).

PACT, *PACT Response to Draft Communications Bill* (London: PACT, August 2002a). Available in PDF format at <www.communicationsbill.gov.uk/ responses_organisations.html> (accessed December 2003).

PACT, *Pact Submission to the ITC Review of the Programme Supply Market* (London: PACT, October 2002b). Available in PDF format at <www.itc.org.uk/uploads/PACT> (accessed December 2002).

Pan, Z., and Man Chan, J., 'Building a Market-based Party Organ: Television and National Integration in China', in D. French and M. Richards (eds), *Television in Contemporary Asia* (London: Sage, 2000), pp. 233–63.

PBS (Public Broadcasting System), 'An Overview of PBS Funding. PBS 2001 Annual Report'. Available at <www.pbs.org/insidepbs/annualreport/fiscal.html> (accessed 2 September 2002).

Peijnenburg, Frank (Head of Acquisitions, NPS), Interview, Hilversum, 31 January 2002.

Phillips, M. (Chairman of the British Television Distributors Association), 'Brit TV: The Global Challenge', Key Address to the BTDA Conference, 20 September 2000. Available at <www.btda.org.uk> (accessed October 2000).

Pieterse, J. N., 'Globalisation as Hybridization', in M. Featherstone, S. Lash and R. Robertson (eds), *Global Modernities* (London: Sage, 1995), pp. 45–68.

Pinna, Lorenzo (Acquisitions Manager, Rai Uno), Interview, Rome, 14 June 2002.

Plunkett, J., 'One Man's Light Entertainment', *C21*, 16 May 2002. Available at <www.c21media.net/features/detail.asp?area=2&article=3307> (accessed December 2003).

Plym-Forshell, Eugen (Acquisitions Executive Nature Documentaries SVT), Interview, Stockholm, 24 April 2002.

Poussier, Dominique (Head of Children's Programmes, TF1), Interview, Paris, 19 March 2002.

Price, D., 'Der Programmrechtemarkt im digitalen Zeitalter', *Media Perspektiven* 7, 2002, pp. 319–33.

Pugnetti, Guido (Head of Acquisitions, Rai Cinema), Interview, Rome, 14 June 2002.

Ramos, Carlos Martinez (Fiction Series Acquisitions, TVE Televisíon Española), Interview, Madrid, 24 June 2002.

Ramos, Inés (Programmer), and Ortega, Carlos (Managing Director, Fox Kids España), Interview, Madrid, 25 June 2002.

RDF Media, *ITC Review of the Programme Supply Market. Written Submission from the RDF Group* (London: RDF, 12 October 2002a). Available in PDF format at <www.itc.org.uk/uploads/RDF_Media.pdf> (accessed December 2002).

RDF Media, *Financial Statements for the Year ended 31 January 2002* (London: RDF, 18 October 2002b).

RDF Media (Holdings) Ltd, *Consolidated Financial Statements for the Year ended 31 January 2003* (London: RDF, 1 July 2003).

Rea, W., 'Land of Opportunity', *Broadcast International*, 7 April 2000, pp. 7–8.

Reding, V., European Commissioner for Education and Culture, 'European Voice Conference on "Television without Frontiers"', Brussels, 21 March 2002.

Redpath, Jayne (Vice President Sales, Granada International), Telephone Interview, March 2002.

Renaud, J-L., and Litman, B., 'Changing Dynamics of the Overseas Marketplace for TV Programming. The Rise of International Co-Production', *Telecommunications Policy*, September, 1985, pp. 245–61.

Richards, M., and French, D., 'Globalisation, Television and Asia', in D. French and M. Richards (eds), *Television in Contemporary Asia* (London: Sage, 2000), pp. 13–29.

Roberts, Patrick (Senior Programme Sales Executive, Channel Four International), Telephone Interview, 18 June 2003.

Robertson, R. 'Globalisation or Glocalisation?', *The Journal of International Communications*, vol. 1, no. 1, 1994, pp. 33–52.

Robertson, R., 'Glocalisation: Time-Space and Homogeneity–Heterogeneity', in M. Featherstone, S. Lash and R. Robertson (eds), *Global Modernities* (London: Sage, 1995), pp. 25–44.

Robertson, R., 'Mapping the Global Condition', in A. Sreberny-Mohammadi, D. Winseck, J. McKenna and O. Boyd-Barrett (eds), *Media in Global Context* (London: Arnold, 1997), pp. 2–10.

Rogers, E., and Antola, L., 'Telenovelas: A Latin American Success Story', *Journal of Communication*, vol. 35, no. 4, 1985, pp. 24–35.

Root, Antony (President, Granada Entertainment USA), Interview, Los Angeles, 20 September 2001.

Rose, D., 'Lords Deal "Blocks" Murdoch Five bid', *Broadcast*, 4 July 2003, p. 1.

Rouse, L., 'Are Imports on the Slide?', *Broadcast International*, 5 October 2001, pp. 38–9.

Rouse, L., 'The Future of Formats', *Broadcast*, 6 June 2003, pp. 26–7.

Roy, A., 'Why Indies are in the Money Again', *Broadcast*, 30 May 2003, pp. 14–15.

Salas, Sonia (Director of Odisea, Multicanal), Interview, Madrid, 25 June 2002.

Saló, Gloria (New Projects Manager, Telecinco), Interview, Madrid, 26 June 2002.

Schiff, Hans (UK Vice President, William Morris Agency, London), Interview, London, 25 October 2001.

Schiller, H., *Mass Communications and American Empire* (Boulder: Westview, 1969), 2nd edn 1992.

Schiller, H., *Communications and Cultural Domination* (New York: ME Sharpe, 1976).

Schiller, H., 'Not Yet the Post-Imperialist Era', *Critical Studies in Mass Communication*, vol. 8, no. 1, 1991, pp. 13–28.

Schiller, H., 'Striving for Communication Dominance', in D. Thussu (ed.), *Electronic Empires* (London: Arnold, 1998), pp. 17–26.

Schlesinger, P., 'Trading in Fictions: What Do We Know about British Television Imports and Exports?', *European Journal of Communication*, vol. 1, 1986, pp. 263–87.

Schlesinger, P., 'On National Identity: Some Conceptions and Misconceptions Criticized', *Social Science Information*, vol. 26, no. 2, 1987, pp. 219–64.

Schosser, Suzanne (Programme Director, SuperRTL), Interview, Cologne, 21 February 2002.

Schwalbe, D., 'Back to the Baby-Boomers', *C21*, 10 January 2002. Available at <www.c21media.net/features/detail.asp?area=2&article=2306> (accessed December 2003).

Scott, M., 'A Vast Market Crammed with Eastern Promise', *Broadcast International*, 30 March 2001, pp. 34–5.

Segal, R., 'On How the Economic Climate is Persuading US networks to Keep Production in the Family', *Broadcast*, 18 January 2002, p. 14.

Seguin, D., 'The Survival of the Biggest', *Broadcast International*, 4 October 2002, pp. 28–31.

Sepstrup, P., *Transnationalization of Television in Western Europe* (London: John Libbey, 1990).

Seymour-Ure, C., *The British Press and Broadcasting since 1945* (Oxford: Blackwell, 1991).

Shed Productions, *Submission to the ITC Programme Supply Review of the Market*, 14 October 2002. Available in PDF format at <www.itc.org.uk/uploads/Shed.pdf> (accessed December 2002).

Shell, Sally (Commercial Director, Wall to Wall Television), Interview, London, 20 August 2001.

Shelton, E., 'American Cream', *Broadcast*, 29 June 2001, p. 15.

Silj, A., *East of Dallas: The European Challenge to American Television* (London: BFI, 1988).

Silverstone, R., *Television and Everyday Life* (London: Routledge, 1994).

Silverstone, R., *Why Study the Media?* (London: Sage, 1999).

Sinclair, J., 'Culture and Trade: Some Theoretical and Practical Considerations', in G. McAnany and K. Wilkinson (eds), *Mass Media and Free Trade* (Austin: University of Texas Press, 1996), pp. 30–60.

Sinclair, J., and Cunningham, S., 'Go with the Flow: Diasporas and the Media', *Television and New Media*, vol. 1, no. 1, 2000, pp. 11–31.

Sinclair, J., Jacka, E., and Cunningham, S. (eds), *New Patterns in Global Television: Peripheral Vision* (Oxford: Oxford University Press, 1996).

Smith, A., 'Towards a Global Culture', in M. Featherstone (ed.), *Global Culture* (London: Sage, 1990), pp. 171–91.

Smith, C., *Review of the Future Funding of the BBC*, Statement to House of Commons by the Secretary of State for Culture, Media and Sport, 21 February 2000. Available in DCMS, Press Release, 21 February 2000, 'Government Announces BBC Licence Fee Rises by £3 million in Return for £1 Billion Savings and Extra Accountability in Digital Age'.

Smith, Paul (Chairman, Celador Group), Interview, London, 5 December 2001.

Smith, R., *The Other Face of Public TV: Censoring the American Dream* (New York: Algora Publishing, 2002).

Sofley, K., 'US Syndication Market in Crisis', *C21*, 1 January 2000a. Available at <www.c21media.net/features/detail.asp?area=2&article=471> (accessed December 2003).

Sofley, K., 'Formats: Pitching to the US networks', *C21*, 1 November 2000b. Available at <www.c21media.net/features/detail.asp?area=2&article=449> (accessed December 2003).

Sparks, C., 'Is There a Global Public Sphere?', in D. Thussu (ed.), *Electronic Empires* (London: Arnold, 1998), pp. 108–24.

Stephens, J., 'Stone Stanley', *C21*, 15 April 2001. Available at <www.c21media.net/features/detail.asp?area=2&article=517> (accessed December 2003).

Stewart, L., 'US Drama Strand Faces the Chop', *C21*, 14 July 2003a. Available at <www.c21media.net/news/detail.asp?area=1&article=7016> (accessed December 2003).

Stewart, L., 'US Viewers Get Double Dose of WNTW', *C21*, 3 March 2003b. Available at <www.c21media.net/news/detail.asp?area=2&article=5632> (accessed December 2003).

Straubhaar, J., 'Beyond Media Imperialism: Assymetrical Interdependence and Cultural Proximity', *Critical Studies in Mass Communication*, vol. 8, no 1, 1991, pp. 39–59.

Straubhaar, J., 'Distinguishing the Global, Regional and National Levels of World Television', in A. Sreberny-Mohammadi, D. Winseck, J. McKenna and O. Boyd-Barrett (eds), *Media in Global Context* (London: Arnold, 1997), pp. 284–98.

Straubhaar, J., 'Culture, Language and Social Class in the Globalization of Television', in G. Wang, J. Servaes and A. Goonasekera (eds), *The New Communications Landscape* (London: Routledge, 2000), pp. 199–224.

SVT, *Facts About Sveriges Television* (Stockholm: SVT, 2001).

Tambini, D., 'Convergence and UK Creative Industries: Flexible Strategy for Future Export Performance', Research Paper, Institute for Public Policy Research (IPPR), January 2000.

TBI (Television Business International), *Television Yearbook 2003* (London: TBI, 2002).

Tettenborn, Sabine (Director of Co-productions, KirchMedia), Interview, Munich, 18 February 2002.

Thomas., A. O., 'Regulating Access to Transnational Satellite Television. Shifting Government Policies in Northeast Asia', *Gazette*, vol. 61, no. 3–4, 1999, pp. 243–54.

Thomas, A. O., 'Transborder Television for Greater China', in D. French and M. Richards (eds), *Television in Contemporary Asia* (London: Sage, 2000), pp. 91–109.

Thompson, J., *The Media and Modernity* (Cambridge: Polity Press, 1995).

Thussu, D., *International Communication: Continuity and Change* (London: Arnold, 2000).

Tiger Aspect Productions, 'Tiger Aspect Submission to the ITC Review of the Programme Supply Market', October 2002. Available in PDF format at <www.itc.org.uk/uploads/Tiger_Aspect.pdf> (accessed December 2002).

Tomlinson, J., *Cultural Imperialism: A Critical Introduction* (London: Pinter Publishers, 1991).

Tomlinson, J., 'Internationalism, Globalization and Cultural Imperialism', in K. Thompson (ed.), *Media and Cultural Regulation* (London: Sage, 1997a), pp. 117–62.

Tomlinson, J., 'Cultural Globalization and Cultural Imperialism', in A. Mohammadi (ed.), *International Communication and Globalization* (London: Sage, 1997b), pp. 170–90.

Torrance, Caroline (Head of International Drama, Granada International), Interview, London, 30 October 2001.

Tracey, M., 'The Poisoned Chalice? International Television and the Idea of Dominance?', *Daedalus*, vol. 114, no. 4, fall, 1985, pp. 17–56.

Tracey, M., 'Popular Culture and the Economics of Global Television', *Intermedia*, vol. 16, no. 2, 1988, pp. 9–25.

Tracey, M., and Redal, W., 'The New Parochialism: The Triumph of The Populist in the Flow of International Television', *Canadian Journal of Communication*, vol. 20, 1995, pp. 343–65.

Tunstall, J., *The Media are American: Anglo-American Media in the World* (London: Constable, 1977).

Tunstall, J., and Machin, D., *The Anglo-American Media Connection* (Oxford: Oxford University Press, 1999).

TVNZ (Television New Zealand), *Annual Report 2002* (Auckland: TVNZ, 2002).

Van den bussche, Peter (Director of Sales, Endemol Entertainment UK), Interview, London, 6 December 2001.

van der Heide, Caro (Head of Programme Acquisitions, VARA), Interview, Hilversum 31 January 2002.

van Diepen, Lisette (Acquisitions Manager, Endemol International), Interview, Hilversum, 1 February 2002.

Van Gompel, R., Van den Bulck, H., and Biltereyst, D., 'Media Systems, Policies and Industries in Transition', in C. Newbold, O. Boyd-Barrett and H. Van den Bulck (eds), *The Media Book* (London: Arnold, 2002).

Varela, Isabel (Head of Acquisitions, Documentaries, Canal Plus España), Interview, Madrid, 24 June 2002.

Varis, T., 'The International Flow of Television Programs', *Journal of Communication*, vol. 34, no. 1, winter, 1984, pp. 143–52.

Varis, T., *International Flow of Television Programmes* (Unesco: Reports and Papers on Mass Communication, 1985), no. 100.

Vaughan-Adams, L., 'Warning Hits Maker of "Robot Wars"', *The Independent*, 4 February 2003, p. 22.

Viljoen, D., *Art of the Deal* (London: Pact, 2002), 3rd edn.

Volkmer, I., *News in the Global Sphere* (Luton: University of Luton Press, 1999).

von Hennet, Thomas (Head of Documentaries, ProSieben), Interview, Munich, 19 February 2002.

Walker, S., 'Back to School', *Television Business International*, August/September 2002, pp. 20–3.

Wall to Wall (Holdings) Ltd, *Financial Statements for the Year Ended 30 June 2003* (London: Wall to Wall, 2003).

Wall to Wall Television, *Submission to the ITC Review of the Programme Supply Market*, 14 October 2002. Available in PDF format at <www.itc.org.uk/uploads/Wall_to_Wall.pdf> (accessed December 2002).

Waller, E., 'Formats: Getting it Right', *C21*, 1 November 2000. Available at <www.c21media.net/features/detail.asp?area=2&article=450> (accessed December 2003).

Waller, E., 'Fox Lines up Two UK dramas', *C21*, 30 October 2002a. Available at <www.c21media.net/news/detail.asp?area=2&article=4604> (accessed December 2003).

Waller, E., 'Endemol Format Delivers for TLC', *C21*, 10 May 2002b. Available at <www.c21media.net/news/detail.asp?area=2&article=3254> (accessed December 2003).

Waller, E., 'More US Format Deals for RDF', *C21*, 13 December 2002c. Available at <www.c21media.net/news/detail.asp?area=2&article=4977> (accessed December 2003).

Waller, E., 'CBS challenges ABC's Version of I'm a Celebrity', *C21*, 2 October 2002d. Available at <www.c21media.net/news/detail.asp?area=2&article=4325> (accessed December 2003).

Waller, E., 'US Networks Retire Top UK Formats', *C21*, 15 May 2002e. Available at <www.c21media.net/news/detail.asp?area=2&article=3289> (accessed December 2003).

Waller, E., 'Inspector Morse Goes over the Wall', *C21*, 20 December 2002f. Available at <www.c21media.net/news/detail.asp?area=2&article=5029> (accessed December 2003).

Waller, E., 'Asian TV Veteran Slams "Degrading Western Formats"', *C21*, 25 March 2002g. Available at <www.c21media.net/news/detail.asp?area=2&article=2856> (accessed December 2003).

Waller, E., 'Englishmen in LA', *C21*, 19 June 2003a. Available at <www.c21media.net/features/detail.asp?area=2&article=6776> (accessed December 2003).

Waller, E., 'TLC Lines up Faking it for March', *C21*, 27 February 2003b. Available at <www.c21media.net/news/detail.asp?area=2&article=5588> (accessed December 2003).

Waller, E., 'TLC Takes More UK Formats', *C21*, 10 March 2003c. Available at

<www.c21media.net/news/detail.asp?area=2&article=5699> (accessed December 2003).

Waller, E., 'TV Corp Issues Profits Warning', *C21*, 3 February 2003d. Available at <www.c21media.net/news/detail.asp?area=2&article=5294> (accessed December 2003).

Waller, E., 'US Deal for New Ragdoll Series', *C21*, 11 June 2003e. Available at <www.c21media.net/news/detail.asp?area=2&article=6659> (accessed December 2003).

Waller, E., 'TVB Looks Beyond the Quiz', *C21*, 12 February 2003f. Available at <www.c21media.net/features/detail.asp?area=2&article=5439> (accessed December 2003).

Waller, E., 'Nothing ventured …', *C21*, 20 August 2003g. Available at <www.c21media.net/features/detail.asp?area=2&article=7429> (accessed December 2003).

Waterman, D., and Rogers, E., 'The Economics of Television Program Production and Trade in Far East Asia', *Journal of Communication*, vol. 44, no. 3, summer, 1994, pp. 89–111.

Weatherford, Jim (Director Asia Pacific, Nelvana International, Japan), Telephone Interview, 6 June 2003.

Wei, R., 'China's Television in the Era of Marketisation', in D. French and M. Richards (eds), *Television in Contemporary Asia* (London: Sage, 2000), pp. 325–47.

Wells, M., 'Anne Robinson's £1m Link with US', *The Guardian*, 10 February 2001.

Wells, M., 'Coming in from the Cold', *The Guardian* 2, 12 May 2002, pp. 6–7.

Wells, P., *Picture-Tube Imperialism? The Impact of US Television on Latin America* (Maryknoll, NY: Orbis Books, 1972).

Westcott, T., 'Tough Sell', *Television Business International*, September 2000, pp. 17–20.

Wildman, S., and Siwek, S., 'The Privatization of European Television: Effects On International Markets for Programs', *Columbia Journal of World Business*, fall, 1987, pp. 71–6.

Wildman, S., and Siwek, S., *International Trade in Films and Television Programs* (Cambridge, MA: Ballinger, 1988).

Willemsen, Yvonne (Project Manager, Teleac/NOT), Interview, Hilversum, 30 January 2002.

Williams, R., *Television: Technology and Cultural Form* (London: Fontana, 1974).

Willis, J., 'On Broadcasting: our Transatlantic Success Story', *The Guardian*, 31 May 1999.

Willis, John (Vice President, National Programming, WGBH), Interview, Boston, 11 September 2002.

Windhorst, Natalie (Programme Buyer, VPRO), Interview, Hilversum, 31 January 2002.

Winstone, K., 'Ellender Assumes the Mantle', 24 May 2002. Available at
    <www.c21media.net/features/detail.asp?area=2&article=3379> (accessed
    December 2003).
Winstone, K., 'Make or Break for Natpe', *Broadcast*, 17 January 2003, pp. 16–17.

Index

Page numbers in bold indicate detailed analysis; *n* = endnote; *t* = table